MW01053274

"Hunter Farrell and Bala Khyllep bring dee ... the urgent task of reframing congregational mission. ... and affirms that God is calling North American Christians to walk alongside others as companions in Christ. I highly recommend this book for classroom use. It is refreshing and accessible. Most important, it is full of faithful wisdom."

Dana L. Robert, Boston University School of Theology, author of *Faithful Friendships: Embracing Diversity in Christian Community*

"Hunter Farrell and Balajiedlang Khyllep have a message for congregational mission leaders: what you do matters. In fact, when mission wanes, the very identity of the church comes into question. The authors provide fresh theological insights for mission as well as practical tools to help God's people recalibrate their ability to participate fully in what God is doing in the world."

Al Tizon, associate affiliate professor of missional and global leadership at North Park Theological Seminary

"Hunter Farrell has written a seminal work for parish mission that promises freedom from the limitations, failures, and even harm of short-term mission trips and parish partnerships. More importantly, he and his companion, S. Balajiedlang Khyllep, provide a vision, a road map, and a vehicle for parishes to revitalize their mission in the world. This is a must-read for every pastor, mission leader, and Christian who longs to participate in the *missio Dei*, because it is accessible, honest, hope filled, and doable."

Donald R. McCrabb, executive director of the United States Catholic Mission Association and partner in the Third Wave of Mission

"Much of what goes by the name 'missions' in American Christianity is captive to the habits of settler colonialism and slaveholder religion, squelching the good news both for those who proclaim it and those who hear it. *Freeing Congregational Mission* offers hope that churches can discover the gospel anew and the world can hear and see God's mission in a way that brings hope and healing for all."

Jonathan Wilson-Hartgrove, author of *Revolution of Values*

"*Freeing Congregational Mission* is a welcoming multicultural, postcolonial, and interdisciplinary work that encourages a critical forward view of God's mission (*missio Dei*) aimed at encouraging more faithful and effective mission engagements. With a distinct focus on the transforming energy of the short-term mission experience, the authors have produced an essential mentoring text to theologically encourage church mission leaders and seminarians who yearn for a more inclusive understanding of God's mission. By examining three core elements necessary to overcome current destructive cultural forces, this book demonstrates how churches, by valuing human diversity, human agency, and ethical behaviors, can learn to model dignity, respect, humility, and love of neighbor related to missions in both local and global contexts."

Marsha Snulligan Haney, intercultural theological education consultant, founder and editor of UrbanMissiology.org

"*Freeing Congregational Mission* is a must-read book for anyone who wants to engage in mission faithfully. In my ministry, I have been to over eighty countries and interacted with both senders and recipients of mission. The criticism of colonial models of mission as well as self-serving mission practices is a common theme. And yet there is the understanding that most mission teams mean very well. This book is the first of its kind that I have seen address this in an open, critical, and sensitive fashion. I will recommend it highly for both academic and mission practitioners' use."

Setri Nyomi, senior lecturer at Trinity Theological Seminary, Legon, Ghana, and former general secretary of the World Communion of Reformed Churches

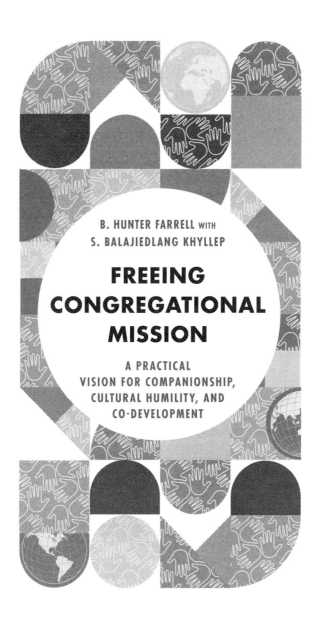

B. HUNTER FARRELL WITH
S. BALAJIEDLANG KHYLLEP

FREEING CONGREGATIONAL MISSION

A PRACTICAL
VISION FOR COMPANIONSHIP,
CULTURAL HUMILITY, AND
CO-DEVELOPMENT

Academic
An imprint of InterVarsity Press
Downers Grove, Illinois

InterVarsity Press
P.O. Box 1400, Downers Grove, IL 60515-1426
ivpress.com
email@ivpress.com

InterVarsity Press® is the book-publishing division of InterVarsity Christian Fellowship/USA®, a movement of
students and faculty active on campus at hundreds of universities, colleges, and schools of nursing in the United
States of America, and a member movement of the International Fellowship of Evangelical Students.
For information about local and regional activities, visit intervarsity.org.

Scripture quotations, unless otherwise noted, are from the New Revised Standard Version Bible,
copyright © 1989 National Council of the Churches of Christ in the United States of America. Used by permission.
All rights reserved worldwide.

While any stories in this book are true, some names and identifying information may have been changed to protect
the privacy of individuals.

Some material in this book is adapted from five works originally written by Hunter Farrell for the Presbyterian
Mission Agency. Used by permission.

Figures T1.1, T1.4, and T1.5 © Paul Joseph Brown, VillageReach. Used by permission.
Figure 8.1 © Sixth Presbyterian Church and S. Balajiedlang Khyllep. Used by permission.
Figure T1.2 © SDI Productions / iStock. Used by permission.
Figure T1.3 © himarkley / iStock. Used by permission.
Figure T1.6 © zms / iStock. Used by permission.
Figure T1.7 © S. Balajiedlang Khyllep. Used by permission.
Figure 4.1 © IDI, LLC

The publisher cannot verify the accuracy or functionality of website URLs used in this book beyond the date of
publication.

Cover design and image composite: David Fassett
Interior design: Daniel van Loon
Image: abstract vector design: © studiostockart / DigitalVision Vectors / Getty Images

ISBN 978-1-5140-0068-7 (print)
ISBN 978-1-5140-0069-4 (digital)

Printed in the United States of America ∞

InterVarsity Press is committed to ecological stewardship and to the conservation of natural resources in all our
operations. This book was printed using sustainably sourced paper.

Library of Congress Cataloging-in-Publication Data
Names: Farrell, Bennett Hunter, 1958- author. | Khyllep, Shankur Balajiedlang, 1982- author.
Title: Freeing congregational mission : a practical vision for companionship, cultural humility,
    and co-development / B. Hunter Farrell with S. Balajiedlang Khyllep.
Description: Downers Grove, IL : InterVarsity Press, [2021] | Includes bibliographical references and index.
Identifiers: LCCN 2021041932 (print) | LCCN 2021041933 (ebook) | ISBN 9781514000687 (print) |
    ISBN 9781514000694 (digital)
Subjects: LCSH: Missions—North America. | Christianity and culture--North America. |
    Postcolonialism—North America.
Classification: LCC BV2063 .F37 2021 (print) | LCC BV2063 (ebook) | DDC 266/.0237—dc23
LC record available at https://lccn.loc.gov/2021041932
LC ebook record available at https://lccn.loc.gov/2021041933

P   25 24 23 22 21 20 19 18 17 16 15 14 13 12 11 10 9 8 7 6 5 4 3 2 1
Y   43 42 41 40 39 38 37 36 35 34 33 32 31 30 29 28 27 26 25 24 23 22

CONTENTS

ACKNOWLEDGMENTS

THIS BOOK BEGAN WITH A LOVE that cares enough to speak the truth. It was the love of Congolese, Peruvian, and Indian mentors, teachers, and friends who dared to ask a question or lovingly disagree—even when they knew it would be difficult for us to hear—that moved us to share their teachings.

We are also grateful to the more than 1,200 US congregational mission leaders—mainline Protestant, Catholic, and evangelical—who participated in our research who not only identified issues that called for reflection, but articulated the need for concrete tools to engage in God's mission in more meaningful and respectful ways. Their honesty and courage give us hope.

We want to acknowledge Jon Boyd and InterVarsity Press colleagues for their seasoned hand in transforming a hope-filled manuscript into this book, and also the Rockefeller Foundation for the generous fellowship they provided to Hunter in 2019 to advance the writing of the book.

Libby Ferda, Sandra Fomete, Michael Haasl, Scott Hagley, Todd Leach, Case Thorp, Doug Welch, and Ken White offered insightful comments on the book and we are grateful to them. Pittsburgh Theological Seminary encouraged us to work on this book and students Rebecca Young, Bill Quinn, and Kelcey Bailey contributed to the project with their research and insights.

From Bala: I am indeed grateful to my mother who set aside a handful of dried rice for mission at every meal (a practice within the Presbyterian Church of India) and for a father who was uneducated but persistently advocated for the education of his children. Their commitment to the mission of the church formed me to have a heart for all God's people. I am grateful for the priceless intercultural lessons learned through living in many parts of India and the United States, especially for the family and friends in Meghalaya, Serampore, South Dakota, and Pittsburgh. I thank my mother-in-law, Anita Miller, who is always ready to proofread and provide insight. And finally, I'm grateful to my wife, Cheryl, and children, Isabet and Indarisha, for breathing joy into the most stressful of times and for challenging and encouraging me every day.

From Hunter. Mission experiences in Congo and Peru served as a place of rich intercultural learning with loving mentors: Dr. Tshihamba Mukome Luendu, Dr. Mulumba Mukundi Musumbu, Rev. Mukuna Tshitebua, Dr. Rolando Perez, Cardinal Pedro Barreto, Yolanda Zurita, Conrado Olivera, and the many mission companions of the Joining Hands Against Hunger Network. A cradle Presbyterian, I left the church in my teenage years. But it was the PC(USA)'s understanding of mission and its deep, if imperfect, mission relationships within the United States and across the globe that drew me back into the church. I will be forever grateful.

While my parents were not missionaries in the traditional sense, my mother's boundary-crossing life and my father's longstanding commitment to serve underprivileged youth in our hometown of Dallas, Texas, served as an invisible compass for me. Our three bilingual and bicultural children, Ndaya, Will, and Andrew, grew up as "foreigners" in contexts not their own and modeled for us how to bloom where one is planted. Their encouragement has been invaluable to me.

Most of all, this book would not be what it is without the daily encouragement of Ruth, my wife, mission companion, and best friend, who learned three languages and lived with me on four continents, all to engage in God's mission as a learner. There is not an insight in this book that she hasn't helped shape or strengthen in some way.

SECTION ONE

THE THREE
STONES

ONE

THE CRISIS WE FACE

It is disgraceful that . . . the impious Galilaeans
[Christians] support not only their own poor but ours
as well, all men see that our people lack aid from us.

ROMAN EMPEROR JULIAN, 362 CE[1]

CHRISTIANS HAVE ALWAYS BEEN a generous people. Since the era of the early church, non-Christians and even the opponents of Christianity (like the Roman emperor Julian, above) noticed Jesus' and his followers' exceeding generosity and particular concern for people living under the weight of poverty and oppression. This lifestyle is embodied in the apostle Paul's call to follow in Christ's example of setting aside self-interest and living in service to others: "Do nothing from selfish ambition or conceit, but in humility regard others as better than yourselves. Let each of you look not to your own interests, but to the interests of others. Let the same mind be in you that was in Christ Jesus" (Phil 2:3-5).

In the United States, the mission of the church has often been considered one of the highest priorities of Christian congregations,[2] whether evangelical, Catholic, or mainline Protestant. Many congregations proudly identified themselves as "mission churches" because of the prayer, funding, and time they poured into God's global mission—sometimes 10 percent,

---

[1]"Letter to Arsacius, High-Priest of Galatia" (June 362), in *The Works of the Emperor Julian*, trans. Wilmer Cave Wright (1913), vol. 3.

[2]Sometimes called the local church or parish, in this book, *congregation* refers to the basic unit of the Christian church that gathers regularly for worship, study, prayer, and participation in mission.

20 percent, or more of their total congregational budget went to missions, local and foreign. "Mission" was all the activities done *for the people outside the church's walls* in the name of Jesus Christ, from the "clothes closet" or soup kitchen for our city's economically disadvantaged to prayer and financial support for overseas missionaries. In obedience to the Great Commandment ("Love your neighbor as yourself") and the Great Commission ("Go and make disciples of all nations"), mission was about reaching out in love to our neighbors across the street and around the world.

In each of these "mission-minded" congregations were the "mission advocates" who lifted up the cause of God's local and global mission—and sometimes even battled the finance committee members, resisting the constant pressure to increase the percentage of the annual budget dedicated to staff salaries, member services, special projects like sanctuary carpeting, or a host of other legitimate operating needs. To these advocates, the mission budget was sacrosanct because it represented why the church existed—its very *essence*. "If we can't support Christ's mission in the world, we shouldn't call ourselves a church" was their attitude.

But over the last few decades, an almost imperceptible cultural undertow has been pulling the church off course. Even some of the most dedicated mission leaders haven't noticed the changes because of the subtle cultural shifts taking place in US society. Somehow, the outward nature of mission, the powerful flow of God's love and grace through our congregations and parishes out into the world, is being short-circuited. And ironically, *we* have increasingly become the beneficiaries of our own mission work. You don't believe me? For just one example, let's take a look at the short-term mission trip phenomenon.

THE ENERGY BEHIND THE SHORT-TERM MISSION TRIP

Just a small blip on the mission radar of most churches fifty years ago, today short-term mission (STM) trips have exploded into a booming industry that *Toxic Charity* author Bob Lupton estimates between $3.5 and 5 billion a year.[3] Nearly two million Americans participate in an STM each year.[4] One

[3]Bob Lupton, "Colonialism or Partnership?," Focused Community Strategies, January 22, 2014, www.fcsministries.org/fcs-ministries/blog/colonialism-or-partnership.
[4]Robert Ellis Haynes, "Consuming Mission: Towards a Theology of Short-Term Mission and Pilgrimage" (Eugene, OR: Pickwick, 2018), 116.

of the largest financial contributions that many congregations and their members make toward the global mission of the church is for these trips to both domestic and international destinations. At an average cost of $1,000 per individual for the typical eight-day trip, a congregation and its members can together spend tens of thousands of dollars to prepare, equip, send, and support one STM group overseas.[5] Yet an increasing number of books and articles—from scholarly missiological journals to popular books like *When Helping Hurts*—are raising critical questions as to the impact of STM trips on both the travelers and the "host communities."

Most of us understand intuitively that crossing the seas to build a house in Tegucigalpa, teach a Vacation Bible School class in Bangkok, or feed and hold babies in Kampala is simply not an effective—and probably not very faithful—use of God's resources. Even the members of the congregation's finance committee are questioning the impact of these expenses! Some critics maintain that this significant investment in our own international travel to distant lands may be decreasing the funds contributed to support long-term mission workers and the work of global partners,[6] yet we continue to invest in this most attractive of congregational mission strategies.

These critiques of STM are not new. But neither scholars nor practitioners seem to be asking the *why* question. How *do* we explain the energy behind the North American church's fascination with short-term mission trips? What is it that keeps the North American church—embedded as we are in a culture that so highly values efficiency and measurable impact—pouring money into a mission strategy that research indicates simply doesn't generate lasting positive impact for the "host community"? If this most popular of US congregational mission strategies isn't helping the neighbors we're called to serve, then why do we keep doing it?

A common answer is because the trips are said to be *transformative* for our congregations. Could it be that the outward mission focus we received from previous generations is being eclipsed by a more modern, inward focus that is "all about us"? Through our research, we've heard from the mission leaders of African American, White, Latinx, and multiracial churches who

[5]Haynes, "Consuming Mission," 117.
[6]Scott Moreau, "Short-Term Missions in the Context of Missions, Inc.," in *Effective Engagement in Short-Term Missions: Doing It Right!*, ed. Robert Priest (Pasadena, CA: William Carey, 2008), 15-16.

feel uneasy about some elements of their short-term mission trips and yearn for the insights and tools they need to channel the transformational energy of STM into strategies that actually deepen trust and relationship and enable diverse Christians to participate in Jesus Christ's transformation of the world.

This transformational energy is the focus of *Freeing Congregational Mission*: the book will challenge our congregations' current repertoire of mission activities and offer case studies, strategies, illustrations for your teaching, and a seven-count toolkit, created by coauthor Balajiedlang Khyllep through our work with Pittsburgh Theological Seminary's World Mission Initiative for congregational mission leaders like you to use to strengthen the faithfulness and effectiveness of your congregation's participation in God's mission.

MISSION STRATEGIES MADE IN OUR OWN IMAGE

It is not just the short-term mission trip phenomenon that reveals this massive shift in focus. Our research with congregational mission leaders reveals several large and growing industries that US local congregations use to engage in mission.

Orphanages are expensive, unsustainable, and abuse-prone institutions that were largely discredited in North America and Europe years ago, yet they represent a major benevolence for about a third of Catholic, mainline Protestant, and evangelical congregations surveyed.[7] In numerous contexts in the Majority World, orphanages often ignore the very people most suited to respond to the child's needs—the child's parent(s). Most "orphans" in fact have at least one living parent.[8] The child's parent(s) and extended family may need only a temporary helping hand to provide for their child, but supporting an orphanage is so satisfying to donors that it has made orphanages a growth industry in numerous Majority World nations, with churches providing financial support and STM volunteers.

More than $3 billion is given annually to *child-sponsorship programs*.[9] Forty-six percent of the Presbyterian Church (USA) congregational mission

---

[7] World Mission Initiative, "Survey of Congregational Mission Leaders," January 2019 (a survey of 649 mission leaders of Catholic, mainline Protestant, and evangelical congregations).

[8] Kathryn E. van Doore, "Paper Orphans: Exploring Child Trafficking for the Purpose of Orphanages," *International Journal of Children's Rights* 24 (2016): 378-407.

[9] Emily Buchanan, "Is Child Sponsorship Ethical?," BBC, May 9, 2013, www.bbc.com/news/uk-22472455.

leaders I surveyed in 2014 personally sponsored a child.[10] Sponsors report finding deep satisfaction in a personalized relationship with a vulnerable child despite the ethical questions that have been raised and the fact that sponsorship is by nature inefficient due to the added administrative costs of "donor care": managing sponsor-child relationships, letter writing and translation, donor gifts and visits, and other activities that one child-sponsorship agency described as "the only way to capture the donors' attention."[11] Are there better ways to care for vulnerable children?

Prepared meal–packaging projects have exploded in popularity among US Christians, especially among mission conference attendees and youth and college groups, as evidenced by the growth in both the number of institutions providing this service and the volume of their operations. Since 2005, Rise Against Hunger (formerly Stop Hunger Now) has mobilized more than 350,000 volunteers annually to package more than 415 million meals in 74 countries "with a mission to end hunger in our lifetime."[12] But packaged meals will never end world hunger. They can save a life when delivered to a disaster zone but ignore the root causes of hunger and can even depress market prices in communities that aren't experiencing a disaster, discouraging local farmers from planting next season's crop and reducing *food sovereignty.*[13]

Rather than understanding mission as joining God in the spreading circle of relationships transformed by God's unconditional love and forgiveness, is our consumer culture twisting our view of the *missio Dei* into a mission marketplace—a "buyers' market" that places decision-making power in the hands of the person paying for the mission program? Our congregations' choices to support these and other mission strategies point to the twin challenges we face as mission leaders.

---

[10]"Re-membering Missiology: An Invitation to an Activist Agenda," *Missiology: An International Review* 46, no. 1 (2018): 44. Article references a survey of 664 Presbyterian Church (USA) mission leaders the author conducted in April 2014: "Congregational Mission Leaders Activities Survey."

[11]Kevin Lewis O'Neill, "Left Behind: Security, Salvation and the Subject of Prevention," *Current Anthropology* 28, no. 2 (2013): 209.

[12]Rise Against Hunger, "How We Work," www.riseagainsthunger.org/our-impact/.

[13]Food sovereignty is a term originally coined by members of the Via Campesina movement to mean that the people who produce, distribute, and consume food should control the mechanisms and policies of food production and distribution, that is, outsiders should not determine that a particular community must grow cash crops for export, rather than the foods that can nourish their community. This concept places farmers and consumers at the center of the food system. Nyéléni Forum, "Synthesis Report," March 31, 2007, https://nyeleni.org/spip.php?article334.

THE AGE OF "SELFIE MISSION"

How many of us haven't "liked" a friend's Facebook or Instagram post of a photo that portrays them engaged in some benevolent activity—serving a meal, building a school, or traveling on an STM trip? How many of us haven't posted this kind of image ourselves? I know I have. Social media provide us with powerful tools to portray ourselves instantly to all of our friends in particular ways.

Somehow the symbol of mission in our era has become a "selfie"—a self-portrait instantly "shareable" and "likeable" by our friends on social media that helps us frame ourselves in a benevolent posture helping the "less fortunate" around the world. Although I don't consider myself wealthy by any measure, my awareness of my bank account, my modest investment portfolio, and my pension fund make me feel a bit uneasy when I engage with economically disadvantaged neighbors, both in my city and globally. Somehow I feel better about my relative wealth when I'm portrayed as helping others. How easy it can be for me to engage in mission-like activities but in actuality do less to advance Christ's mission in the world and more to lessen the feelings of guilt I experience when I see news reports of most of the world struggling for survival. Perhaps you've seen this response in your own church—or felt this way yourself.

If the primary beneficiaries of our most popular mission strategies are not economically disadvantaged communities but *us*—we who are among the wealthiest and most comfortable Christians in the world—what has happened to our understanding of God's mission? Would our ancestors in the faith who sent career missionaries to a hundred countries and built hospitals, schools, and churches around the world and in the United States *even recognize* the strategies we call "the mission of Jesus Christ" today? Why is this important contradiction in US congregational mission practice an "elephant in the room" that no one seems to be talking about?

Perhaps as a mission leader you've been aware of this trend in US culture in general—the shift toward self-centeredness. Experts describe it as an "epidemic of narcissism." According to national studies, traits related to narcissism are increasing across our society: more superficial values, greater materialism and self-centeredness, less concern for others or interest in helping the environment, and lower empathy.[14] Though the "millennial generation" is often blamed for possessing a sense of entitlement and self-centeredness, the cultural shift is not limited to young adults. One of the most frequently repeated concerns I have heard from congregational mission leaders is their uphill battle for the attention and participation of their church members in an age of distraction—Netflix, the Food Channel, and online shopping. Can it be that "selfie mission" is quietly replacing mission in the way of Jesus Christ, who "though he was rich, for [our] sakes he became poor, so that by his poverty [we] might become rich" (2 Cor 8:9)?

Because these subtle changes are cultural—not doctrinal—*selfie mission* can be seen in evangelical and mainline Protestant congregations and in Catholic parishes across the country—the cultural undertow is pulling us *all* off course. It can be seen in the impact of our mission work in communities around the world. In fact, it is such a part of church culture in this country that it has become *normalized*. Rather than understanding mission as our joining with what God is already doing in the world (the *missio Dei,* or mission of God), we often frame mission as all we do to respond to a world in need. Mission can become our task list—a set of problems to be solved, needs to be fulfilled, and checks to be written—rather than the spreading circle of relationships rooted in Jesus Christ.

At the heart of this crisis in our understanding of mission is the question, *Whose mission is it, anyway?* As long as "mission" is merely the sum of *our* benevolent activities, we will never enter into the kind of mutually healing relationships exemplified in Scripture: from Jesus, the teacher who calls his disciples "friends," to Paul's surprisingly mutual relationship with those to whom he was sent as an apostle. When *selfie mission* serves more our own interests and not the world that God so loves or when we begin to think of it as *our* mission rather than God's, *it* is antithetical to the self-giving mission of Jesus Christ that consistently points to God. I have talked with many congregational mission leaders who have long sensed these significant yet subtle changes in mission and have struggled to steer their church toward strategies that transform both mission partners and themselves. This tendency toward selfie mission is the first, more obvious element of the crisis

---

[14]Jean M. Twenge and W. Keith Campbell, *The Narcissistic Epidemic: Living in an Age of Entitlement* (New York: Simon & Schuster, 2010), 99.

confronting us as mission leaders. The second element of the crisis is deeper
and comes from our mission history. If selfie mission is the more visible tip
of the iceberg of the crisis confronting our congregations today, the more
substantive challenge is what lies below it.

FREEING MISSION FROM ITS COLONIAL PAST

The current crisis in our US congregations' understanding and practice of
mission requires a hard look at the historical underpinnings of the modern
European missionary movement. As we assess that beautiful and troubling
history, we see that our congregations' contemporary understanding of
mission is built on the theological and cultural assumptions of European
colonialism. Let me start with a full disclosure: having spent three decades
of my life either serving as a missionary in Africa and Latin America or
supervising hundreds of missionaries around the world, you won't find me
throwing stones at the missionary enterprise. I've visited too many missionary cemeteries in Korea and West Africa to not appreciate the lives offered up by our missionaries, from whatever nation or Christian tradition.

It is clear that the modern missionary movement significantly advanced
the spread of the gospel of Jesus Christ. The church was planted on five
continents and grew to the point that today there are more believers in the
former "mission fields" (Africa, Asia, and Latin America) than in the traditionally "churched" Global North (Europe and North America). The Bible
was translated into hundreds of languages that were preserved through
tireless literacy work over many years. Missionary-founded schools, teachers'
colleges, technical institutes, and universities educated millions. Clinics,
hospitals, and medical schools were built and made a massive contribution
to global health. Human rights, including women's rights, were advanced.
The positive impacts generated by the modern European missionary
movement are difficult to overstate.

But there is also an underside to our mission history. Beginning in the
late fifteenth century and continuing to the 1960s, European (and, later,
American) missionaries made the fateful decision to board colonial ships
and fully participate in the colonial enterprise—an economic and political
system that subjugated entire continents, stole land and natural resources,
exterminated millions of Native Americans, enslaved millions of Africans,

and imposed European languages and ways of thinking on nations around the world. By doing so, they unintentionally dealt a blow to Christ's mission that has had enduring, negative consequences for the church's engagement in God's mission. There were notable exceptions: for example, Dominican friar Bartolomé de las Casas in the West Indies, African American Episcopal missionary Alexander Crummell in Liberia, and the three Methodist missionaries who were imprisoned in Angola in the 1960s for their anticolonial work there provide examples of missionaries who challenged the colonial system.[15] But modern mission history is filled with examples of missionaries blessing the colonial enterprise with its Eurocentric assumptions of White racial superiority. These assumptions were constructed on what social scientists call "unilinear cultural evolution"—the widely accepted theory that there is only one road that leads from "savagery" to "barbarism" to "civilization," and that is *our way*.[16] For that reason, any reference to "culture" in modern American parlance can be misconstrued to refer to the ballet, opera, or symphony—powerful symbols of supposedly superior European cultures.

Having served in missions for almost three decades, I am intimately acquainted with the "missionary halo" that has been placed on my head by many American Christians due to our culture's profound respect for missionary sacrifice and dedication. In my experience, few people are more trusted or revered in many US churches than a missionary. Yet in some ways, the missionary halo can be so shiny that it blinds us from seeing that for more than four centuries, the church's mission provided the theological justification for brutal colonial policies: genocide, enslavement, and the exploitation of other nations' resources, generally along lines of racial difference.[17] The propagation of the Doctrine of Discovery by Pope Nicholas V in a series of papal bulls beginning in 1452 stated that, because our missionary activity was necessary to save those we perceived to be "savages," European Christians were justified "to invade, search out, capture, vanquish, and

[15]Sandra I. Sousa, "'Now We Don't Have Anything': Remembering Angola Through the Lens of American Missionaries," *Configurações: Revista de Ciências Socias* 17 (2016): 119-37, http://journals.openedition.org/configuracoes/3286.

[16]See "unilinear cultural evolution," Oxford Reference, www.oxfordreference.com/view/10.1093/oi/authority.20110803110706530.

[17]I am grateful to Pittsburgh Theological Seminary student Tony Igwe for this insight during a February 2020 class discussion.

subdue all Saracens [Muslims] and pagans whatsoever . . . and to reduce their persons to perpetual slavery and to convert them to [the European rulers'] use and profit."[18] This proclamation represents the church itself drawing what would become a nearly indelible line between "White" Europe and a colonized world of people of color. It is a troubling vision filled with assumptions of White superiority and violent ethnocentrism that remain with us to this day and that we will examine in more detail in chapter two— and one reason that our mission history prevents us from seeing African American, Asian American, Latinx missionaries or any missionaries of color. As a White/Euro-American, middle class, educated American, I seemed to "fit the bill" of this cultural expectation almost perfectly: people who looked like me were the ones portrayed as missionaries in Sunday School materials and story books, while missionaries of color—or even the thousands of new immigrants to the United States who work as missionaries in this country— have been invisibilized by the racist lens through which the church has looked at mission for more than five hundred years.

Before leaving this section, it should be noted that the enduring colonial assumptions of White superiority impact nearly all of us in the American church—Black, White, Brown, and multiracial—but in differentiated ways. These assumptions of "mission from a position of power" produced patterns of paternalism in mission: assumptions about the perceived superiority of the European missionary's beliefs and capacities over the person who welcomed the missionary—and powerful reactions against the assumptions. These patterns of paternalism can be present in any church that has been formed by these historical forces, whether you have been privileged or exploited by them. One purpose of this book is to describe the impact of these assumptions on the ways our congregations engage in mission and propose a more faithful way. Churches of all racial/ethnic groups are invited to appropriate the insights about our shared, racialized mission history and will need to apply the insights to their own context.

In summary, this is the twin challenge we face as Christ's church in a broken and hurting world: a self-glorifying, "selfie" mission that places us, rather than God, in the center of mission and the enduring assumptions of

---

[18]Nicholas V, "Romanus Pontifex," Papal Encyclicals Online, www.papalencyclicals.net/nichol05 /romanus-pontifex.htm, originally published January 8, 1455.

a colonial mission based on power. These, I will argue, are at the root of the crisis that our US congregations face. It's not our fault, of course—culture and history shape us in unseen ways. But God has given us minds and hearts so that we can critically reflect on the ideas presented in this book like the Bereans described in Acts 17:11, who "examined the scriptures every day to see whether these things were so." I have been brutally honest with you in these opening pages, and I'm grateful you are still reading. Because, despite the massive challenge before us, *you* are a vital part of why I feel so hopeful about our shared future.

REASONS FOR HOPE

In thirty years of learning from and working with US congregational mission leaders, I remain deeply hopeful about our current predicament for two reasons. In the first place, the last century has seen a significant shift in leadership: a century ago, mission leadership was the exclusive purview of "mission elites" who strategized, prioritized, and allocated resources. They were the faith mission agency leaders, Protestant denominational executives, the superiors of Catholic missionary orders, and the leaders of the ecumenical movements. Today, the landscape of mission has been "flattened": mission leadership has been decentralized to the point where every local congregation can serve as a mission agency, and its lay and clergy mission leaders have become the primary mission decision-makers. This change has triggered an explosion in the diversity of skills, perspectives, and insights available to God's mission: increasingly, Christians see themselves as "missionary disciples," to use the words of Pope Francis, "sent ones" who carry their missionary vocation to school, work, community life, and even the public sphere. While the networking and coordination of so many dispersed decision-makers remains a major challenge of this emerging missionscape, the massive potential energy of thousands of congregations in the Global South and Global North working to address the root causes of hunger, disease, conflict, injustice, and human suffering and to share their faith in Christ is deeply encouraging and is already manifesting itself in the congregational experiences that will be highlighted throughout the book.

A second reason for hope is the quality and commitment of so many US congregational mission leaders themselves. While some leaders have not given much thought to the crisis we face, many have expressed their deep misgivings about current congregational practices and are open to rethinking the foundations of how congregations engage in God's mission. In the vast majority of conversations I've had with congregational mission leaders, I often encounter an initial defensiveness as I inquire about current mission practices. But this is often followed by a Spirit-filled moment when the conversation shifts and the mission leader expresses a desire to take the congregation deeper into more faithful and effective mission practice. This vulnerability—a willingness to critically assess current practice and to invest time and work in improving the ways we engage in God's mission—fills me with great hope.

For these reasons, this book is designed for *congregational mission leaders*: the people who lead their congregation into mission. Nationally, the vast majority are lay leaders—often unpaid—although some larger congregations employ a professional missions pastor or director. Congregational mission leaders can also include youth and women's leaders who deeply desire to get their people out of the pews and into the community and the world, the members of a congregation's mission or outreach committee who make decisions about where to allocate funding, and pastors and priests in small and medium congregations who understand that it is the space of mission that transforms people and congregations. These are the leaders for whom this book is designed.

A WAY FORWARD

In response to the twin challenges, this book calls for a reformation in the way US congregations understand and engage in God's mission. In the Kasai region of south central Democratic Republic of Congo, the Luba and Lulua peoples understand that "three stones make home"; that is, three selected, carefully positioned foundational stones create the *diku*, the hearth or cooking fire, that is the center of family life in that region and in thousands of communities across the Majority World. The Congolese hearth provides food for the family and serves as the symbol of home: the family gathers, stories are retold, values are passed down to the next generation, visitors are welcomed, food is shared and hospitality practiced. In fact, in the Tshiluba language of the region, the term for "family" is *bena diku*, "the people of the hearth"—that is, the people who share food from the same cooking fire.

Different from my own Euro-American, individualistic cultural orientation,[19] many Luba and Lulua see a world in which family is the primary lens of identity: "I am because we are" as South African bishop Desmond Tutu famously summarized African ways of thinking, referring to it as "Ubuntu theology."[20] Congolese worldviews focus on "we": community, connection, and relationship. If Western culture is tempted to understand mission as a house we build, as evidenced in our emphasis on short-term mission construction projects, Luba and Lulua Christians might envision mission as "the gathering place"—the *diku*. Mission is the place where God's self-offering in Jesus Christ becomes the Eucharistic meal that gathers the people of every community to be fed and sent out to share both their resources and their brokenness in service to God's mission to the world.

With the power of connection that this circle of three stones embodies, we will argue that much of our struggle as mission leaders is caused by poorly placed foundational stones: a mission theology that is more narcissistic and colonial than it is shaped around Jesus' model of "mission from a position of weakness," an insufficient understanding of cultural differences and how to navigate them, and a lack of awareness regarding critically important learnings from development studies.

In section one of the book, we will lay out this critique and propose, identify, and describe the three foundational stones on which a more faithful and effective understanding of mission can be built. Acknowledging both the vestiges of an empire-serving model of the colonial era and the self-serving model currently in vogue in our culture, the book will challenge leaders to consider instead a *theology of companionship*—the "sharing-bread-with" relational nature of the Trinity that puts us on the road with Jesus and his followers in every time and place.

The second stone is especially needed in our world of increasing cultural diversity: instead of allowing our congregations to default to their own

---

[19]Which Dutch social researcher Geert Hofstede found to be the most individualistic culture in the world in an exhaustive series of studies in seventy countries.
[20]Desmond Tutu, *No Future Without Forgiveness* (New York: Doubleday, 1999), 31: "Ubuntu . . . speaks of the very essence of being human. [We] say . . . 'Hey, so-and-so has ubuntu.' Then you are generous, you are hospitable, you are friendly and caring and compassionate. You share what you have. It is to say, 'My humanity is caught up, is inextricably bound up, in yours.' We belong in a bundle of life. We say, 'A person is a person through other persons.'"

cultural assumptions (perhaps "time is money," "rugged individualism," or "it's all about the bottom line," etc.), we can offer our congregations the power of *cultural humility* required to understand our neighbors and to communicate God's love with greater respect and clarity. To Jesus of Nazareth, context mattered greatly. He went to great pains to translate the power, mystery, and tenderness of God's love into the everyday gestures and rituals and words so that the people of first-century Palestine could understand this love and share it with their neighbors. The second stone challenges us to grow in cultural humility so that God's mission becomes a space where the learnings generated by cultural difference open the door to a new rhythm of prayer and praise, a deeper understanding of Scripture, and the personal transformation and congregational renewal we seek.

The third stone invites us to incorporate into our mission work the principles of development studies that can reframe the mission encounter from "modernization" or "social improvement" to *empowering co-development.* Giving a hungry person a fish is a good thing. Charity and benevolence are faithful responses to people in need. But most mission leaders innately sense that there is more to Christ's mission than mere giving. Teaching others to fish, as the Chinese proverb reminds us, is a much more powerful gift than merely giving a fish because it empowers them to face their future. But a quick inventory of our churches' mission activities reveals the unsettling truth that much of our mission work is limited to charity. One mission leader confided to me that he believed his church was "addicted to fish giving": Is it possible that our congregations struggle to see mission as more than mere charity work simply because charity feels so good? While generous giving is biblical and good, giving too much or for too long can hurt a community as surely as overwatering a plant. Yet when congregational mission leaders engage in the difficult, but important, work of opening their people's eyes to powerful, sustainable co-development, communities living in poverty and injustice are allowed to "own" the change process itself, become agents of their own development, and grow into all God created them to be. The results can be earth-shaking!

A cooking fire requires three selected, well-placed stones to serve as a foundation for the meal God is preparing for us. If the stones are poorly selected or placed, our shared meal could end up on the ground! But with these three foundational stones in place, we are ready to gather with God's family around the hearth and share in God's mission: the world change movement built on relationship, respect, and mutual empowerment. This is the spreading circle of relationships in Jesus Christ that is the *missio Dei*.

In section two, we will apply the learnings of the three foundational stones to some of US congregations' most popular mission activities, according to our research: leading short-term mission trips, caring for children at risk, and reforming congregational mission programs from a committee that allocates funds to a movement. We will reflect on the strengths and weaknesses of these popular mission strategies and present ways that mission leaders can engage in missional jiu-jitsu, "flipping" the legitimate desires of our people to connect with others and to make a difference in the world toward more faithful and effective mission strategies. We will include illustrations of what mission companionship, cultural humility, and co-development look like in the mission practice of innovative leaders. Throughout the book, we will offer a number of tools for mission leaders, designed by coauthor Balajiedlang Khyllep, who works with Pittsburgh Theological Seminary's World Mission Initiative. Bala brings a big heart for God's mission and years of intercultural and church experiences from Northeast India, the plains of South Dakota, and western Pennsylvania. The toolkit includes a short-term mission orientation curriculum and daily reflection guide, a training exercise in planning development projects, and a guide to navigating crosscultural differences, among other tools.

WHY THIS BOOK?

This call for a reformation in congregational mission is, for me, the result of thirty-five years of work in intercultural mission. Working first with the Latinx community in downtown Washington, DC, then in Democratic Republic of Congo and Peru for fourteen years, and, later, as the director of Presbyterian World Mission for a decade gave me opportunities to hear how the Christians of the Global South (our global partners) understood God's call to mission—and how our US churches' efforts could help or harm them. Some US congregations engage in faithful and effective work, but my experience is that most of us could do much better. Many congregations, building on faulty foundations, engage in God's mission in ways that can be perceived as demeaning and paternalistic to local and global communities and that are counterproductive to the congregation's own stated goals. Yet they appear to be unaware of it, and the practices continue year after year—often in a new locale. "No one ever told us this!" is the most common response when they are enabled to hear from mission companions in a more direct and meaningful way.

But my research and experience suggest that many congregational mission leaders see the contradictions inherent in their congregation's mission program and long to free their congregations of an understanding and practice of mission that fails to make the difference in the world that God intends. My heart broke as I listened to the mission director of a large congregation speak of her role as more closely akin to that of a "social director on a cruise ship" than that of a leader of Christians committed to sharing faith and to addressing the root causes of poverty, human trafficking, and migration: "I spend more time entertaining mission enthusiasts than challenging or teaching them and am evaluated [by the congregation's senior leadership] by how much the members enjoy their mission activities, rather than how effective our mission work is."[21]

At its worst, mission can become a commodity to be bought and consumed. Robert Haynes's *Consuming Mission* shows how STM participants "spend" their time, money, service, and sacrifice to purchase personal growth experiences in a highly transactional way that results in the commodification of Christ's mission.[22] This central contradiction is perhaps the greatest challenge facing congregational mission leaders in this country today. How can mission leaders help their people swim against the tide of the colonial mission's legacy and current US culture to discover that *our* "life in Christ" is intrinsically bound together with that of our neighbors near and far? This book will attempt to both describe the problem and provide concrete tools for congregational mission leaders to lead with integrity and impact.

It is hard to take an honest look at how our mission practices impact other communities—and ourselves—but we stand arm in arm with Christian mission leaders from around the world, and many of them deeply desire to walk with us on this path. The mere possibility that different members of the

---

[21]Mission director (anonymous), personal interview, October 22, 2009.
[22]Robert Ellis Haynes, *Consuming Mission: Toward a Theology of Short-Term Mission and Pilgrimage* (Portland: Wipf & Stock, 2018).

body of Christ could work together across geographic, cultural, and theological differences to address the root causes of injustice, poverty, and broken relationships moves me to gather these stories of contrition, confession, and powerful transformation. These stories show what the church of Jesus Christ can be and do when we carefully reflect on the foundational stones we place around the fire God has kindled. As we gather together around the fire like Jesus' followers on the road to Emmaus, we will break bread as companions ("bread sharers") and our eyes will be opened to see Jesus among us—and in each one.

None of us can reach the destination by ourselves. The work of leadership in a time and place where there are no maps is exceedingly difficult. But you play a key role in how your congregation understands and engages in God's mission, and, by reflecting together, we can make the journey together as companions. Are you willing to take your place in the spreading circle of relationships rooted in Jesus Christ and lead your people on this life-giving journey?

FOR REFLECTION

1. Have you seen examples of the kind of "selfie" or colonial mission that we suggest creates the "crisis in mission" facing US congregations today?

2. The mission of the church used to be one of the highest priorities of Christian churches across the country—evangelical, Catholic, and mainline Protestant. How have you seen your congregation's engagement in mission change over the past years? What reasons would you give for this change?

3. Can you recall a mission experience that left you wondering who the primary "beneficiary" was?

4. As you consider your own congregation and your leadership role, what are the opportunities you have to shape the ways your congregation understands and engages in mission? Teaching? One-on-one conversations? Mission funding–allocation conversations? Accompanying your church members into missional experiences and reflecting on those experiences?

TWO

UNCHECKED BAGGAGE

History shapes mission, whether the missionary—and
those who are evangelized—are aware of it or not.

JOSÉ MÍGUEZ BONINO[1]

WHOSE MISSION?

A FEW MONTHS AFTER I arrived in Congo as a twenty-three-year-old mission volunteer, a delegation from a local congregation near the city of Kananga invited me to a meeting of their development committee. My excitement grew along with my sense of the role I might play—finally, *someone* recognized me as a potentially valuable contributor! *This is what I came for,* I thought. As I sat with the committee late one afternoon, I could hardly keep still—I so badly wanted to share with them my ideas. Although French was a first language for none of us, looking back on those days, the bigger communication barrier was not the language but the underlying culture that shaped the ways we communicated. My American ear was accustomed to "plain speak," the direct discourse our culture is known for: when I disagreed, I said so clearly, sometimes interrupting a committee member to get my point across, no matter their age. My Congolese counterparts, to the contrary, seemed to me to speak in a circular fashion, using an image, proverb, or story from time to time to get their point across. Needless to say, most of their points were lost on me!

---

[1]José Míguez Bonino, "How Does United States Presence Help, Hinder or Compromise Christian Mission in Latin America?," *Review and Expositor* 74, no. 2 (1977): 173.

But as I listened, I grew incredulous: what they seemed to be saying was they wanted their church to lead the village in the clearing of a field covered with rocks and two trees and the building of the goalposts so that their youth could host a soccer match. Their proposal took me completely by surprise. I had read the health statistics and knew that Congo—and our region in particular—suffered from extremely high infant mortality (the percentage of children who die before their second birthday), and I thought they would want to do something to clean up their community's water source. Even my untrained eyes could tell the water was contaminated and probably responsible for the village's poor health. As I look back on that conversation, I see that I didn't have the knowledge of Congolese ways of communicating to be able to appropriately express my disagreement, so I just disagreed—clearly and passionately! I was frustrated that we were wasting time with a mere soccer field when we could have been preventing children from dying in the village! I tried to convince the committee members to support the water project, but to no avail. Theirs *was* the only village in the area that didn't have a soccer field, and I wondered if pride had trumped reason.

But it was clear the group had made their decision—the enthusiasm was palpable as they defined the tasks, divided up responsibilities, and made plans for a community workday the following Saturday. That evening, I struggled with what to do: *Could I support this effort in good conscience?* According to my way of thinking, it clearly ignored the village's primary need: reducing infant mortality. After praying about the challenge, I decided to go along with the group. The following Saturday, the village turned out en masse as the church leaders organized the village into work groups: the women of the church distributed drinking water and prepared a *bidia* (cassava and corn meal porridge) and goat meat feast that would be remembered for years, the children cleared the field of hundreds of rocks and stones, and the men felled and uprooted two trees—all to prepare a soccer field for what I discovered was the area soccer championship scheduled for the very next day! Evidently, the village had never before won the area championship.

On Sunday afternoon, as the visiting teams—and more fans than I could have imagined—assembled around the new soccer field, I looked around and realized the only thing missing was our village's soccer team. When the young men of the team arrived and saw the now-impressive field and the huge "home" crowd, they were overcome with joy and pride. The home team played with what people said was an unprecedented level of enthusiasm and crushed the visiting team 4-0. Frankly, the visiting team never had a chance! The celebration lasted into the night. As I left to catch a ride back to Kananga, a village elder shook my hand and smiled: "Let's talk again next week. We want to talk with you about our water source."

That night back in my apartment, I puzzled over the turn of events. Two elements stood out with painful clarity: the village elders' capacity to know what their own community needed most and my own assumptions about what I knew. The elders had seen clearly what was invisible to me: the primary need for the community to believe in itself since they would be unable to organize themselves around the need for clean water (or anything else) if they couldn't imagine their community working together to enact change. Back in the United States, highly paid strategic planning consultants coach their Fortune 500 clients to begin the complex process of organizational change with a few "quick wins"—smaller outcomes that validate the direction of the change process and prepare the team for the longer struggle ahead.[2] The village leadership seemed to have mastered this technique.

More troubling for me was the second element: in my inflated sense of self-importance, *I had assumed that I knew best*. I turned this observation over and over in my mind. What a curious assumption—*that a newcomer like me would know more than the community leaders about what the community needed*. Where did that come from? Though my intentions were good, I knew the basic assumption was completely illogical: I was young and inexperienced, had only basic French, was completely ignorant of the complexity and nuance of the local culture, and had never planned or directed a project like this even in my own context—much less a foreign cultural context. Yet I was convinced that my approach was superior! *What a strange assumption*, I thought. I would ponder this odd contradiction in my heart for some time before I would begin to see that there were deep historical reasons for my erroneous perception of my own personal and cultural superiority and for my need to guide the village church's process of development.

---

[2]Margaret Reynolds, "3 Reasons Strategic Leaders Use Quick Wins to Drive Long-Term Performance," Vistage Research Center, November 5, 2013, www.vistage.com/research-center/business -leadership/3-reasons-strategic-leaders-use-quick-wins-to-drive-long-term-performance/.

It was as if I were carrying around a piece of unchecked baggage—a heavy suitcase filled with the values and assumptions of previous generations that I'd never taken the time to unpack, examine, and decide to keep or discard. The precious gift of this discovery was an opening window on the God who had been in Congo long before I or any other foreign missionary got there, who was working through local leaders and the local culture to bring blessing to people with me or without me, who had called me to walk with God and the Congolese to bring them—and me—into deeper discipleship and the abundant life promised by Jesus Christ (Jn 10:10).

This contradiction drew my attention to the theology that undergirded my engagement in mission—whose mission was it, anyway? My head knew it was God's mission from start to finish. But my heart kept whispering that it was *my* mission—that God needed me "to be God's hands and feet" to save the world that God so loves. The bottom line, insisted my heart: *if I don't do this, it won't get done.* That painful, but important, night of prayerful reflection pushed me to begin to unpack some of the assumptions I was making about mission. To understand God's mission and my part in it, I needed first to study up on how that mission had developed over time. What I discovered shocked me and required me to critically examine many assumptions I was making about God's mission and people. The events of history weren't my fault, certainly. But I began to see that my deepest frustrations and failures in both local and global mission were often directly related to the assumptions that were shaped by the curiously close relationship between the European movement to colonize much of the Global South from the fifteenth to twentieth centuries, on the one hand, and the development of the modern missionary movement, on the other. Let's look historically at how our missionary ancestors got on the wrong boat in their well-intentioned but fundamentally flawed efforts to join in God's mission—and how they were used for God's glory and the blessing of the world anyway!

THREE ERAS OF CHRISTIAN MISSION

As we reflect on how the good news of Jesus Christ has spread across national and linguistic barriers over the past two thousand years, it may be helpful to divide the growth of the movement initiated by Jesus himself into three eras: the early church (from the first chapter of Acts of the Apostles to roughly 400 CE), the imperial church (from the fifth through the fifteenth centuries), and the colonial period (from the fifteenth to the twentieth centuries).[3] Our read of history will show us why we desperately need a reassessment of our theology of mission today.

The early church: Growth through persecution and migration. In the Gospels, Jesus of Nazareth shaped his revolutionary message around ancient Jewish culture and traditions, proclaiming what God desires of humankind: selfless service, support and advocacy for the poor and oppressed, a life of sacrificial love, and renewed human relationships where husbands loved their wives more than they loved themselves and parents respected their children. Jesus made such an impact on the lives of the people he encountered that he initiated a spreading circle of loving human relationships that grew outward from Jerusalem after Pentecost.

For almost three centuries after Christ's death and resurrection, the underground Christian church generally responded to Roman state persecution with growth,[4] and the resulting outward migrations pushed the people whose lives had been transformed by Jesus into new ethnic and linguistic communities. The apostles and earliest Christians were scattered out from Palestine throughout the Roman Empire and beyond. Early Christian legend states that the apostles traveled to such distant lands as Egypt (Mark), India (Thomas), Ethiopia (Matthew), and Persia (Simon the Zealot). While today we tend to think of missionaries as professionals who travel internationally to do specific tasks (Bible translation, education, health, evangelism, etc.), mission historian Jehu Hanciles points out that the primary missionaries of those early centuries were migrants and refugees who carried their faith in Jesus Christ with them, understood their primary identity to be as a missionary, and ministered out of the weakness of their social location as foreigners, newcomers, and cultural outsiders yet turned the world "upside down" (Acts 17:6).[5] This posture of the missionary from a position of

---

[3]Dale Irwin and Scott Sunquist's *History of the World Christian Movement* (Maryknoll, NY: Orbis, 2001) follows the development of the Christian movement from a small band of followers of Jesus of Nazareth to the development of world Christianity.

[4]Around 195 CE, the church father Tertullian made his famous observation of this period: "The blood of the martyrs is the seed of the Church" (*Apologeticus*, chapter 50).

[5]Jehu Hanciles, *Beyond Christendom: Globalization, African Migration and the Transformation of the West* (Maryknoll, NY: Orbis, 2009). The brilliance of Hanciles's book lies not in its recognition of the protagonism of refugees and migrants in the spreading of the gospel in early church

weakness and vulnerability—the missionary as servant—is profoundly biblical and mirrors Jesus' paradigm against which we must evaluate all subsequent mission activity, including our current mission practice.

In that first era, the missionaries were in general less powerful than the people with whom they shared the good news of Jesus Christ: they were refugees and cultural outsiders, often poor, and lived on the underside of empire. They spoke the local language with a foreign accent and were forced to rely on local friends to understand the local culture. They could not rely on their own power or status but had to look to God as their source of strength. The daily threat of persecution for following a subversive religion honed their sense of call and identity as messengers of Jesus Christ. Of course, the dynamic of this early period reflected the content and tone of the New Testament writings, which were recorded during this era: the upside-down nature of the realm of God where "the last shall be first," a God who "has filled the hungry with good things and sent away the rich empty-handed," where it seems impossible for the wealthy to enter the kingdom of God, and where women were the first witnesses to the resurrection. A repeated theme of the New Testament writings is the believers' call to rejoice in suffering in the name of Christ (Mt 5:10-12; Rom 8:18-25; Heb 11:1-12:3; Jas 1:2-4; 1 Pet 4:12-19; and much of the book of Revelation).

The imperial era: The imperial church and early Christendom. In the early fourth century CE, after Roman emperor Constantine's conversion to Christianity and Emperor Theodosius's subsequent declaration of Christianity as the official religion of the empire, the patterns of the growth of the Christian movement changed in significant ways. Beginning in the late fourth century, as the new official religion of the realm, Christianity followed the military extension of the empire, reaching into England and Ireland, Germany, across North Africa, into Eastern Europe and the Middle East.[6] As kings, chiefs, and rulers accepted the faith of their Roman conquerors, that faith was imposed on their subjects and Christianity would continue as the state religion of the nations that grew up out of the former Roman Empire. The history is much more nuanced than this: to be sure,

---

history but in his documentation of this reality throughout the history of the church, including the present age.

[6]Kenneth Scott Latourette, *A History of Christianity* (New York: Harper & Row, 1953), 1:381-407.

many parents raised up their children in the way of Jesus and many Roman Catholic monasteries, convents, and missionary orders preserved and extended Christianity into new communities through friendship and service. But by and large, the transmission of Christian faith followed the lines of political domination, moving from ruler to subject, from the powerful to the powerless, from top to bottom.

It is important to note the significant change in the dynamic of the transmission of Christian faith. If, in the era of the early church, faith was transmitted "up" the social ladder from the poor who first embraced it to the rich and from the people to their rulers, in the era of the imperial church, faith was transmitted "down," imposed by the rulers of Christendom on their subjects, who were then instructed in the faith by official priests and chaplains. In this second era, many missionaries were perceived as "agents of the empire" and drawn into a powerful political system that bestowed on them political power in the eyes of those they went to serve. Many were "professionals," employed by the empire to evangelize and catechize the masses in return for territories and resources assigned to their religious orders. The missionaries' social location and their ministry from a position of relative power changed the texture of Christian mission in an era of mass "conversions" and rulers' shifting politico-religious alliances. This pronounced shift toward *mission from a position of power*—when combined with the Europeans' difficulty in understanding hundreds of ethnic groups who thought, spoke, worshiped, and lived in ways culturally different from theirs—would open the door to a weakening of missionary solidarity with the people they were sent to serve. But this significant change in direction was not over yet. We now turn our attention to that period which has done so much to complicate Christians' efforts to love their neighbor across cultural difference—and our understanding and practice of Christian mission—up to the present day.

The modern era: European colonialism and the wrong ship. European Christendom's responses to early encounters with "foreign" peoples in Africa, the "New World," Asia, and the Pacific would mark the third period of Christian mission: the era of European colonialism.

Colonialism is defined as Europe's project of domination of other countries for its own economic gain that developed between the fifteenth and twentieth centuries. According to historian Philip Hoffman, in 1800 Europe

controlled 35 percent of the world's territory; by 1914, it controlled 84 percent.[7] To understand the violence, theft, genocide, and pain the colonial
movement generated in much of the world, we need to acknowledge that,

> the fundamental decisions affecting the lives of the colonized people are made
> and implemented by the colonial rulers in pursuit of interests that are often
> defined in a distant metropolis. Rejecting cultural compromises with the
> colonized population, the colonizers are convinced of their own superiority
> and their ordained mandate to rule.[8]

Beginning in 1517, Portuguese ships under Henry the Navigator ventured
south and east along the coast of West Africa and soon reached the mouth
of the Congo River, the Cape of Good Hope, and eventually India and Japan
in an insatiable quest for new sources of raw materials and markets for Portuguese goods. As the highly profitable trade grew, other European nations
eagerly followed suit: the Spanish, English, Dutch, and French each sought
their own cut of the lucrative trade routes. New technologies in navigation
and sailing opened the way for the "discovery" (at least from the European
point of view) of new lands and peoples; the military advantage gained by
their possession of gunpowder, firearms, and cannons quickly transformed
the initial encounters into violent ones.[9] As mentioned in chapter one, the
fifteenth-century Doctrine of Discovery provided theological justification
for European colonial armies to claim sovereignty over distant lands and
force their peoples to produce the precious metals, crops, and raw materials
needed for Europe's burgeoning economies.

While European nations colonized people groups on six continents,
the impact of this military, economic, political, and cultural violence on the
Americas—as one example—illustrates some of the sinister elements of
the period. Beginning in the late fifteenth century, the disease, violence, forced
servitude, and massive cultural dislocation brought by the early *conquistadores*

---

[7]Philip T. Hoffman, *Why Did Europe Conquer the World?* (Princeton, NJ: Princeton University Press, 2015), 2-3.

[8]Jurgen Osterhammel, *Colonialism: A Theoretical Overview*, trans. Shelley Frisch (Princeton, NJ: Markus Wiener Publishers, 2005), 15.

[9]It is impossible to read the conquistadores' chronicles of Moctezuma's initial encounter with Hernán Cortés near Mexico City and Atahualpa's with Francisco Pizarro in Cajamarca, Peru—both bathed in religious language and symbolism—without a profound sense of regret at this beginning of an intense period of history virtually unparalleled for the scope of human suffering, loss of life, and cultural upheaval.

to the indigenous peoples of the New World began a demographic implosion that was arguably unprecedented in world history in its scope and savagery.[10] Historians estimate that between 25 and 95 percent of the estimated population of 57 million indigenous people in the Americas were killed or died of disease in the first decades of Spanish and Portuguese colonialism.[11] These massive figures may keep us from seeing how the violence and profound dislocation were experienced by the exploited people themselves. I had a chance to learn about the impact of this reign of terror on one indigenous community in Peru when I worked as a missionary there.

The Spanish forced tens of thousands of indigenous men to work in the silver mines of Potosí (in today's Bolivia) in the *mita*,[12] the policy that legalized forced labor in the New World and made possible the extraction and theft of some 22,695 metric tons of silver between 1545 and 1823,[13] worth more than $12.5 billion at today's silver prices.[14] The rich silver deposits of Mexico, Peru, and Bolivia could not be economically exploited without access to abundant mercury (as part of a simple—and highly dangerous— chemical process to refine silver ore into more purified silver). Once mercury was discovered near the city of Huancavelica, Peru, tens of thousands of indigenous men were rounded up and sent to Santa Barbara and forced to work the mine, often until they died.

I spent several months in 2005 living in the community of Santa Barbara in the central Andes Mountains of Huancavelica, Peru, and the people of Santa Barbara still talk of the immense human suffering inflicted on their

---

[10]Multiplying the massive impact of the physical devastation of the *Conquista* was the cultural violence: the brutal suppression of native languages and cultural understandings, the violent eradication of indigenous religious beliefs and practices, and even the destruction of systems of cultural understanding that could have helped the indigenous populations "make sense" of the upheaval of their world.

[11]Gustavo Gutierrez, *Las Casas: In Search of the Poor of Jesus Christ*, trans. Robert R. Barr (Eugene, OR: Wipf & Stock, 2003), 461-66.

[12]The Spanish colonial authorities turned the Incan Empire's *mita*, or system of collective labor where able-bodied community members contributed their labor to projects for the common good, into an exploitive system of forced labor that subsidized Spanish mining through the provision of cheap labor.

[13]Kris Lane, "Potosi Mines," Latin American History, Oxford Research Libraries, https://oxfordre .com/latinamericanhistory/view/10.1093/acrefore/9780199366439.001.0001/acrefore -9780199366439-e-2.

[14]James Anderson, "How Much Is a Ton of Silver Worth?," SD Bullion, August 15, 2019, https:// sdbullion.com/blog/how-much-is-a-ton-of-silver-worth-weigh.

ancestors in "la mina de la muerte" (the mine of death). Historian Guillermo Lohmann Villena notes that in the first decades of mercury extraction, more than seven thousand individuals were killed by accidents, sickness, overwork, or mercury poisoning.[15] A plaque in the Santa Barbara mine memorializes one miner's testimony to the surreal human suffering: "Santa Barbara, mine of death. In your bowels the breath of life was extinguished each day and we never knew if we were still breathing or merely living in an interminable nightmare."

Beyond the theft of valuable minerals, the death of so many indigenous workers caused a severe labor shortage in the mines and plantations that were expected to generate such a lucrative profit for the colonial powers. This period of rapid economic expansion saw the beginnings of the transatlantic triangular trade, formed around the transportation of sugar, tobacco, and cotton from the Americas to Europe; rum, textiles, and guns from Europe to Africa; and the forcible capture and enslavement of an estimated 12.5 million Africans to fill Europeans' need for cheap labor in the Americas.[16] The "triangular trade" became a global vortex that wreaked havoc in communities across Africa and the New World: lands and resources were stolen, millions of human beings were enslaved, entire civilizations were destroyed. For much of the Majority World today, this is the "bad news" of the gospel brought to them by the European colonial era.

DUE DILIGENCE

From European perspectives, colonialism *developed* their colonies.[17] But if history is more than the victor's telling of the tale, we also need to listen to the voices of those exploited by this transnational movement. While mines were dug; plantations hacked out of the bush; and cities, roads, and ports built, the overarching logic of the colonial system was extractive and exploitative: Europeans sought ways to extract valuable natural resources

---

[15]Guillermo Lohmann Villena, *Las minas de Huancavelica en los siglos XVI y XVII* (Lima: Pontificia Universidad Católica del Perú, 1999), 87.

[16]"Trans-Atlantic Slave Trade—Estimates," Slave Voyages, https://slavevoyages.org/assessment /estimates.

[17]But as we will see in chapter three, the verb *develop*, in the sense of human and community development, cannot take a direct object: no one can "develop" someone else. A community develops itself through its participation in specific processes, using needed inputs available to it.

from the colonies as cheaply as possible without the free or informed consent of local populations.

These political and military actions would be considered theft by any legal system. To justify the subjugation of distant populations and the exploitation of their resources, a new, dangerously seductive narrative began weaving together implicit assumptions of White racial superiority with the presumed duty of the White race to "civilize" and "Christianize" the darker-skinned peoples of the world and to "develop" them commercially. Rudyard Kipling's poem "The White Man's Burden" (1899) illustrates the strange and toxic mixture of White superiority and benevolence required to justify the bald theft of natural resources from the colonized nations and the murder of millions:

> Take up the White Man's burden—
> Send forth the best ye breed—
> Go, bind your sons to exile
> To serve your captives' need;
> To wait, in heavy harness,
> On fluttered folk and wild—
> Your new-caught sullen peoples,
> Half devil and half child.[18]

This use of the Christian religion to theologically justify notions of cultural and racial superiority added an insidious element of cultural violence that would have a devastating and enduring impact on people across the Global South. Nigerian writer Chinua Achebe spoke eloquently to the cultural damage wrought by the imposition of the colonial masters' religion on African cultures in his award-winning novel *Things Fall Apart*:

> The white man is very clever. He came quietly and peaceably with his religion. We were amused at his foolishness and allowed him to stay. Now he has won our brothers, and our clan can no longer act like one. He has put a knife on the things that held us together and we have fallen apart.[19]

---

[18]Rudyard Kipling, "The White Man's Burden" (1899), The American Yawp Reader, www .americanyawp.com/reader/19-american-empire/rudyard-kipling-the-white-mans-burden-1899/.
[19]Chinua Achebe, *Things Fall Apart* (London: Wm. Heinneman, 1958), 124-25.

Indeed, some institutions, social systems, and cultural traditions in Africa, Latin America, the Middle East, and Asia have "fallen apart" as a direct result of colonialism. Colonialism is clearly not the sole reason for poverty and injustice in the Global South—there is a long list of reasons including national leadership, corruption, ethnic conflict, natural disasters, and more— but as we begin to see the enduring impact of the colonial structures, massive loss of natural resources, terms of trade, imposed political structures, and the paternalistic assumptions that undergird them, we begin to understand that a significant and enduring reason for the low quality of life indicators (life expectancy, infant mortality, access to clean water, etc.) in much of today's Global South is the colonial system.

As we reflect on this third era of mission history, we must be careful when we apply today's ethical standards to yesterday's logics and actions:

> Our belief in the integrity and value of all human cultures is quite a recent development. From the early 20th century, anthropologists have taught us to try to understand all societies in their own terms. Before then, Europeans believed that all peoples could be placed somewhere along a single spectrum from primitive superstition to modern civilisation and rational ways of thinking. Such ideas profoundly influenced Christian missionaries, who frequently assumed that part of their job was to move people along the spectrum so that they would become civilised, "just like us."[20]

Still, the vehement protests of the iconic Dominican friar Bartolomé de las Casas and others against the Spanish colonial abuses suggest that even in the late fifteenth century there were those who critically examined the church's violent mission through the lens of Scripture and found it woefully lacking. But the Dominicans' reading of Scripture was perhaps not so extraordinary: How many other missionaries of that era saw the horrendous reality as European colonialism crushed the indigenous people of the Americas but allowed the benefits of their position as protégés of the colonial regime—their privilege—to silence them? We (and the missionaries of every generation) must constantly be aware of our position in the economic and political systems of our day and ask: *Is our privilege blinding us from seeing those whom the system exploits as God sees them?*

---

[20]Brian Stanley, "Spreading the Word: The Missionary Expansion of Christianity," British Library, www.bl.uk/sacred-texts/articles/spreading-the-word-the-missionary-expansion-of-christianity.

Anticolonial sentiments have been expressed in forums as diverse as the United Nations General Assembly, the media, and academia (postcolonialism is a prevalent theme in school textbooks and popular literature across the world). From James Michener's *Hawaii* to Barbara Kingsolver's *The Poisonwood Bible*, from Teju Cole's "White Savior-Industrial Complex"[21] to the immensely popular and biting "White Savior Barbie" parody on Instagram and Twitter,[22] so much has been written in the United States over the last fifty years about the negative impacts of colonial mission that many American Christians have closed their ears to what feels like a single-minded critique of Christian faith. While our churches have clung to the heroic narrative—in some ways accurate—of iconic US and European missionaries pouring out their lives in exemplary self-sacrifice, a surprising number of US Christians, unchurched Americans, and many people in other countries have a much more nuanced view of missionaries. In the traditional European view, Western missionaries are seen as selfless individuals who loved the people, learned local languages, and built schools and clinics, but may have been used by a system that exploited the very people they went to serve. The more critical view is that missionaries often acted as ethnocentric Westerners who imposed their own values on subjugated peoples around the world in ways that destroyed local cultures.

After thirty years of missionary service, I find these historical facts to be profoundly disturbing and quite painful. Perhaps you do as well. Because these facts draw a direct line between the White supremacy so imbedded within the colonial mindset and my own misguided assumptions about the Congolese village's soccer field. Yet the simple acknowledgment of their reality makes available to us one of the most powerful of Christian practices: confession. By naming, admitting, and repenting from our ancestors' and our complicity in the patterns of racial assumptions, behaviors, and ways of speaking that constitute systemic racism, we are freed from the burden of assuming "we are better than" or that "we can develop our neighbor." As we reflect on ways to engage in God's mission in the twenty-first century, we will have to guard against our own defense mechanisms that seek to shut

---

[21]Teju Cole, "The White-Savior Industrial Complex," *The Atlantic*, March 21, 2012, www.theatlantic.com/international/archive/2012/03/the-white-savior-industrial-complex/254843/.
[22]Damian Zane, "Barbie Challenges the 'White Saviour Complex,'" BBC News, May 1, 2016, www.bbc.com/news/world-africa-36132482.

down the source of this bad news (if you feel like throwing this book out the window, don't do it!). To Whites like me, it can feel as if our history, our way of life, our "place at the table" is threatened as never before. But the God who guarantees us a place at the table is with us as we strip away the storied traditions of our often mythical mission history and look more intently at mission in the way of Jesus Christ.

To see Christ's mission clearly, we will have to be very aware of the complex minefield that lies before us—the profoundly negative consequences of the decision by European missionaries to board colonial schooners to reach the distant shores they would evangelize. It was a costly decision with long-lasting consequences that requires of us deep attentiveness: confession in the face of White superiority and the systemic racism that enables it, and a valuing of Jesus' missional postures of humility, listening, respect, and empowerment. American novelist Teju Cole speaks for many mission critics when he challenges US Christians who seek to make a difference in the world: "If we are going to interfere in the lives of others, a little due diligence is a minimum requirement."[23]

MISSION AND THE ROOTS OF RACISM

Both literally and figuratively, we could say that the early European missionaries boarded the wrong ship: by aligning themselves with a racist colonial system, they extended their mission into previously unreached destinations, to be sure, but also provoked widespread and lasting negative reactions among Muslims ("the Saracens" in the language of the Doctrine of Discovery), Hindus, Buddhists, African primal religionists, and indigenous peoples around the world. Though it is uncomfortable, we need to pause and reflect on the massive moral injury done by the colonial movement and the church's complicity with it. Among the manifold legacies created by this unholy alliance between the colonial rulers and the church that US Christians must deal with today are (1) a widespread distrust of American mission efforts and motivations, whatever the race/ethnicity of the missionary and (2) our own unexamined assumptions of perceived cultural and racial superiority as we engage with others in God's mission.

---

[23]Teju Cole, "The White Savior Industrial Complex," *The Atlantic*, March 21, 2012, www.theatlantic.com/international/archive/2012/03/the-white-savior-industrial-complex/254843/.

As I look back to that early intercultural encounter with the Congolese village church and their soccer field project, I see now that my own implicit, unexamined assumptions—the mental "map" that I unwittingly carried into every conversation and encounter with Congolese neighbors in those years—were powerfully shaped by assumptions of White racial superiority that linger on from the colonial period. I assumed my culture had provided me with the "right answers" to almost any question the Congolese could ask—didn't my country's stronger economy, more powerful military, more "exceptional" history, more "developed" culture, more "civilized" ways justify this perspective? Even as I write these words, it causes me pain to see the blind pride, the misguided sense of exceptionalism, and, yes, the racism that undergirds these assumptions—*my* assumptions. Perhaps you have sensed these assumptions at play deep within your heart as you interact with local and global mission partners—assumptions that guide your words and actions in unintended ways. This is, I believe, an important question for all of us formed in American society, no matter what our race or ethnicity. As antiracism educator Dr. David Campt notes, "The same invisible cultural forces that shape racist behaviors in the majority population also influence the ways Black and Brown brothers and sisters respond to these behaviors: we all have the virus."[24]

It is as if we were each paddling across a river in a canoe. All of us are impacted by the force and direction of the current: some are unaware of the current and are carried downstream, never reaching the other side; others note the river's power and direct their canoe strategically across the current in a way that allows them to get to the other side. Whether we are the descendants of the exploiters or the exploited or a mixture of both, all of us formed by this shared mission history must stop and examine the unchecked baggage we carry so that we don't perpetuate the colonial "mission from strength" model.

A powerful gift that comes to us as we participate in God's mission is being drawn into intercultural relationships where we are invited to rethink our "unchecked baggage." Deep companionship with local and global mission partners teaches us how to think critically about the mental map

---

[24]David Campt, presented at Pittsburgh Theological Seminary's McClure Lectures, October 28, 2020.

with which we grew up and to work to "decolonize" our participation in God's mission: In what ways do my words and actions reveal the underlying assumption that I know what's best for a given situation? Of course, it's not my fault that the cultural map I inherited was so flawed. But I have talked with dozens of congregational mission leaders who have found it has been interactions with their mission companions over the years that helped open their eyes to see the incompatibility of the gospel of Jesus Christ and the racialized assumptions of superiority we encounter in our society.

THE OTHER SIDE OF THE LEDGER: COLONIAL MISSION'S POSITIVE IMPACTS

There is another side to this perspective, and it's important to note it. On the positive side, the modern missionary movement shared good news of God's love with people in countries and cultures literally around the world. The Bible was translated into hundreds of languages, and significant numbers of people became literate not just in the colonial languages but their own mother tongues. Schools, universities, clinics, and hospitals were built and millions of people were educated and healed. Doctors, nurses, teachers, and administrators were trained. The church was planted and grew in new cultural contexts, and thousands of leaders were formed in Bible schools, catechist schools, pastoral institutes, and seminaries. The role of women, children, and ethnic minorities was vastly enhanced in many countries,[25] and human rights were advanced.[26] Medical care for the blind, lame, infirm, hearing impaired, and lepers was provided, often free of charge. Important innovations in tropical medicine were made by Christian missionary doctors who saved the lives of millions of people.

Renowned Yale mission historian Lamin Sanneh vigorously defended the missionary movement against its anticolonial critics in his book *Translating the Message: The Missionary Impact on Culture*, noting that the act of translating the Christian Scriptures into the vernacular languages of dozens of colonized countries constituted a significant contribution toward cultural

---

[25]Western missions pioneered education for women in countries like Syria and Lebanon, India, Korea, and Japan.

[26]William Reyburn provides an articulate defense of Christianity as a historically unique promoter of universal human rights. Some other historians and social scientists would argue that the trend toward the universalization of Western understandings of human rights that Christianity injected into non-Western societies is yet another enduring legacy of the colonial era.

preservation and renewal.[27] In addition to preserving these language and cultural groups, the gospel message injected into the stratified colonial context a revolutionary message of hope built on the radical notion of the equality of colonizer and colonized. Historically, the Christian worldview has provided to hundreds of millions of individuals a way of understanding the world based on an all-powerful God who deeply identifies with their hardships, disappointments, and pain; forgives them their wrongdoings; and joins them to a large and growing family—the family of Jesus Christ. This transnational movement, which claims a higher allegiance than kinship, nationality, or race, stretches around the world and includes colonial masters and subjects, slave owners and slaves, kings and serfs. It is this utterly illogical, counterintuitive, countercultural yet essential tenet of the Christian message that would set the stage for Christian participation in justice movements including the abolitionist movement, the civil rights movement, workers' rights, women's rights, environmental justice, the anti-apartheid struggle in South Africa, and churches' work for justice for Palestinians— wherever Christians lived out their calling to solidarity with the "other." This is the undeniable and profoundly disruptive dimension of Christian faith that prevents it from merely reinforcing the societal status quo or from functioning as "the opiate of the people."[28]

This solidarity was directed not merely toward persecuted Christian brothers and sisters but to groups of poor and oppressed people because of their shared humanity. These examples are richly documented in missionary biographies from Spanish Dominican priest Bartolomé de las Casas's stand against the Spanish genocide of the New World's indigenous peoples to African American missionary Rev. William Sheppard's courageous defense of Congolese workers against the rubber barons' exploitation under Belgian King Leopold in the late nineteenth century. The enduring, positive impacts of the missionary movement during the colonial missionary era were multiple and well documented.

In addition, it is also important to note that the positive impacts of God's mission have not flowed in only one direction, as the colonial notion of

---

[27]The work of the United Bible Society and its national counterparts, Wycliffe Bible Translators (known as the Summer Institute of Linguistics in many countries), and other organizations has continued this key missionary strategy over the years.

[28]Christian Smith's *Disruptive Religion: The Force of Faith in Social Movement Activism* (New York: Routledge, 1996) provides a helpful theoretical framework for this dimension of religion in general.

"the White Man's Burden" supposed. Paralleling the growth of the church in the Acts of the Apostles, the planting of the church in diverse cultural contexts around the world forced colonial missionaries and national believers to rethink Christian faith in new contexts and express it through new languages as they discovered that faithful responses to issues both personal and public would necessarily be different in Rome and Accra, in Canterbury and Mumbai, or in Edinburgh and Kinshasa—wherever Christians reflected on Scripture through a different cultural lens. Each time believers from different cultural backgrounds brought their perspectives on Scripture into the growing circle of the Christian church, new, rich sources of insight were added to the church's understanding of Christian faith.

A second element of the "reverse impact" of the missionary movement on US domestic society is carefully documented in David Hollinger's *Protestants Abroad: How Missionaries Tried to Change the World but Changed America*. In it, he shows how US Protestant missionary families of the early twentieth century were so transformed by their long-term mission experience—"embedded" as they were in local communities—that they returned home and made a profound impact on US society: they advanced human rights, multiculturalism, and the fight against racism with a degree of influence and impact far out of proportion to their numbers. Protestant missionaries and their adult children returned to the United States to lead the struggle against the internment of Japanese Americans during World War II, support the civil rights movement, leverage their expert knowledge of the languages and cultures of Asia to humanize US foreign policy in Thailand and China, and open the eyes of the next generation to the dangers of US exceptionalism and parochialism.[29]

To understand the power of this long-term commitment and the intentional commitment to locate oneself among people who are culturally different, let's listen to Duncan Green, Professor in Practice at the London School of Economics and strategic adviser for Oxfam-Great Britain, one of the world's leading development agencies. Green, like many of his colleagues in the world of international development, is no friend of the missionary

---

[29]Hollinger's research uncovers the fascinating role of returned US missionaries and their adult children in avoiding US foreign policy blunders in Thailand and, in the cases of "the loss of China" and the tragic war in Vietnam, pointedly raises the question if history might have been very different if the mission-formed Americans' advice had been heeded.

movement. But he shared this frank and insightful assessment of the impact of what he calls missionary "embeddedness" after meeting with a group of Catholic missionaries in Ireland at a meeting organized by Misean Cara:

> Missionaries exemplify *long termism* and a deep knowledge of context—the room was full of priests, religious sisters and lay people who had spent decades in the same community, learning the language and becoming deeply immersed in local culture—the kind of *embeddedness* that [we] lament has been lost from the aid and diplomatic sector. They value people and relationships, not blueprints and policy documents.
>
> Missionaries also model another idea I've been talking about in recent years—they are living proof that one alternative to the *dead hand of the project* is to directly support leaders instead. Find charismatic individuals who are likely to make change happen and support them to do so without having to concoct endless project proposals to justify the grant. Oh wait, isn't that what missionaries are?
>
> Their deep and permanent roots in communities should make them ideally placed to do advocacy, something that Misean Cara is encouraging its 90 member organizations to explore.[30]

It was perhaps this very embeddedness—the commitment of thousands of Western missionaries to locate themselves in distant towns and villages for many years, to learn their languages and cultures, to accompany the people in their struggles—that gave the missionary movement the power to effect such deep change.[31] For all these contributions of our missionary forebears we give thanks to God. The fact that God continues to use frail, fallen people to change the course of history continues to inspire hope for all of us.

UPSTAGING GOD

True missionary embeddedness—because it grows out of the spreading circle of relationships through Jesus Christ—invites us to set aside our own power for the sake of the companions we are called to serve. It also serves

---

[30]Duncan Green, "Are Missionaries Naturally Suited to 'Doing Development Differently' and Advocacy?," From Poverty to Power, June 29, 2019, https://oxfamblogs.org/fp2p/are-missionaries-naturally-suited-to-doing-development-differently-and-advocacy/, italics mine.

[31]It is curious that there has not been more robust collaboration between missiology and the church-planting movements in the United Kingdom and the United States (Fresh Expressions, V3, 1001 New Worshiping Communities, and a host of denominational programs).

as a fertile space where we can examine our own power and privilege relative to the people we desire to serve. Why is it so important to have this awareness? In my own missionary service in Africa and Latin America, though my language and cultural skills were inferior to that of my hosts, I was almost always the most powerful person in the room: I was often the best educated and one of the few people with a dependable salary, health benefits, social security, and a pension. If I got seriously ill, my mission agency would medevac me to a US hospital for expert care. If I saw a pressing need, I could contact a US church and ask them to help. Over the years, innumerable Congolese and Peruvian friends approached me to intercede with a US church to help them get funds, a scholarship, or needed medical care for themselves or a loved one. In the eyes of my host communities, it was my social location and knowledge of English that made me a powerful broker of foreign material resources. My timely support could literally save a life or open a door on a new future for someone. In the Congo, where average annual income was less than $400, Batumane Bampele, a member of my Congolese church's youth group, put it starkly: "You foreigners are like gods to us."[32] This unmerited economic advantage bestowed on me by my social location often gave me a sense of entitlement and created dangerous blind spots in my vision. To show you how unaware we can be of our own blind spots, I need to share a story.

After four years of work in the Kasai region of DR Congo, I accompanied two Congolese seminary colleagues on "mission itineration"—a three-month trip to visit sixty-six congregations in four US states. My colleagues, Professor Mulumba Mukundi and student Kihani Masasu, and I gave a similar presentation in each church: I showed some slides of our seminary and the people of the surrounding communities, described the context and my work, and then introduced Dr. Mulumba, who spoke on the seminary's progress and challenges as it tried to prepare students to minister in our context. Kihani was a gifted singer and he would share a word of testimony, perform a song he had composed, and teach the congregation to sing it.

We repeated this presentation in each church. Kihani had made some indirect comments about my part of the presentation, but I hadn't really

---

[32]Barbara Tasch, "The 23 Poorest Countries in the World," *Business Insider*, July 13, 2015, www .businessinsider.com/the-23-poorest-countries-in-the-world-2015-7?IR=T.

listened or thought to follow up with him about it. It wasn't until late in the itineration that he paused after we finished lunch at a rest stop in central Texas. "Pastor," he said quietly, "it seems that all your photos and your words show us in our poverty." I was puzzled and made an awkward response. I knew that the Kasai's cultural conventions insisted on showing foreigners the best parts of one's community—similar to a cultural pattern with which I was raised—but the notion is quite a bit stronger in the Kasai's strongly collectivist cultural context. So his question stayed on my mind all afternoon.

That evening, as we gave our presentation to a church in Austin, I saw my slides—and my description of the iconic African "mission field"—with new eyes. I saw that my descriptions of Congo and its church were saturated with the hardships I had encountered: a repressive government, no electricity or running water, the worst poverty I'd ever experienced, the difficulty of running a seminary with over a hundred students on a shoestring budget. These hardships had somehow become the key messages of my part of the presentation: extreme poverty, difficult work, frustrating conditions. I had to admit I had silently enjoyed the grateful adulation I received in each and every church—folks would line up to thank me for my service: "I don't know how you do it," many would comment as they shook my hand warmly after the presentation. Strangers would embrace me. Kihani's words helped me to see that I had somehow worked my way into the center of the picture: I had become the story's hero; the White savior. To be sure, people were delighted with Kihani's musical ability and were intrigued with Professor Mulumba's work. But they absolutely loved their fellow countryman who was "toughing it out" for the Lord in Africa. Suddenly, the story I was sharing seemed less about God's mission than about my own. Maybe you recognize yourself in the mission story I grew to enjoy telling.

For me, the story of God's mission had been formed by years of Sunday school lessons, sermons, Bible studies, and mission conference keynote addresses—even my elementary and secondary schools' history lessons were filled with a particular version of world history that foregrounded the accomplishments of my people and invisibilized the achievements and contributions of local Christians and missionaries of color. I remember my high school US history teacher's sense of outrage when the new textbooks arrived and included for the first time marginal inserts from the perspectives of

African Americans, Native Americans, Latinx, and women: "They've changed our history!" was her accusation. Indeed. Mission, in our telling of the tale, was done almost exclusively by US missionaries—we knew there were British, German, and French missionaries out there, but in the many hundreds of mission stories I heard in my growing up years, I can't recall a single story about a Latin American or African missionary. The story of Christian mission, I would argue, was all about us.

Yet mission historian Jehu Hanciles's exhaustive research shows that in Africa—the continent where the Christian church grew the fastest in the last century—even though the initial outreach was done by European missionaries, the phenomenal growth of the church was largely due to tens of thousands of African catechists, lay workers, women's leaders, evangelists, pastors, youth leaders, and priests who understood the implications of the gospel message for their people and translated it into their heart languages and cultural understandings.[33] This is truly the untold story of the colonial age of mission. I find Hanciles's insight tremendously hopeful as we watch the number of US long-term missionaries decrease each year. With the shift in the center of Christianity from the Global North to the Global South in our lifetime, should it surprise us that God has been doing "a new thing" (Is 43:19) for a long time?

Even so, in my three decades of teaching, preaching, and interacting with congregational mission leaders across the country, I've observed that many are still reading the lines supplied them by the colonial period's script. These stories of the "Great Age of Mission"[34] coincided with the closing years of the colonial period and almost always had a White American missionary at the center. These stories tell part of the larger story of God's mission, but because they are the only stories most of us have heard, we are tempted to believe the story of God's mission is "all about us"—that we are indispensable parts of God's story.

This script is part of the "unchecked baggage" that most US Christians carry into mission—the subconscious values and assumptions of White

---

[33]Hanciles, *Beyond Christendom*, 112-36.

[34]In reference to noted Catholic mission historian, Lawrence Nemer, SVD, *The Great Age of Mission: Some Historical Studies in Mission History*, Studia Instituti Missiologici Societatis Verbi Divini 100 (Sankt Augustin, Germany: Steyler Verlag, 2013).

racial superiority passed down to us for the past five hundred years. Few of us have intentionally stopped, unpacked the bag, and examined its contents. While African American, Latinx, Native American, and Euro-American Christians may carry this baggage and react to it in different ways, because our cultural lenses have been formed by these scripts of White racial superiority, when we engage with others across lines of cultural difference (race/ ethnicity, nationality, income, language, gender identity, etc.), we have to be aware of the ways our shared mission history may have sown seeds of cultural superiority, leading us to rely on top-down practices of mission that fail to respect others as companions.

In doing so, we can inadvertently upstage God and step on our mission partners. Perhaps you've felt the awkwardness of being whisked up to the front row when you enter a church in many places in the Global South— sometimes even asked to speak or preach! More troubling are those instances when a US visitor takes on responsibilities (whether medical care, construction, or education) for which they are not qualified. This was graphically illustrated by the case of the well-intentioned, but unqualified, young American woman whose efforts to care for malnourished children in Uganda escalated into a court case and made headlines around the world when 105 children allegedly under her care died.[35] While her guilt or innocence has not been established by a court, my point is that the open door of hospitality in many communities of the Global South can dovetail with our assumptions of power and privilege in unhelpful and even dangerous ways. These dynamics can form a "perfect storm" when unexamined, but racist notions of privilege and perceived superiority combine with our lack of cultural awareness and what we misread as the host community's silent acquiescence.

A Scriptural understanding requires us to reconsider Jesus' countercultural practice of engaging in mission from a position of weakness, vulnerability, and mutuality: he was the servant who washed his friends' feet; the God-man who called his disciples "friends"; the One who, "though he was rich, yet for your sakes he became poor, so that by his poverty you might

---

[35]Nurith Aizenman, "U.S. Missionary with No Medical Training Settles Suit over Child Deaths at Her Center," National Public Radio, July 31, 2020, www.npr.org/sections/goatsandsoda/2020/07 /31/897773274/u-s-missionary-with-no-medical-training-settles-suit-over-child-deaths-at-her -ce#:~:text=Renee%20Bach%2C%20an%20American%20missionary,died%20in%20the%20 charity's%20care.

become rich" (2 Cor 8:9). I am convinced that if we don't intentionally work to untangle the racist colonial script we inherited about God's mission, we will continue to act out of a position of power and an implicit sense of entitlement. The *missio Dei* will be understood as merely an expression of our personal benevolence or, worse, as an instrument of our country's foreign policy, but in any case not the power of God to redeem, heal, and reconcile our very broken world: "For the message about the cross is foolishness to those who are perishing, but to us who are being saved it is the power of God" (1 Cor 1:18). The *missio Dei* will be "all about us" and not about God. Because our assumptions about mission and about people who are racially and culturally different from us are so subtly, yet profoundly, shaped by the colonial period, there is an urgent need to reset this first stone—a theology of mission that reflects the way of Jesus—in our common home's hearth as we gather around the fire God has kindled.

Perhaps, if you haven't already started this process of reflection, it may be time for you to unpack and examine your own "unchecked baggage." Several recent books can be helpful to leaders and church groups interested in stripping away the layers of varnish that often hide the relationship between Christian mission and systemic racism.[36] Tool 1, located at the end of chapter three, can provide a practical exercise for you to use with your congregation's leaders, your mission/outreach committee or to orient a short-term mission team. The tool invites your mission leaders and participants to consider how they perceive and portray your mission companions.

Willie James Jennings, professor of systematic theology and Africana studies at Yale Divinity School, gives hope to those of us who struggle to "decolonize" our journey in God's mission: "Missionary, merchant, soldier. The Holy Trinity of colonialism that shaped our world. . . . But by discerning the merchant and soldier inside of us, we free the missionary of resistance inside of us."[37] To be able to resist the historic patterns of "mission from a

---

[36]Mark Charles and Soon-Chan Rah's *Unsettling Truths: The Ongoing, Dehumanizing Legacy of the Doctrine of Discovery* (Downers Grove, IL: InterVarsity Press, 2019) explores the intertwined histories of colonialism and Christian mission. Jemar Tisby's *The Color of Compromise: The Truth About the American Church's Complicity with Racism* (Grand Rapids: Zondervan, 2019) documents the American church's support of and complicity with systemic racism in this country.

[37]Willie James Jennings, presented at Pittsburgh Theological Seminary's Schaff Lecture, May 13, 2017.

position of power" and our culture's growing fascination with self-satisfaction, we need to build a robust, Christ-centered theology of mission. Let us look at the contours of the first stone.

FOR REFLECTION

1. When you recall the three eras of the history of Christian mission, how do you assess both the strengths and weaknesses of each era?

2. What do you find most encouraging about the way the church has engaged in mission throughout the centuries? Most troubling?

3. What did the church give up when it accepted the power and privileges accorded it by the colonial governments?

4. Can you perceive ways in which the Doctrine of Discovery may have influenced your congregation's understanding of mission?

5. *"As I look back to that early intercultural encounter with the Congolese village church and their soccer field project, I see now that my own implicit, unexamined assumptions—the mental 'map' that I unwittingly carried into every conversation and encounter with Congolese neighbors in those years—were powerfully shaped by assumptions of White racial superiority that linger on from the colonial period."* Can you identify an experience in mission work when your words or actions were shaped by assumptions of White racial superiority or your reactions against those assumptions? Describe the situation and how you might act differently.

THREE

THE FIRST STONE

A Theology of Companionship

A S STATED IN CHAPTER ONE, when we look at the ways our con-gregations understand and practice mission, we mission leaders are in a challenging place. We are struggling to faithfully lead our people into God's mission, but we are hindered by two blind spots: the present and the past. The first blind spot is the daily pressure of our culture's growing tendency toward materialism, affluence, and a degree of narcissism that stands in opposition to the essence of the gospel message. The second blind spot was created by Christian mission's historical legacy of colonial power and its underlying logic of White superiority: that our ways—our civilization—were better than ev-eryone else's. In the second chapter, we unpacked some of the assumptions we carry into mission that were formed by our mission history.

We described this twin challenge to faithful participation in the *missio Dei* as a riptide of historical and cultural forces that is imperceptibly pulling all of us—evangelicals, mainline Protestants, and Catholics alike—away from the mission of Jesus Christ. Unless we have the tools and the courage to lead our local churches in a critical reflection on this first stone—the theology of mission undergirding our current mission practice—we will not be able to lead them into mission in the way of Jesus Christ, a movement that so impacted the women and men he met that they went out and turned the world "upside down" (Acts 17:6). Now we will describe an understanding of mission that comes to us from Jesus' model of mission as companionship. Let's begin with a true story.

MISSION AS COMPANIONSHIP

When the name of the new pastor was announced by the Pastoral Nominating Committee to the members of First Presbyterian Church of Brooklyn,
Iowa, the entire congregation was taken aback. "A pastor from West Africa?
Serving *our* church in the cornfields of rural Iowa? *Really?*" Even the most
supportive church members had their doubts. The community had been
settled by German and English settlers during the westward expansion in
the nineteenth century; furthermore, as farming jobs became fewer,
Brooklyn hadn't seen the arrival of many Latinx or African American residents. In fact, in the more than one-hundred-year history of the congregation, no African American or African had ever preached from the pulpit
of First Presbyterian–Brooklyn.

But the report of the Pastoral Nominating Committee vibrated with excitement as it talked about the group's interviews with Ben Nti, a gifted
candidate who immigrated to the United States from Ghana a decade before
and who brought uncommon spiritual maturity and leadership skills, along
with a deep love for people. Perhaps most surprisingly to the Midwest
farming community, Pastor Ben considered himself and his family to be
missionaries sent by God from Ghana to Iowa. Perhaps this was precisely
what the struggling church needed!

While the typical pastoral search committee is charged with finding "the
strongest candidate" available, in a very real sense, Pastor Ben was the
weakest candidate the committee interviewed. He was a cultural outsider
whose Ghanaian-accented English required the Iowans to listen carefully to
his words; an African immigrant whom visitors to the church would not
infrequently assume to be the church's janitor; a foreigner whose lack of
familiarity with the local "ways things are done" in Iowa would surely limit
his efforts to lead and grow the church through a time of unsettling economic and cultural change. Yet God enabled the congregation to recognize
Ben Nti's calling to lead them as their pastor and they unanimously voted to
call him as their pastor.

Pastor Ben set about learning as much as possible about the people he
was called to serve. He sought out an older member who had farmed in the
community his entire life and asked him to teach him what it meant to be a
farmer. Folks laughed when the pastor said he was going to "farm school,"

but they grew to love his earnest desire to know them in all their peculiarities. When a group of men in the church informed Pastor Ben that their custom was to forgo Sunday services during the fall hunting season, they were surprised when their new pastor challenged them to remember their primary calling as Christians was to love and worship God—so he invited them to a weekly Thursday evening service to bless the hunt, and the Thursday evening worship service grew in attendance.

Because Pastor Ben and his family trusted in an all-powerful God, God used his perceived "weaknesses" to surprise the Iowan community with a leader whose lack of familiarity with their local traditions gave him the courage to question old practices, whose profoundly West African belief in the power of prayer challenged the congregation's American secular doubts, and whose deep humility disarmed them and moved them to open their hearts to him. Pastor Ben and his wife, Edna, and son, Praise, certainly were not perfect, but they had a crystal-clear understanding of themselves as missionaries: imperfect people called to cross lines of difference to share God's love with a particular group of people—the people of Brooklyn. They sought to do that following the model of Jesus Christ, and their missionary strategy can perhaps best be described as a theology of companionship. We understand a theology of companionship to consist of a circle that circumscribes four key elements:

1. Mutual accompaniment

2. Shared vulnerability

3. Centeredness on the sending God

4. Mission from the margins

MUTUAL ACCOMPANIMENT

Jesus' mission was built on human relationships. The Nti family came alongside the people they were called to serve, breaking bread with them, joining them in their celebrations and moments of grief, and immersing themselves in Brooklyn ways of life. Their actions from the first day signaled not "We are here to grow the church" or "We are here to change you" but rather "We are here with you." The people of Brooklyn quickly understood that the Nti family's ministry was not primarily about completing tasks, objectives, or a strategic plan (though these components would come in due time), but was built on loving relationships with the members of the community.

This missional style is time-intensive and requires stepping into the rhythm of life of the community. The word *companion*, in fact, comes from the Latin *com* ("with") and *panis* ("bread"): "one with whom we break bread." To eat with someone is to invite that person into your personal space, to share together. Sharing a meal requires that you "let down your guard"—it is a space that opens you up to be known more deeply by your companion. The Ntis shared innumerable meals with church and community members and demonstrated a commitment to walk with them through moments of personal tragedy, to celebrate their successes, and to accompany them through the uncertain economic times affecting the area.

In the New Testament, the first description used of the earliest Christian community is "the Way."[1] All four Gospels view Jesus' ministry as a mission on the road: most of Jesus' encounters—the healing and miracle narratives that show the tenderness and power of the Son of God—take place as he moves from place to place. Jesus meets the Gerasene demoniac after he crosses over the Sea of Galilee (Mk 5). He is walking with the disciples through Samaria on the road from Judea to Galilee when he meets the woman by the well (Jn 4). Jesus' life-changing encounter with Zacchaeus happens as he is walking through Jericho. On the road between Samaria and Galilee, Jesus meets the ten lepers and heals them all (Lk 17:11-19). Mission in the way of Jesus often occurs in chance human encounters on the road, at the grocery store, or at school, and it is deeply sensitive to context.

Once they are touched, healed, transformed, a common desire of the people who encounter Jesus is to be in relationship with him: the Gerasene demoniac "begged [Jesus] that he might be with him" (Lk 8:38). The Samaritan woman immediately began to draw others to Jesus. The disciples themselves leave their former lives behind to be able to walk with Jesus. People just wanted to be with Jesus.

Perhaps this was the sense of the clarion call offered by Bishop V. S. Azariah of India, one of the very few delegates from the Global South to the

---

[1]Acts 9:2; 19:9, 23; 22:4; and 24:14, 22 refer to the early Christians and to their new faith and consequent lifestyle as "the Way." If the exodus (in Greek, "the way out") represented a particular people's (the ancient Israelites) road out of slavery into liberation, "the way" represents the path to liberation opened by Jesus Christ for all people.

famed Edinburgh Missionary Conference of 1910. After lauding the foreign missionaries in India for their sacrificial commitment, he said, "Through all the ages to come the Indian Church will rise up in gratitude to attest the heroism and self-denying labours of the missionary body. You have given your goods to feed the poor. You have given your bodies to be burned. We also ask for *love*. Give us FRIENDS!"[2]

In her reflection on Bishop Azariah's words, Boston University mission historian Dana Robert notes the centrality of crosscultural friendship in the creation of World Christianity and cites numerous friendships between missionaries and national Christians throughout the twentieth century to show how friendship has functioned as the bridge that binds culturally different Christians together, providing a counterweight to what she describes as the naturally racist bearing of the colonial missionary movement:

> Indeed, without friendship as clear witness to Christ-like love, the inequities and racism of the colonial era might have prevented the spread of Christianity across cultures. Azariah's cry was a complaint, but it was also a prophecy. For some missionaries, lifetime cross-cultural friendships were a vital witness against racism and colonialism, and a sign of the inbreaking reign of God. Jesus said, "No one has greater love than this, to lay down one's life for one's friends." (Jn 15:13)[3]

Sometimes other languages capture this sense of the sweetness of human relationship in ways we are not accustomed to in English. In the Tshiluba language of south central DR Congo, there is a beautiful verb that describes this tender longing to remain in a visitor's company. The verb *kushindikija* means "to accompany home," but it is understood in the context of Lulua[4] village culture where, after you have enjoyed a prolonged time of a shared meal and fellowship, it is not uncommon to walk your guest home. But *kushindikija* is the verb used when the host walks the guest home and then the guest, desiring to extend the time together, walks the host back to her or his home. If the fellowship is sweet enough, this can continue for quite a

---

[2]Quoted in Brian Stanley, *The World Missionary Conference, Edinburgh 1910* (Grand Rapids: Eerdmans, 2009), 125.

[3]Dana L. Robert, "Cross-Cultural Friendship in the Creation of Twentieth-Century World Christianity," *International Bulletin of Mission Research* 35, no. 2 (April 2011): 100-107, www.international bulletin.org/issues/2011-02/2011-02-100-robert.html.

[4]A large, Tshiluba-speaking ethnic group in south central DR Congo.

while, if only to extend the time spent together. Companions earnestly desire to be in each other's company. This is the power of longer-term mission companionship: we visit each other, send emails to each other to see how companions are faring, pray for one another, and study Scripture and worship together via Zoom. Our love for one another draws us into each other's lives to the point of taking risks for one another. We discover we are succeeding in breaking down our congregation's normal expectations of "mission as project" when we see our members express concern about how recent heavy rains or a new law may have affected our mission companions and when we receive concerned communications from our companions when tragedy befalls our community or nation. These indicators point to the beginnings of the first element of companionship: mutual accompaniment, mission as a commitment to walk together.

SHARED VULNERABILITY

Why then do we not understand mission primarily as friendship, following Bishop Azariah, Dana Robert, and authors Christopher Heuertz and Christine Pohl,[5] who helpfully lift up the relational nature of Jesus who called his disciples "friends"? In an age where we "friend" and "unfriend" people on Facebook with the click of a button and where we have countless friends with whom we haven't spoken in years, I believe the mission of the triune God, whose very essence is relationship, requires a different term that suggests greater intensity, intentionality, and directionality than friendship. To be someone's *companion* suggests unusual openness, vulnerability, and the innate understanding that your own journey is intrinsically bound together with that of your companion.

Companionship requires a sense of mutuality, shared agency, and shared direction: both parties agree to walk together in the same direction of their own volition. Companionship is more than *being with*: it connotes an intentional *walking together* with a shared destination in mind, though neither party may know exactly where the path is leading them. Companionship is more intimate—more purposeful—than friendship. This is how I understand the desire of the disciples and others whose lives were transformed

---

[5]Christopher Heuertz and Christine Pohl, *Friendship at the Margins* (Downers Grove, IL: InterVarsity Press, 2010).

by Jesus to be his *companions*: friends who break bread together, share what they have together, and purpose to walk together—to grow in their common humanity. The desire to accompany your companion, especially in their moments of vulnerability, is a characteristic of mission as companionship. When a friend asks if he can accompany me as I await test results in my hospital room, I know that he desires to be my companion, to walk with me in my moment of deep vulnerability. This is the space of companionship.

Once I had mastered the basic greetings of the Tshiluba language in DR Congo, I made a point of greeting just about every person I passed on the street: "Muoyo muanetu!" ("May your life be strengthened, my brother or sister!"). But one day, I was walking with a close friend, Congolese pastor Kashama Lengulula, and I remember greeting many people on the road. But Pastor Kashama stopped me and said, "To address someone as your sibling means you will share with them everything you have. This is what it means to be family." I stood in awkward silence, thinking about all I had to lose from the new relationship. Among my Congolese friends and coworkers, in fact, I was the only person with a salary paid in dollars, a bank account, or a retirement plan. Yet to claim to be family carried serious consequences—to share with them all I had. In the Eucharist, Jesus' followers break bread together and declare to the world the astounding truth that they—rich and poor, male and female, Congolese and American—are one family and will share with each other everything they have: "the whole group of those who believed were of one heart and soul, and no one claimed private ownership of any possessions, but everything they owned was held in common" (Acts 4:32).

Projects, tasks, agenda, and deadlines all have their place in the work of mission, but, as Bishop Azariah pled with the missionary statesmen gathered in Edinburgh, *mission as companionship* recognizes that the first calling of God's mission is the call into relationships of mutuality and vulnerability with people—individuals in all their uniqueness with needs, desires, gifts, and hopes. *Mission as companionship* is similar to "mission in partnership,"[6] but partnership can suggest a transactional relationship as from the business world where relationships are guided by business interests and the profit

---

[6]General Assembly Council, Presbyterian Church (USA), "Presbyterians Do Mission in Partnership," 2003, www.pcusa.org/site_media/media/uploads/global/pdf/presbyterians_do_mission_in_partnership.pdf.

motive. Likewise, "mission as accompaniment" builds on the same themes of mutuality and shared witness and is characterized by its focus on our commitment to walk together with the other.[7] Rafael Malpica Padilla of the Evangelical Lutheran Church in America and Kimberly Lamberty, a Catholic mission educator and leader, have deepened our thinking with their work on "mission as accompaniment," which I fully affirm.[8] But whereas the word accompaniment focuses on the activity, I believe the word companion is more helpful as it points to the human relationship out of which the many activities of accompaniment naturally flow.

The difference between the sense of connection one finds in many of our local congregations and the often more intense bonds that characterize many twelve-step groups (such as Alcoholics Anonymous [AA]) is the *shared vulnerability* that members feel. People in recovery are so aware of their need for each other that they are willing to accept the risks that come with vulnerability. At your first AA meeting, you introduce yourself simply, "Hi, I'm Hunter and I'm an alcoholic." Perhaps your addiction has been the most tightly held, shameful secret of your life—perhaps you have lied about it for years to everyone in the world, including yourself. Yet you can enter into the community of healing in complete vulnerability only through the "truth telling" of confession: "I am one of you and I can't do this without you." Your greeting signals your willingness to "drop your guard" and be vulnerable with gathered strangers simply because you believe they are on the very road that leads to healing and, perhaps, they will be willing to walk with you. The group's immediate response—a hearty, "Hi, Hunter!"—signals your instant acceptance by your new companions: "We understand. We're just like you. Welcome." At the very start of the encounter, confession is offered and the group responds with a communal assurance of pardon and welcomes you into fellowship. In a moment, pretenses are cast aside and broken, vulnerable individuals are enabled to connect deeply as companions on the road to healing.

---

[7] Rafael Malpica Padilla, "Accompaniment as an Alternate Model for the Practice of Mission," *Trinity Seminary Review* 29, no. 2 (2008): 87-98; and Kim Lamberty, "The Art of Accompaniment," *Missiology* 43, no. 3 (2015): 324-38, doi:10.1177/0091829614563062.

[8] Malpica Padilla's important work on accompaniment has been developed by the ELCA's Global Mission Unit: "Accompaniment," 2013 ELCA Glocal Mission Gathering, https://download.elca .org/ELCA%20Resource%20Repository/Accompaniment_(full).pdf?_ga=2.5813687.525219377 .1611330594-334092837.1611330594. See also Lamberty, "Art of Accompaniment."

After the deep sharing of the meeting, communion with the "Higher Power" and with your new companions is sealed with the ritual of shared coffee and snacks. American novelist James Baldwin wrote, "Love takes off the masks that we fear we cannot live without and know we cannot live within."[9] No wonder twelve-step groups have generated such a powerful wave of healing and wholeness over the decades. How would our churches' witness deepen if we entered each missional encounter with such courageous vulnerability—a willingness to name our own brokenness, our addictions, and our needs?

In part because of the top-down spread of the gospel during the imperial and colonial eras (fourth through twentieth centuries), many pastors and missionaries are hesitant to set aside the power that our people ascribe to us: we cling to our titles, our prerogatives, our status. In contrast, though he was one of the better-educated people in the town of Brooklyn and certainly had seen more of the world than the average local resident, Pastor Ben humbled himself upon arriving in Iowa and adopted the posture of a learner. He asked the men of the church to teach him to hunt. He placed himself under the mentorship of a local farmer to teach him the joys, hopes, and fears of farmers' lives. He sought out and developed a special filial relationship with the congregation's former pastor who had retired after thirty-eight years of ministry in Brooklyn just before Ben was called. By submitting himself to the community as a learner, Pastor Ben embodied a respect for the people and traditions of Brooklyn, showing he was a person they could trust. Pastor Ben was able to incorporate what he learned about the community into his teaching, preaching, and friendships, further deepening the bonds of trust and their shared sense of companionship.

While many of us understand Jesus as the Son of God to have been omniscient, all-knowing, it is surprising to see how deeply committed he was to the posture of learner. Jesus spent the first three decades of life earning the right to be heard by the people of first-century Palestine: he learned their language; communicated using the cultural conventions of parables, proverbs, and vivid stories; and grounded many of his theological claims by citing the Hebrew Scriptures. Even as the fully grown Messiah, it is remarkable how

---

[9] James Baldwin, *The Fire Next Time* (New York, NY: Dial Press, 1963), 109.

many times he set aside his agenda to stop and engage with someone, taking his cues from his conversation partner.

In the healing of the Syrophoenician woman's daughter, we see Jesus' capacity to take on the role of the learner in an extreme way that appears to alter his mission agenda in a way that can challenge our own understanding of Jesus Christ: the Son of God appears to learn from this Gentile woman!

> Now the woman was a Gentile, of Syrophoenician origin. She begged him to cast the demon out of her daughter. He said to her, "Let the children be fed first, for it is not fair to take the children's food and throw it to the dogs." But she answered him, "Sir, even the dogs under the table eat the children's crumbs." Then he said to her, "For saying that, you may go—the demon has left your daughter." So she went home, found the child lying on the bed, and the demon gone. (Mk 7:26-30)

This text from Mark's Gospel presents a surprising, almost scandalous, account in which we see Jesus submitting himself as a learner to the foreign woman—whose social location places her clearly outside his mission agenda. Though she was utterly powerless in the sociopolitical context of the times, the Savior recognizes the wisdom of her challenge—that the mission of God necessarily extends beyond the people of Israel—and he submits his logic to hers. The Syrophoenician woman's daughter is healed, and Jesus appears to change course, immediately traveling into the Gentile territory of the Decapolis. He actually appears to enlarge his mission to include non-Jews as a result of the Syrophoenician woman's lesson. It would take Jesus' disciples some time to process this powerful opening of God's mission: Peter's vision in Caesarea and the subsequent Council of Jerusalem (Acts 10–11; 15) show the Jesus movement struggling to understand how inclusive God's realm truly is. Can we follow in the way of Jesus Christ and adopt a position of vulnerability, showing ourselves to be learners in relationship with the people to whom God sends us? This posture can change the entire direction of our participation in the *missio Dei*, even as it did Jesus'.

Vulnerability and a teachable spirit lie very close to the heart of what God requires of us to be God's companions: "to do justice, and to love kindness, and to walk humbly with your God" (Mic 6:8). Why is it that Jesus insists repeatedly on the necessity to "become like children" in order to enter into the realm of God (Mt 18:3)? Why does the realm of God belong to children (Mk 10:14 and parallels)? This willingness to present oneself to the community as a learner is an essential element of mutual interdependence in our theology of *companionship*.

Beginning in the 1970s, Fuller Theological Seminary mission linguistics professors Thomas and Elizabeth Susan Brewster developed a model of language and culture learning called Language Acquisition Made Practical, popularized as the LAMP method. The method stirred controversy among seasoned missionaries and profoundly impacted thousands of new missionaries with the simple yet profound thesis of their booklet *Bonding and the Missionary Task*: the most effective way a missionary can minister is to present themselves as learners, working to learn the language of the people they are sent to serve.[10] For years, missionaries had viewed language learning as the often difficult, but necessary, requirement for long-term mission service. The Brewsters upended that logic and posited the very process of language learning as ministry from a position of vulnerability. It also creates a powerful sense of belonging as missionaries learn to depend on the host community for necessities and look to them for the ways to speak and act in ways the community can understand (communications scholars call this "receiver-oriented communication"). More importantly, their embodied vulnerability serves as an invitation into missional companionship that says, "Where are you going? May we walk with you?" This heart attitude is a radical departure from the colonial era's model of imposed faith and coercive relationships.

When my wife, Ruth, and I first traveled together to DR Congo (then Zaire), the Reverend Dr. Tshihamba Mukome Luendu, the leader of the national Presbyterian Church, drove us to the Lulua village of Tshimana, where we spent our first months in language and culture learning, following the Brewsters' LAMP method. When we submitted ourselves to the community, every person in Tshimana instantly became our teacher—especially the children, who were thrilled! No one in Tshimana had seen a foreigner interested in learning their language, and we never lacked willing volunteers who would teach us, correct us, and encourage us. From the start of our time there, Ruth and I sensed the importance of the deep connections that were forming between the people of Tshimana and us, but only later would we get a sense of how Congolese neighbors viewed those connections. For years after this

---

[10]Thomas Brewster and Elizabeth Susan Brewster, *Bonding and the Missionary Task: Establishing a Sense of Belonging* (Pasadena, CA: Lingua House, 1983).

"bonding experience" we were often introduced to Congolese church audiences as *bena Tshimana*, "people of Tshimana," the traditional label for the village's kinship group. The audience would often roar with delighted approval. By adopting the role of learner, a space was created where the people of the region could invite us to be their companions on the journey. Without the Brewsters' insights and Dr. Tshihamba's strong support, we would not have been able to exit off the highway of "missionary as expert" long enough to see the alternate route that "bonding" opened up for us: a sense of belonging and companionship in Christ. The road the Brewsters pointed out was slower, to be sure, but it led us much deeper into companionship relationships than would have been possible for us without the bonding experience.

Companionship requires recognizing that each person brings strengths and gifts but also concrete needs and personal brokenness to the space of encounter. Children became our teachers. Missionary professors became students. When Ruth and I were praying to have children, members of the church's youth group showed up unannounced one evening and held an all-night prayer vigil in our house (four months later, we adopted our son, Will). Though none of us knew exactly where we were headed on our shared road, Congolese companions and we understood at a deep level that our life in Christ was somehow inextricably bound up together. Australian indigenous artist Lilla Watson's celebrated quote succinctly summarizes the mutuality of a commitment to learning in mission as companionship: "If you have come here to help me you are wasting your time, but if you have come because your liberation is bound up with mine, then let us work together."[11]

In his reflection on Watson's quote, Franciscan contemplative priest Richard Rohr describes this mutuality as "authentic solidarity":

> Authentic solidarity involves a pilgrimage of voluntary displacement from our position(s) of privilege—whether that be class, race, gender, physical ability, nationality, religion—and appreciation for traits that our culture deems not "normal" or valuable. Only through relationships can I discern what kind of service is really needed, if I'm the one to offer it, and whose needs I am meeting. It's not about "I'm helping you" but "We're walking and learning together."[12]

---

[11]"About," Lilla: International Women's Network, https://lillanetwork.wordpress.com/about/.
[12]From his September 20, 2019, daily devotional on the Center for Action and Contemplation Facebook page, www.facebook.com/CenterforActionandContemplation/.

Many of us find it much easier to serve the other rather than to walk with them. In the soup kitchen or homeless shelter, it is safer to stay on "our side" of the service counter. Roles are clear and prescribed, and unanticipated needs can be "referred" to the proper resource. In contrast, a theology of companionship requires us to be "all in," bringing to the table of God's mission everything we are, following Jesus' model of the shared vulnerability of companionship.

CENTRALITY OF THE SENDING GOD

While on the road with his mission companions, Jesus did not seek the spotlight for himself, but consistently pointed others to God the Father, the One who had sent him (cf. Jn 5:19-23; 8:21-29). Jesus' followers are called to do the same (Col 3:16-17). In his ministry in Iowa, Pastor Ben avoided claiming credit for the occasional successes of ministry but consistently gave credit to God. He modeled a style of engagement that pointed to a powerful God rather than to his own strengths, skills, and resources. Ben insisted he was the messenger and not the message.

This is important because a theology of companionship consists of more than a mutual bond formed between two people who are journeying in the same direction. There is always a larger presence in a missional companionship relationship because the two parties have an expressed commitment to seek to discern and follow not their own path, but *God's*. Thus, even as the Father sends the Son, and the Father and Son send the Spirit, the 1952 International Missionary Council conference in Willingen, Germany, noted the third movement: "Father, Son and Holy Spirit sending the church into the world."[13] Thus, the triune, sending God is at the center of every companionship relationship. Companionship is not merely attaching oneself to another and going wherever our partner wants, as some forms of postcolonial mainline Protestant mission have insisted. "Doing whatever our mission companion wants" is ultimately as paternalistic as refusing to do anything a companion suggests, because it doesn't take their initiative seriously; rather, we accept or reject it merely because they are different from us. Instead, it is the mutual redirecting of both companions back onto the path of God's good

---

[13]Quoted in David Bosch, *Transforming Mission: Paradigm Shifts in Theology of Mission* (Maryknoll, NY: Orbis, 1991), 373.

intentions for the world—the path that necessarily leads us into the very nature of God: justice, compassion, healing, mercy, forgiveness, and peace.

Often, Christians in the Global South are surprised by the deeply secular assumptions of their US mission partners. We often seem to them to be reticent to talk about God, to be uncomfortable sharing our testimony, to not fully rely on the power of prayer. We are quick to see the visible—the empirical—but slow to see God's action in all things. US Christians are often affected by the growing secularization of US academic, political, and public life. That is why Pastor Ben's centering of each conversation around God made such a deep impression on his congregation. He consistently saw the hand of God in the happenings of Brooklyn in ways that surprised his people. Several members commented on Pastor Ben's reliance on prayer. Tony Hilpipre, a church member who had served on the committee that recommended Pastor Ben to the Brooklyn congregation, recalls discovering how secular his own life had become when he spent time with this pastor who exuded a level of spiritual maturity and made prayer the hallmark of the congregation's shared life:

> [Pastor Ben] brought a spiritual presence, a spiritual maturity, to our church. He has become so special to me. His focus on prayer and how prayer works in our lives has helped me to gain an awareness of God at work in even the everyday occurrences. My awareness of God is now greater than ever. We get together twice a week to go over our community, our country, and our church, and then to just pray. His insights, his "whole-world Christianity" is just so refreshing in our busy world.
>
> I think about some of the things we were lacking when Ben came: our sense of relationship with each other and with God. And my relationship with God has never been stronger. We were so closed off [from] our . . . community before, but Ben saw this immediately. We have many elderly attendees, but he is helping us to "grow young" through Bible study for 16 to 29 year olds! Pastor Ben sure rubs off on us—I constantly have "God-moments" that enable me to see God at work.[14]

Pastor Ben's spirituality and holistic worldview—his ability to see the mighty acts of God in the events of everyday life in rural Iowa—caused the

---

[14]Tony Hilpipre, personal interview, September 16, 2019.

congregation's understanding of mission to shift and center around the sending God. Under his leadership, they began to think of themselves as missionaries in their own right, mission companions called by God to reach out to their community and the world beyond. Pastor Ben has much to teach us about a theology of companionship, and I believe his "whole-world Christianity" points us to a reclaimed vision of Christian witness, especially in a postmodern age.

In some traditions of Western Christianity—and through their global missionary efforts, a large swath of the "mission churches" of the Majority World—"the winning of souls for Christ," or personal evangelism, has historically been considered the most important focus of Christian faith. In some circles it is considered the primary objective of mission activities because its impact is eternal. Given the troubling history of the colonial era and the difficulty of distinguishing colonialism from the missionary movement, many have understandably reacted against the church and the gospel it proclaims. Christianity has been perceived to represent the imposition of faith and a closed-minded moralism that are a poor reflection of the ministry of Jesus Christ. Perhaps you have met people who have been deeply wounded by the church—whether by judgment and exclusion, through physical or emotional abuse at the hands of clergy, or simply because of the church's greater focus on the doctrinal boundaries that defined "who's in and who's out" than on sharing the life-giving good news of God's love for everyone in Jesus Christ. Indeed for many mainline Protestants and Catholics, evangelism—the sharing of God's love with others by communicating in words and actions what God did for us in the life, death, and resurrection of Jesus Christ—has become a dirty word, the "E-word." According to some authors, even US evangelicals (for whom evangelism has traditionally been understood to be an essential identity marker) have become more reticent to share their faith with others due to pressure from an increasingly secular culture.[15] While there are several explanations for these trends, many US Christians today feel uncomfortable with the E-word because it connotes an imposition of Christian beliefs and behaviors and a moralistic superiority. The language of "winning souls," "conversion," and

---

[15]Evangelical author Michael L. Simpson terms this *evangelical timidity*. See *Permission Evangelism* (Colorado Springs: Cook Communication Ministries, 2003), 46.

"discipling others" is increasingly contested in a context of religious and cultural pluralism.

So what is the place of evangelism in Christian mission today? Once our eyes are opened to the pain inflicted by the impositional evangelism of the colonial era of missions, our reaction is often an awkward, postmodern silence. But because Scripture points us to Jesus Christ, and Christ points us to the triune God, we understand *mission as companionship* to include a willingness to share a witness with bold humility to what we have experienced of God in Christ. In the wake of the development of the "Social Gospel" and subsequent reaction by US evangelicals in the first half of the twentieth century, the concept of evangelism tended to divide US Protestant traditions: evangelicals have tended to understand the communication of the unique, saving work of Christ to be essential to Christian identity and the first priority of Christian mission, while a number of mainline Protestants tend to understand evangelism more broadly to be living a lifestyle that exhibits gospel values.

US evangelical churches that generally identify with the National Association of Evangelicals (NAE) affirm Christ's uniqueness as the way to God and the central importance of personal evangelism: sharing the "saving knowledge" of Jesus' life, sacrifice on the cross, and resurrection for all sinners. Indeed, one of the four theological statements that a person must affirm to be considered an evangelical by the NAE makes reference to evangelism: "It is very important for me personally to encourage non-Christians to trust Jesus Christ as their Savior."[16] This understanding of evangelism as encouraging others to trust Christ as savior is one of the essential characteristics of US evangelicals and can distinguish them from some (but not all) of their Catholic and mainline Protestant counterparts.

Mainline Protestant churches that identify themselves with the National Council of Churches of Christ in the USA and the World Council of Churches, on the other hand, tend to affirm evangelism as bearing witness to salvation through Jesus Christ but are reticent to condemn other religious traditions, as seen in the statement affirmed at the San Antonio Conference

---

[16]"NAE LifeWay Research Evangelical Beliefs Research Definition," LifeWay Research, 2015, http://lifewayresearch.com/wp-content/uploads/2015/11/NAE-LifeWay-Research-Evangelical -Beliefs-Research-Definition-Methodology-and-Use.pdf.

of the Commission on World Mission & Evangelism (CWME) (1989): "We cannot point to any other way of salvation than Jesus Christ; at the same time we cannot set limits to the saving power of God. There is a tension between these affirmations which we acknowledge and cannot resolve."[17]

This statement affirms the Christian belief that Jesus Christ is the only way to salvation yet acknowledges that this affirmation does not deny that God can use other religious traditions to bring people to God in ways we do not fully understand. The San Antonio statement led to a later expression in "Religious Plurality and Christian Self-Understanding," a paper adopted at the Athens CWME Conference (2005): "Thus we affirm that salvation belongs to God, God only. We do not possess salvation; we participate in it. We do not offer salvation; we witness to it. We do not decide who would be saved; we leave it to the providence of God."[18] The Athens paper reminds us that it is God who saves. But an affirmation of personal evangelism—of the importance or necessity of communicating the content of God's saving action in Christ—is not generally emphasized in this tradition of US Christianity.

Mainline Protestants tend to understand evangelism as suggesting a coercive, argumentative spirit rather than witness—the joyful sharing of God's good news in deed and, more rarely, in word. While this can be an important distinction, are we losing something in this delineation between evangelism and witness? As a mainline Protestant missionary who was profoundly reevangelized by Christians in Congo, I wonder if we are throwing out the baby with the bathwater and may have lost something of the content of the gospel even as we testify to its power.

Perhaps all US Christians—evangelical, Catholic, Orthodox, and mainline Protestant—might listen to many Catholic and Protestant Christians in the Majority World, who witness in less secularized cultural contexts and tend to practice personal evangelism much more frequently and more naturally than their US counterparts: the Ethiopian Evangelical Church Mekane Yesus (8.7 million members), the Korean Methodist Church (1.5 million), and the

---

[17]"Your Will Be Done: Mission in Christ's Way," Commission on World Mission and Evangelism Conference, San Antonio, Texas, 1989.
[18]Conference on World Mission and Evangelism, "Preparatory Paper No. 13: Religious Plurality and Christian Self-Understanding," World Council of Churches, March 2005, www.oikoumene .org/en/resources/documents/other-meetings/mission-and-evangelism/preparatory-paper-13 -religious-plurality-and-christian-self-understanding.

Presbyterian Community of Congo (1.25 million) invest significantly more of their time and resources in evangelism, evangelism training, open air preaching, revival meetings, and healing ministries than do their respective mother churches (the Evangelical Lutheran Church in America, the United Methodist Church, and the Presbyterian Church [USA], respectively). I have heard comments from leaders of all three of these Global South churches who note that an essential part of the church's holistic witness is to point people to the gift of hope we have in the knowledge of God's outpouring of love through Jesus Christ: "Why would you hide from someone you love the free gift of a loving God?," asked the Rev. Iteffa Gobena, the former president of the Mekane Yesus Church.[19] "Your church isn't the United Way," retired president of Peru's United Bible Society and former member of Peru's national congress, Pedro Arana, once reminded me. "Why is it so hard for you to share what God has done in your life?" These leaders perceived that it is often difficult for their Euro-American Christian counterparts to speak with friends of God's loving actions in their life, to pray for healing, or to thank God publicly for God's blessings. African American, Latinx, and Asian American Christians have responded to secularization in differentiated ways, but because our book is directed primarily at Euro-American Christians, this challenge to a more holistic witness is important to note.

Companionship invites us to be intentional about creating opportunities to share with others our own stories of what God has done in our lives, pointing to God through Christ, "the author and finisher of our faith" (Heb 12:2 KJV), and companions will regularly dedicate part of their time together to shared prayer, Bible study, worship, and testimonies (faith sharing). This element helps US mission companions avoid the commodification of mission (mission as a product that can be purchased) and rather bring their whole selves into it—not just their identities as planner or organizer but as witness, counselor, worshiper, and prayer companion. An encounter with Christians who are more comfortable sharing the story of what God in Christ has done for them may be a transformative moment where more secularized Christians' faith can find its voice. Especially when the objective is not to change someone's mind but to give praise to

---

[19]Personal interview, January 16, 2015, Addis Ababa, Ethiopia.

God, the result is a song that arises from a thankful heart as American Baptist minister Robert Wadsworth Lowry's hymn "How Can I Keep from Singing?" declares.

Pastor Ben Nti helped the Iowa Presbyterians to grow spiritually and become more accustomed to sharing their faith in a secularized context. In a similar way, as we walk together with mission companions, our own spirituality and desire to share God's love will be deeply affected by our mission companions and we find we are better able to incorporate authentic evangelism and witness in a more holistic practice of mission.

MISSION FROM THE MARGINS

Companions are people who commit to walking together on the road, sharing with each other from a place of vulnerability in ways that point to the sending God—these are three of the elements that constitute a theology of companionship. But we need to reflect on a final element of companionship that flows out of Jesus' ministry: the presence, perspective, and leadership of those forced to live in the margins of society.

Because the *missio Dei* was most clearly embodied in the ministry of Jesus Christ, our discipleship requires us to keep before us at all times that group of people to whom Jesus directed much of his mission, with whom he spent most of his time, and for whom he expressed a special love: the people whom poverty, oppression, and exclusion have pushed to the margins of society. Of course, Scripture testifies to the fact that God is redeeming the whole creation (Rom 8), and, of the whole creation, God has special pleasure in loving and redeeming human beings who, different from the rest of the created order, are capable of choosing to obey God and serve in God's mission of the healing of the world. "We love because he first loved us," says 1 John 4:19. But a critical aspect of God's love—inescapable if we are faithful to the witness of Scripture—is that, while God loves every person, God has a particular love for the poor, the excluded, the sick, and the oppressed (the widow, orphan, and foreigner, referred to repeatedly in the Old Testament). Psalm 68:5 speaks of God's very identity in terms of God's particular concern for the poor: "Father of orphans and protector of widows is God in his holy habitation." This insight into the very character of God is supported by the more than two thousand verses of Scripture that testify to God's special love for those who have been marginalized.[20]

Throughout Scripture, God is shown to act decisively in history through the people of God to give "those who have been excluded from the banquet of life"[21] access to the abundant life Jesus named in John 10:10. The texture of religious life in the Old Testament points us to an essential part of the *missio Dei*: the removal of barriers to abundant life for those excluded from the table. Among the missional practices prescribed by the sending God are the care for widows, orphans, and foreigners, who were not protected by the institutions of society; the practice of gleaning, that is, intentionally leaving some of the harvest for hungry people to use; the giving of alms to provide for the needs of people struggling with hunger; the practice of jubilee (the regular practice of freeing prisoners and slaves and forgiving debts); and the doing of justice as an intrinsic part of the spiritual life.

Old Testament theology builds a strong case for the centrality of God's concern for the widow, orphan, and stranger, which calls on God's people to protect those marginalized by society—people who risk falling through the cracks of an unjust society unless God and God's people advocate and do justice for them. Because of God's character, God's people are called to replicate this special love for the oppressed: "For the LORD your God . . . executes justice for the orphan and the widow, and loves the strangers, providing them food and clothing. You shall also love the stranger, for you were strangers in the land of Egypt" (Deut 10:17-19).

In the New Testament, Jesus, Matthew, Luke, Paul, and James in particular continue this central theme and lift up God's eternal concern for the poor and marginalized. In the opening chapters of the Gospel of Luke, the author frames Jesus' ministry, using two seminal passages. In Mary's Magnificat, Luke understands the mission of God to turn the world upside down by restoring the marginalized to their rightful place at the banquet of life: "He has brought down the powerful from their thrones, and lifted up the lowly; he has filled the hungry with good things, and sent the rich away

---

[20]"A List of Some of the More Than #2000Verses in Scripture on Poverty and Justice," *Sojourners*, https://sojo.net/list-some-more-2000verses-scripture-poverty-and-justice.

[21]Daniel Hartnett, "Remembering the Poor: An Interview with Gustavo Gutierrez," in *America: The Jesuit Review*, February 3, 2003, www.americamagazine.org/faith/2003/02/03/remembering -poor-interview-gustavo-gutierrez.

empty" (Lk 1:52-53). In Jesus' inaugural sermon at Nazareth, Luke insists on the upside down nature of God's mission as he portrays the very heart of God's mission as restoring those marginalized by poverty and powerlessness: "The Spirit of the Lord is upon me, because he has anointed me to bring good news to the poor. He has sent me to proclaim release to the captives and recovery of sight to the blind, to let the oppressed go free, to proclaim the year of the Lord's favor" (Lk 4:18-19). Matthew 11 recalls Jesus' understanding of his whole ministry as he tells John the Baptist's disciples to report back to him the essence of what Jesus came to do: "The blind receive their sight, the lame walk, the lepers are cleansed, the deaf hear, the dead are raised, and the poor have good news brought to them" (v. 5). Jesus' coming marks the beginning of the fulfillment of God's promise to show favor to the poor and marginalized. Jesus' ministry symbolically and concretely removes barriers from poor and oppressed people's entry into the abundant life God intends for all. In the summary of his apostolic commissioning to go to the Gentiles in Galatians 2, Paul notes that the church leaders in Jerusalem "asked only one thing, that we remember the poor, which was actually what I was eager to do" (Gal 2:10).

From his inaugural sermon at Nazareth as recorded in Luke 4 and throughout his mission as portrayed in all four Gospels, Jesus Christ understands his mission to be as wide as the world but directed in a special, intentional way to the poor and marginalized. He chooses to spend most of his time with the poor, develops deep relationships with them, directs his healing touch to them most frequently, risks scandal by insisting on sharing table fellowship with them, frees them of their demons, and restores them to fullness of life by treating them as equals and by declaring the "year of the Lord's favor" (Lk 4:19), a reference to the Year of Jubilee when land—precisely what the poor needed to sustain life—was returned to them. In short, Jesus Christ was sent by the Father and anointed by the Spirit "to bring good news to the poor" (Lk 4:18). Our understanding of mission as companionship is incomplete unless it takes seriously God's abiding concern for the marginalized—and also something more.

Jesus' ministry not only removed barriers to restore to the center of his realm those pushed to the margins by injustice; he also consistently acted in ways that empowered them, giving them an unanticipated degree of agency in their own healing and restoration. He commissioned the Gerasene de-moniac (Mk 5:1-17 and parallels) to become his witness. Jesus restored to health and wholeness the woman who suffered hemorrhages for twelve years—and publicly credited her faith for her healing (Mk 5:24-34 and par-allels). By using empowering dialogue with the Samaritan woman (Jn 4:1-42) or a surprisingly powerful question to Bartimaeus, the man born blind (Mk 10:46 52) "What do you want me to do for you?"—Jesus steadfastly refuses to assume complete responsibility for an afflicted person's healing, but en-gages them and evokes their faith to be part of their own healing process. In all four Gospels, Jesus frequently includes the sick and afflicted, safeguarding their agency as co-healers with him. This profound commitment to a mission of mutuality invites us to consider the concept of co-development, which we will discuss in depth in chapter five.

The biblical witness to Jesus' special relationship with the poor and op-pressed finds expression in the beliefs and practice of many of our churches. Particularly since Vatican II, many portions of the social doctrine of the Catholic Church examine with deep sensitivity the ways particular public policies will affect the most vulnerable. On timely issues of economic justice, climate change, or immigration, the US Catholic Bishops' Conference con-sistently asks the question, "How will this policy affect the most vulnerable in society?"

While the conflict over the Social Gospel[22] in the United States has di-vided evangelicals and mainline Protestants for a century, recently we have seen a growing confluence of shared concern for the poor and oppressed among US Protestants—and a recognition of the importance of their in-clusion in mission efforts. The Lausanne Covenant (1974), strongly influ-enced by evangelical leaders John Stott, Billy Graham, Samuel Escobar, and Carl F. H. Henry—and by Latin American leader René Padilla's clarion call

---

[22]In the early twentieth century, liberal Protestants in the United States reacted to the growing poverty, alcoholism, and child labor of the industrial age by articulating the Social Gospel in an attempt to apply Christian faith to the problems of the poor. Fundamentalists reacted against what they perceived to be the loss of the spiritual dimensions of the gospel. The resulting conflict opened up a chasm between evangelicals and liberal Protestants, pushing both groups to sharpen and limit their focus—evangelicals generally focused solely or primarily on "spiritual needs" and liberal Protestants solely or primarily on social needs—in ways that distorted the holistic nature of the gospel preached by Jesus and divided the American church.

address[23]—marked the resurgence of a US evangelical commitment to social justice, increasingly seen in evangelical pronouncements and mission practice to the present day.[24] Since the Social Gospel debates, mainline Protestants have often framed their public theology in obedience to their understanding of the biblical priority of caring for the poor and vulnerable, and their ecumenical theological affirmations frequently address concerns of social justice and the root causes of poverty, violence, human trafficking, and exclusion.

Increasingly, US Catholics, evangelicals, and mainline Protestants would agree with British theologian N. T. Wright in the leadership role of the poor, the oppressed, the marginalized: "When God wants to change the world, he doesn't send in the tanks. He sends in the poor in spirit, the meek, the humble, the brokenhearted, the mourners, the hungry for justice, the peacemakers. They are the ones through whom the world gets changed."[25] The apostle Paul put it this way:

> Consider your own call, brothers and sisters: not many of you were wise by human standards, not many were powerful, not many were of noble birth. But God chose what is foolish in the world to shame the wise; God chose what is weak in the world to shame the strong; God chose what is low and despised in the world, things that are not, to reduce to nothing things that are, so that no one might boast in the presence of God. (1 Cor 1:26-29)

To be clear, God works through all people. But Scripture repeatedly witnesses to the upside-down nature of the mission of God, who works in especially powerful ways not through the noble or the powerful but through those who have been shoved to the margins by poverty or injustice.

We American Christians must exercise our witness in the light of Jesus' responses to two of the men of wealth described in juxtaposed texts in Luke 18 and 19. The rich young ruler, who couldn't be Jesus' companion because

---

[23]Latin American evangelical leader C. René Padilla's prescient keynote address at Lausanne 1974 has enduring relevance for American Christians today: "Evangelism and the World," www .lausanne.org/wp-content/uploads/2007/06/0134.pdf.

[24]René Padilla provides a helpful analysis of the early years of this shift in his "Evangelism and Social Responsibility: From Wheaton '66 to Wheaton '83," *Transformation: An International Journal of Holistic Mission* 2, no. 3 (1985): 27-34.

[25]Premier Christian Radio, "#38 Lockdown livestream: Tom answers questions on Facebook live," June 11, 2020, in *Ask NT Wright Anything*, podcast, www.premierchristianradio.com/Shows /Weekday/Ask-NT-Wright-Anything/Podcast/Ask-NT-Wright-Anything-38-Lockdown-livestream -Tom-answers-questions-on-Facebook-Live.

he couldn't bear to part with his wealth, is contrasted with Zacchaeus, whose paradigmatic encounter with Jesus resulted in radical generosity ("Look, half of my possessions, Lord, I will give to the poor") and a commitment to concrete acts of justice that appear to be a kind of reparation ("and if I have defrauded anyone of anything, I will pay back four times as much"). Living in one of the wealthiest nations in the world, US Christians must necessarily encounter the living Christ in their *metanoia* (in New Testament Greek, "turn around, "about-face," "conversion") because to turn and follow Jesus Christ necessarily requires that we turn around in our relationship with the poor and oppressed. In summary, the question is not "Will we include the poor and marginalized in our mission?" but rather "Will we join in God's mission with and through the poor and marginalized?" Companionship gives us a hunger to join with the marginalized on the road of God's mission.

"As the Father has sent me, so I send you," says Jesus in John 20:21. To participate in the mission of God in the way of Jesus Christ, we must do as Jesus did: we must walk with those who have been sidelined by poverty and injustice and understand ourselves to be graciously included by God as their co-missioners. The upside-down circle of mission companionship requires not merely the presence and participation of those the world considers "weak" and "foolish", but their agency and leadership. Mission companionship is the place where those of relatively less power and privilege are given the first word in planning and needs assessment and the last word in decision-making. Biblically speaking, mission that is not primarily concerned about bringing good news to the poor and empowering them to exercise their God-given leadership in the processes of their transformation is an incomplete version of God's mission. This is an essential tenet for engaging in mission in the way of Jesus Christ and is impossible for us to ignore.

A theology of companionship joins four commitments: to walk together in intentional, mutual accompaniment; to share from a place of vulnerability; to keep the triune God at the center of the relationship; and to elicit the presence and leadership of those who have been marginalized. The power of the upside-down circle of companionship arises from God's preference to use the vulnerability of the weak to reveal God's glorious strength, "that no one may boast." This keeps us focused on God's mission, not our own. These four commitments keep us from upstaging God. We end this chapter with Tool 1, a tool that you can use to help your members reflect more deeply on their mission companions.

FOR REFLECTION

1. Think of a recent mission experience (a short-term mission trip, service in a local soup kitchen, joint project, etc.). Can you identify specific elements of the mission activity that would change if your congregation affirmed the four elements of mission as companionship?

2. Which element of companionship (mutual accompaniment, shared vulnerability, a centeredness on the sending God, or mission from the margins) would be the most challenging for your congregation to adopt? Why?

3. In our American context, some congregational mission leaders have worked to deepen their people's understanding of mission beyond the traditional "one-way street" in which economically advantaged partners offer products and services to "needy partners." Imagine changing one recent mission activity so that your church was not the "giver" or "teacher" but "receiver" and "learner" *with* mission companions. Describe the activity and how it would differ from your traditional mission practice.

4. A Peruvian pastor once said to the American church, "You're not the United Way, why is it so hard for you to share what God has done in your life?" Do you think sharing one's faith story is important for Christian witness? Is it possible to engage in mission without sharing this story? Given the history of mission, what are the limitations, if any, when one shares one's testimony?

TOOL 1

WHAT'S IN A PICTURE?

Guidelines for Representing Others Through Photography

BACKGROUND

Has a friend ever posted an unflattering photo of you on social media? Photography has become one of the easiest and most powerful ways to share our stories. With the rise of social media and advancement of technology, everyone now has the ability to take high-quality photos and share them publicly. Because it's so easy to take and post photos, we rarely pause to reflect on the underlying ethical considerations. Every photo tells a story: a well-taken photo can help a cause or clarify a mission need or activity for others, while a poorly taken one can lead to misunderstanding and even greater prejudice toward others. In order to navigate the weighty decision to snap a picture, we advocate holding to the standard of the Golden Rule. If we focus on loving our neighbors as ourselves, how does that inform our photography? When in doubt, we suggest asking yourself, "How would I feel if someone portrayed me in this way?" This is an important question to ask when taking photographs and when deciding to use or share them.

OBJECTIVE: To help church mission leaders and short-term mission travelers visually represent (photograph and display) others in ways that demonstrate dignity, respect, and love of neighbor.

ACKNOWLEDGMENT: The guidelines below are adapted with permission from Global NGO VillageReach and offer some succinct best practices for photography (www.villagereach.org/wp-content/uploads/2020/07/VillageReach-Photography-Guidance-1.pdf).

QUESTIONS TO CONSIDER WHEN TAKING AND SELECTING PHOTOGRAPHS

Motive. *What is the purpose in taking this picture? Why is this person(s), scene or action compelling to you? What story or stories are you trying to portray?* Visual representations of poverty should not be the reason an image is compelling. Representing the context of your work is accomplished by showing the complex, multi-layered reality of the communities with which you work.

Substitution. *Would I consent to this photograph if it was a picture of me, my child or loved one? Would I want my community or neighborhood depicted in this way?* Examine the photo for both obvious and subtle elements that would make you question the picture if it were of you, your family, or your community.

Position. *Does the composition or angle of this photo disempower or marginalize the subject?* Depending on the angle of the photograph, the subject can appear either vulnerable and powerless or having power and agency. Body position where the subject is directly facing the camera with direct eye contact is the most empowering position.

Context. *How does the context or the environment give meaning to the subject of the photograph? What does this expanded meaning communicate to the viewer?* Meaning in an image does not come only from the primary subject, but also from the environment in which they are presented. Think about the environment of the photograph and what it may communicate.

Power. *Who is the "doer" in the image? How does the subject dis/empower vulnerable groups?* Whenever possible, truthfully and accurately portray the people we work with as both doers and receivers of an action. Avoid photographs that reinforce the traditional stereotypes of "givers" and "receivers."

Tone. *Does the emotional tone and message of the image elicit equitable emotions such as empathy, compassion, understanding, or shared humanity? Or does the image rely on "top-down" emotions such as pity, guilt, or sympathy?* Even subtle facial expressions can play a significant role in the viewers' conscious and unconscious reading of an image.

Consent. Informed consent is the active permission of a photography subject, acknowledging and accepting the potential consequences of their participation. Informed consent includes an understanding of how and where these photographs will be used. Every individual has a right to clearly understand what their consent entails and to refuse to be photographed. You must respect this right. If you sense any reluctance or confusion, refrain from taking the photo. No payments or other forms of compensation should be given in exchange for photography consent.

Remember that these tips are not an exhaustive list of the things to consider when taking and using photos in mission work. When in doubt, rely on the Golden Rule–inspired question: "Would I want to be photographed in this way?"

TRAINING EXERCISE FOR MISSION PARTICIPANTS

To help your congregation's mission leaders and participants understand the concepts of ethical representation, you can use the following one-hour program with your group. This will help participants apply the ethical concepts presented in these guidelines so they can better represent others through the many pictures they're going to take during a trip or experience.

Opening "ice-breaker" (10 min.). Invite participants to name a time when they have been in a photo that made them feel embarrassed either about how they looked or how the photo depicted the situation. Ask them to share how it made them feel and what could have been done differently to that image to avoid the negative feelings.

Review core concepts from VillageReach photography guidance (15 min.). The facilitator should review the full document and prepare to share the above summary of the VillageReach guidelines and talk through the major points with the group.

Evaluation of pictures (30 min.). Before the group gathers, make a copy of each of the following six photos, not including the captions. Captions are for the leader's reference only when moderating the discussion. Label each photo from one to six for easy identification and place them on a table in your gathering room. Instruct participants to walk around the table in silence, look carefully at each photo, and answer these questions about each photo:

- What do you observe in the photo?

- How does each picture empower or disempower the people in the image?

- Does the image reinforce traditional stereotypes of "benevolent givers" and "passive receivers"? What would you change to make that picture embody the dignity of your mission companions?

- After everyone has finished, have them share their responses with the group. Use the captions provided on each photo to help participants stretch their awareness and to deepen the group's conversation.

Application (5 min.). Think through your ministry context or your upcoming mission trip, especially how you can respectfully represent the people you encounter, being sensitive to cultural cues as to when taking pictures is acceptable. It's always important to ask your host if it's acceptable to take any pictures wherever you go, especially if you want to take pictures of children. If at all possible, explain how you would like to use the pictures.

Realizing that photos of White people working alongside people of color can project an image of "White savior," it's important to think about how you would approach taking these pictures. How would you portray your group in relationship with your mission companions? What would you include or not in the pictures? How will these images be shared on social media? Close the session with a prayer.

Figure T1.1. Health clinic in Africa, church providing health care for the community, mother accompanies daughter from clinic visit, maternal love and care for child, worn infrastructure, etc.

Figure T1.2. White worker provides food to child of color, other workers of color present in photo's margins, stereotypical presentation of benevolent White worker providing for needy child, etc.

Figure T1.3. Foreign volunteer cuddles and kisses children, children appear awkward (where are their parents?), stereotypical presentation of "White savior" caring for needy children of color, etc.

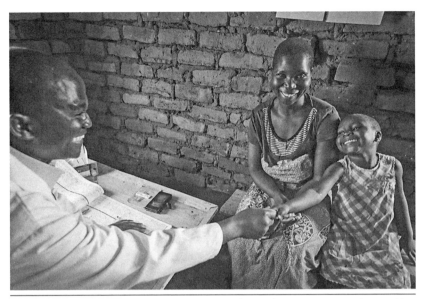

Figure T1.4. Moment of mutual delight between African physician, young patient, and her mother; child expresses trust and joy; physician exudes care, delight, and sensitivity (carefully grasping child's outstretched finger); mother appears relaxed and trusts the physician's relationship with her child, etc. Could child be imagining herself as a physician someday?

Figure T1.5. "Circle of care" around African children: mothers support their children surrounded by (health?) workers, camera angle foregrounds personhood of children and their mothers, warmth and joy, etc.

Figure T1.6. The boy looks sad and dirty. He seems to be homeless and seems to be begging for something. He is alone without anyone with him (Where is his family? Where is he in this picture? Is he at his own neighborhood or refugee camp?). The photo was taken from a top-down angle with a boy looking up that portrays the boy as powerless to the viewers.

FOUR

THE SECOND STONE

An Invitation to Cultural Humility

ONE DAY I HAD AN all-day meeting at a mission hospital an hour away from the seminary where my wife, Ruth, and I worked in DR Congo. Ruth decided to visit a sick friend and invited two young Congolese boys to go with her for some fun exploring the hospital grounds. The boys seemed to enjoy the day, and at the end of the hot afternoon they sat, watching some of the hospital personnel playing tennis. One of the employees asked the boys if they would each like to have a tennis ball. The boys' eyes lit up and they eagerly accepted.

When we returned home, Ruth asked the boys if they wanted her to write their names on the balls so people would know whose they were. They did. Then seven-year-old Mikobi asked if she would write his brother Tshejo's name on the ball too. She thought how nice that was and wrote "Tshejo." Then, Mikobi asked if she would write his friend Dilunda's name on the ball. Something stopped her in her tracks—maybe it was a fear that there would be confusion over whose ball it really was. So Ruth paused and said, "Mikobi, this is *your* ball." He looked at her, confused, and finally said, "Mamu, if my friends had gone on the trip wouldn't they have gotten a ball?"

Mikobi's words caused us to realize that in years of interactions with Congolese friends, we had never heard from their children the often-repeated protest of American two-year-olds: "That's mine!" Items that, to us, should have been personal possessions were shared with much greater freedom among Congolese families than we were accustomed to. Yet don't we in

North America hear our two-year-olds scream "that's mine!" every day and simply ascribe it to human nature? The "that's mine!" response is, in fact, not a biological response but a culturally conditioned one. It is indeed learned— and we're the ones who taught them. "This is Daddy's. This is yours." We teach our children the rigorous rules of private property first; then, we struggle for years to teach them how to share.

For Mikobi, sharing came first. He received a prized possession and naturally wanted to share it. Which of these two cultural understandings seems closer to God's desire for how we live together as a people—as a global community? Jesus tells the rich young ruler clearly what is lacking in his nearly perfect life: "Sell all that you own and distribute the money to the poor, and you will have treasure in heaven; then come, follow me" (Lk 18:22). All cultural perspectives, including our own, are limited and imperfect. But Mikobi's words—growing out of his Congolese cultural values—held up a mirror to our own deeply held, but invisible, individualistic assumptions and opened our eyes to a more biblical way of understanding our relationship to our possessions and to our neighbor. Suddenly we became aware that our perspective on Scripture was obscured by our own cultural assumptions and needed the light of our Congolese companions' perspective. Without companions who see from different cultural vantage points, we might lose our way on the road of God's mission.

A DIVERSE WORLD

The second foundational stone for our practical vision is often underestimated and sometimes completely overlooked by many US Christians as we venture into local and global communities. In a world of increasing cultural diversity, loving our neighbor who is culturally different from us often requires understanding and communicating effectively with them in terms they can understand. This skill set is especially needed when we consider that cultural difference is present in all of our lives almost all the time: though we will discuss a more precise definition of cultural difference later in the chapter, for now we should bear in mind that cultural difference includes economic status, language background, nationality, race/ethnicity, sexual orientation, gender identity, and religion. Each of these elements of cultural difference shapes the lens through which we see the world.

We live in a context of growing cultural diversity across the United States—Latinx are a growing presence in cities and rural communities from North Carolina to Arkansas to California. Minneapolis is home to more than one hundred thousand Somalis. Small towns across the country have become home to people from around the world as the foreign-born population of the country has grown to 44.5 million—resulting in its largest share of the US population since 1910.[1]

There was a time when mission suggested that missionaries travel long distances and live in a specific location for decades, learning the language and local ways of thinking. Today, most middle-sized American cities (especially but not limited to cities with a university or industry or increasing construction) have people of dozens of nationalities living and working in them. Larger cities can be home to people of more than a hundred nationalities.

In addition, a large number of new immigrant groups in many cities and towns were evangelized by Catholic and Protestant missionaries many years ago and have come to the States with their faith and a deep sense of identity as missionaries. Sixty-one percent of legal immigrants to the United States in 2012 were Christians; in addition, among the approximately 11.1 million unauthorized immigrants living in the country, a 2011 Pew Research Center study estimates 83 percent of them are Christian.[2] Burmese Baptists (the spiritual descendants of American Baptist missionary Adoniram Judson), Latin American Catholics and Pentecostals, and Brazilian, Indian, and Nigerian Methodists have migrated to the United States in recent years, strengthening struggling churches, even as they bring a renewed commitment to prayer, evangelism, church planting, and, in many cases, a more holistic view of the gospel that brings together social justice and evangelism. Diversity and opportunities for serving and witnessing across cultural difference are abundant today across the breadth of our country even without leaving the country.

---

[1] Jason Lange and Yeganeh Torbati, "U.S. Foreign-Born Population Swells to Highest in Over a Century," Reuters, September 13, 2018, www.reuters.com/article/us-usa-immigration-data /u-s-foreign-born-population-swells-to-highest-in-over-a-century-idUSKCN1LT2HZ.

[2] Pew Research Center, Religion and Public Life, "The Religious Affiliation of U.S. Immigrants: Majority Christian, Rising Share of Other Faiths," May 17, 2013, www.pewforum.org/2013/05/17 /the-religious-affiliation-of-us-immigrants/#affiliation.

The rapid growth and accessibility of international air travel and the rising levels of disposable income among US Christians have made international short-term mission trips a major and growing component of the mission program of many US congregations, whether small or large. Robert Wuthnow estimates that almost one-third of all US mission funding is used to pay for short-term mission trips.[3] Among very large congregations, Robert Priest found that "94% of megachurch (that is, churches with average Sunday attendance of 2000 or more) high school youth programs organize short-term mission trips abroad for their youth, with 78% doing so one or more times per year."[4] Overall, Priest and his coauthors estimate that 1.5 million US Christians annually go on short-term mission trips,[5] many of them beyond national borders. If in years past a congregation's experience of intercultural mission was often mediated through "their" missionary, today local church members in Middle America engage interculturally through short-term missions, outreach to international students from dozens of countries who are studying at a local college, and relationships and financial support of projects with global partners. In addition, within US churches, there is an increasing diversity that calls for leadership with the ability to navigate cultural differences: "The percentage of multiracial congregations in the United States nearly doubled from 1998 to 2012, with about one in five American congregants attending a place of worship that is racially mixed."[6]

As a result of all these factors, there has never been a time in the history of the American church when the need for skills in cultural proficiency has been greater. Unless congregational mission leaders are able to help their people communicate more effectively across cultural differences, we limit our love—and the effectiveness of our witness—to groups who mirror our same cultural values and patterns. US cultural patterns tend to prioritize

---

[3]Robert Wuthnow, *Boundless Faith: The Global Outreach of American Churches* (Berkeley: University of California Press, 2009), 180.

[4]Robert Priest, "U.S. Megachurches and New Patterns of Global Mission," *International Bulletin of Missionary Research* 34, no. 2 (2010): 98.

[5]Robert Priest, "Introduction to Theme Issue on Short-Term Missions," *Missiology: An International Review* 34, no. 4 (2006): 431-50.

[6]"Multiracial Congregations Have Nearly Doubled, but They Still Lag Behind the Makeup of Neighborhoods," Baylor University, June 20, 2018, www.baylor.edu/mediacommunications/news .php?action=story&story=199850.

values such as efficiency, achievement, and individual freedom, even as we struggle to understand the people of other cultural traditions who tend to prioritize relationship, group harmony, and community. Among the greatest challenges to faithful and effective mission is effective intercultural communication—having the cultural proficiency to navigate around the misunderstandings, mistakes, confusion, hurt feelings, and broken relationships that litter the field of our churches' interaction with local and global companions. For these reasons, in this section, we will first look at the culture concept and then build a framework with the concepts of cultural proficiency and cultural humility, evaluate their importance, and offer specific tools to grow a congregation's ability to navigate cultural difference.

Although ethnocentrism has characterized much of the colonial era of the history of Christian mission, intercultural encounters have the power to open up a space of grace-filled transformation for all who enter with a learner's heart. If the ethnocentrism resulting from colonial assumptions creates barriers to our loving well, this chapter will argue that cultural humility can serve as a powerful antidote to reduce those barriers. How many times have I watched as an American visitor has surprised and delighted a congregation abroad by greeting them in their native language? What a simple but powerful way to communicate, "I love and respect you and am here to learn from you." How can we develop this prayerful attitude of cultural humility? First, we must understand the depth of the chasm caused by cultural difference in our diverse world.

THE CULTURE CONCEPT

Cultural difference is something each of us is simultaneously aware of (*That's not how I would do it*) and surprisingly ignorant of (*It didn't occur to me that they might feel this way*). In my work with colleagues in different countries, I've heard many definitions of the culture concept. Kihani Masasu, my Congolese seminary student, focused on how culture identifies, or characterizes, a social group: "It's what makes us 'us' as opposed to 'you.'"[7] Peruvian anthropologist Luís Mujica highlighted the implicit nature of culture: "It's everything you don't know you know";[8] that is, culture includes the innu-

---

[7]Personal interview, February 12, 1990.
[8]Personal interview, May 22, 2001.

merable, unwritten "rules" every group of people develops to determine how you greet, who you can kiss, how you explain misfortune, or how you bury the dead. Pastor Mukuna Tshitebua, a Congolese pastor and mentor of mine, insisted on the changing nature of cultural patterns—a group's customs today are shaped by, but not identical to, how their ancestors lived: "The ways of our people are a river, not a lake."[9] I experienced the changing nature of US culture when our family returned to the States from Peru after ten years there (with only brief trips to the States during that period). We were living in Peru when the Twin Towers in New York City were destroyed on September 11, 2001, and, upon returning to the States seven years later, we realized that the theme of security had become much more central to US ways of thinking. September 11th proved to be a culture-altering experience in the life of the American people that deeply affected our shared view of the American people's vulnerability in what we perceive to be an increasingly dangerous world.

Beginning with Gary Weaver,[10] many authors have used the iceberg metaphor to help describe the fact that, while there are many visible aspects of culture symbolized by the smaller, more visible portion of the iceberg (food, dress, behavior, speech, etc.), there is a much larger, submerged portion that includes a social group's shared values, attitudes, assumptions, and beliefs, all of which have a deep, if not hidden, impact on the visual aspects of culture. Trying new foods, wearing culturally appropriate clothing, learning a local greeting—these actions deal with the more superficial aspects of a culture and represent important first steps. Learning about a different culture is a long journey, but, like a series of switchbacks up a hill, at each turn we can look back and realize how far we have come, and because it is motivated by our desire to love our neighbor, we find it difficult to turn back. Shannon Garrett, a Pittsburgh Theological Seminary student, discovered this on an intercultural trip to Cuba: "I tell people now that I'm back I can't 'un-see' Cuba—I can't 'un-know' what I know about Cuba now. So I think I will always be concerned about the people of Cuba now."[11]

---

[9]Personal conversation, June 16, 1988.

[10]Gary Weaver, ed., *Culture, Communication and Conflict: Readings in Intercultural Relations* (Boston, MA: Pearson Publications, 2000).

[11]Personal interview, April 22, 2019.

If ten people are located in different places in a soccer stadium and witness a fight between two players, each one will observe the events—frustration, provocation, response, a shove, and a red card—from her or his own perspective. Some of the factors will be which team they are supporting, what role they are playing (official, player, coach, spectator), their physical location in the stadium, whether they were paying attention, and so on. Each witness's perspective on the incident is limited and deeply influenced by these factors. As the father of a Major League Soccer player, it is hard for me to see my son's errors impartially, and any criticism on Twitter of his performance during a game elicits an immediate, defensive reaction in me. I can't help it—it's just that my perspective is so heavily influenced by my social location in relationship to him: I am his father.

Likewise, every human being has a cultural perspective: from an extremely hierarchical perspective or a flat, more democratic perspective; a concern for the long-term game or a tendency to favor short-term advantage; valuing the individual's rights and responsibilities or viewing things through the lens of the "common good." Culture, then, is a way that groups of people make sense of or interpret what goes on around them. These different interpretations represent people's efforts to deal with the basic problems of human life: how we will eat, communicate, protect ourselves from the elements, and so on.

In summary, we could define *culture* as "the changing set of shared and implicit values, attitudes, practices and systems of meaning that characterize a group of people and help them make sense of the world." This simplified definition recognizes that the culture concept refers to how a group—not an individual—makes meaning of different situations; that cultural patterns are constantly changing; that much cultural knowledge takes the form of unstated, implicit assumptions among members of a social group; and that, while the visible elements of culture include artifacts and behaviors, these more superficial elements often point to the underlying values, attitudes, and beliefs held by a group of people.

But many people have been on the wrong end of the misuse of the culture concept: my Gaelic-speaking, Irish immigrant ancestors would have been among those stereotyped by the English-speaking community of nineteenth-century Philadelphia as lazy and untrustworthy. At that time, to be Irish was to be condemned to membership in an unalterable biological category with inescapable behavioral consequences, hence the "No Irish Need Apply" sign that for years served as a barrier to employment, economic well-being, and dignity. This harmful tendency to stereotype continues in our present day, negatively impacting people of color, people living in homelessness, LGBTQ persons, people with differing abilities, and many others. So while we may tend to think of all Americans as having a common "American culture," we recognize that a gay Latino male's social location will give him a perspective that a straight White female would not necessarily share. This is the nuance of cultural difference: all may be American, but there are definite differences in how people from these groups live based on their experiences, understood through the lens they inherited from their ancestors.

For that reason, we will need to use caution and recognize the limitations of the culture concept. To speak of "US culture" as if it were a monolithic set of values, beliefs, speech, and behaviors would be grossly inaccurate and could "whitewash" the lived experience of race, as White dominant culture is often used normatively in the United States. The significant variation across the cultural patterns of the large social group we call "Americans" is breathtaking: upper-middle income, African American professionals in suburban Atlanta; young, Latinx students in Denver; members of a predominantly White retirement community in the Midwest; recent immigrants from South Sudan in Sacramento; gang members in a major city—each group is unique in some ways from other social groups within the United States, and within each group there is also individual variation. Therefore, when we talk about cultural patterns, we need to be aware that we run the risk of reducing the God-created complexity and beauty of human variation into simplistic stereotypes.

Cultural anthropologists see patterns across large groups of people precisely because these patterns are scientifically verifiable—that is, they exist and provide pathways for thinking and speaking about members of a given social group. In addition, every individual also exercises agency—the God-given ability to reflect critically on one's cultural patterns, to innovate, to refrain from certain behaviors, and to adopt others. This nuance, of course, renders our conversation more complex, but it also keeps us honest—*none of our analytical categories determine an individual's behavior.* History is full of creative, innovative individuals and even people who have stood up against harmful cultural practices of their own people. Let's examine cultural patterns to see in more detail some of their rich dimensions.

FIVE DIMENSIONS OF CULTURAL DIFFERENCE

Given the complexity of the culture concept, one of the challenges of becoming more skilled at communicating across cultural difference is that few of us take the time to study it more deeply. To develop our capacity to communicate well with the thousands of cultural groups around the world would, at first glance, seem like an impossible task! Yet by identifying some of the specific dimensions of culture that can be observed in the patterns of all social groups, we take the first, important steps in unpacking cultural complexity into a specific, observable spectrum—and develop the tools of analysis that will help us in whatever cultural context we find ourselves.

Hofstede, Hofstede, and Minkov identified six specific dimensions of cultural difference in their often-cited book *Cultures and Organizations*.[12] We'll look at four of these dimensions to help us think about cultural difference, and we will add a fifth dimension, *indirect versus direct communication*, that is at the root of much intercultural misunderstanding and conflict. These cultural dimensions are summarized in Tool 2 at the end of this chapter.

Individualistic versus collectivistic. Hofstede defines this dimension of cultural difference thus: "Individualism pertains to societies in which the ties of individuals are loose: everyone is expected to look after him- or herself. And his or her immediate family. Collectivism . . . pertains to societies in which people from birth onward are integrated into strong, cohesive in-groups, which throughout people's lifetime continue to protect them in exchange for unquestioning loyalty."[13] Again, Hofstede describes the general tendencies; we will have to provide the nuance and note the exceptions of individual behaviors.

Especially in US White dominant cultural patterns, children are generally taught from birth to take care of themselves and not be dependent on others (individualistic orientation). In many other cultural traditions,

---

[12]Geert Hofstede, Gert Jan Hofstede, and Michael Minkov, *Cultures and Organizations* (New York: McGraw-Hill, 2010).
[13]Hofstede, Hofstede, and Minkov, *Cultures and Organizations*, 92.

interdependence (giving up a measure of personal independence for the good of the family or community) is more highly valued than individual freedom. The implications of this simple but fundamental difference in cultural orientation shape one's perspective in surprising, far-reaching ways. In a more individualistic cultural orientation, competition is often rewarded and the employer-employee relationship is a contract between parties and can be terminated when the contract has been satisfied rather than binding employer and employee together, like a family bond, as seen in a more collectivist orientation.

The contrast between these two orientations can generate some significant misunderstandings. A US child-sponsorship agency may find that it is impossible to provide financial support for only one sibling in a family without creating significant family conflict in a more collectivist context, where the well-being of the group is prioritized over that of any individual. For collectivist-oriented people, group harmony is often prized over individual fulfillment. A Congolese colleague of mine—raised in that generally more collectivist orientation than my own US White dominant culture—appeared embarrassed when a foreigner publicly commented on the new shirt he was wearing. My colleague tried to signal to the foreigner to keep quiet and even denied that the shirt was new. Later, he explained privately that new clothes or purchases could be perceived as separating him from the group and he didn't want to make his friends feel bad. He used a phrase in the Tshiluba language I had not heard before, literally: "I didn't want to throw myself ahead of the others." I was struck by his remarkable sensitivity to managing potential jealousy. In my more individualistic cultural orientation, I feel individual pride in wearing a new shirt as it contributes positively to my personal prestige and self-image. In fact, while some cultural traditions ensure every individual is free to earn and possess as much as they like, others value ensuring that everyone has enough; some foster individual achievement, while others ensure survival. You can imagine the starkly different cultural lenses we're looking through when we differ even in our understanding of what it means to be "outstanding": for some, it is the highest compliment; for others, if is a sign of selfishness and immaturity.

Power distance. This is "the extent to which the less powerful members of organizations and institutions (like the family) accept and expect that power is distributed unequally."[14] Latin American cultures, according to Hofstede, perceive a more hierarchical structure to societies (see Tool 2): there have been and can be real consequences for "speaking truth to power." In US White dominant culture, folks tend to believe that the world's playing field is level. In my family, we believed that, if a person worked hard enough, he or she could become president of the United States someday. This, in fact, is not entirely accurate, but because we operate on the assumptions of this "level playing field," anthropologists consider us to be part of a "low power distance" cultural tradition—that is, the distance between the more powerful and less powerful members of society is perceived to be less than that of high power distance societies. In Euro-American cultural patterns, students may respect their teachers but feel empowered to (respectfully!) question them and even disagree with them in front of other students—a behavior you will see less frequently in France and quite rarely in Malaysia or Guatemala. As my children have grown up, they tend to call my friends by their first name and treat my wife and me more as equals. Patients feel empowered to ask direct questions about a doctor's diagnosis, and most don't hesitate to argue publicly with their elected representatives—sometimes with painful clarity.

Because of the Euro-American cultural focus on individual rights, we may grow impatient when people struggling against oppression seem to believe their voice doesn't matter: it may be that their lived experience has taught them that there are real and painful consequences for raising their voice. We may recognize power distance differences but not appreciate how deeply it may impact communication and relationships. For example, we are frustrated when it feels impossible to elicit what we perceive to be an "honest answer" when evaluating a joint activity with colleagues from higher power distance cultural traditions, even when we sense something has gone wrong. It may be that it's not honesty that's missing from the answer but directness and that the experience serves as an invitation to learn how to communicate more indirectly. We can be blind to the fact that what we seek is an American cultural answer: quick, direct, and explicit. Our challenge is to allow our mission companions to communicate in their own ways, even when it

---

[14]Hofstede, Hofstede, and Minkov, *Cultures and Organizations*, 61.

creates frustration for us. You can imagine that our ways of communicating are causing our companions no small amount of frustration as well.

The intercultural difference in the perception of power distance is a major challenge to congregations working locally or globally because power distance is perceived and acted on at a deep level of the "cultural iceberg," to return to Weaver's analogy. It takes culturally proficient leaders who have reflected on their own assumptions about mission to cross the chasm of the perceptions of power distance: only those who have begun to (1) identify and critically examine our natural, colonial-era assumptions and (2) to reflect on the power dynamics present in most mission encounters will be able to communicate respectfully and effectively. So enduring was the impact of the European colonial era that when a US dominant cultural group connects with local mission companions in a community of the Global South, it is possible for a US church group to initiate contact, assess needs, and propose, plan, fund, implement, and evaluate a project before they realize they haven't really heard their companions' voice.

Uncertainty avoidance. This has been described as "the extent to which the members of a culture feel threatened by ambiguous or unknown situations."[15] I was in a hurry to return to my home in Lima, Peru, after several weeks spent in a high-elevation, Quechua-speaking community in the Peruvian region of Huancavelica. I hopped into one of the *colectivos*—the cars that carry four passengers on the all-day trip to descend twelve thousand feet to sea level—and found myself seated between two men whom I perceived to be business associates. One was a young Norwegian with a briefcase, the other a middle-aged indigenous man, whom I'll call Juan Luís, from Saqsamarca, the indigenous community adjacent to the area where I was working. As the three of us made small talk at the start of the long journey, the Norwegian grew frustrated and exclaimed, "I can't believe they turned me down!" He quickly summarized what he described as his four wasted days scouring Saqsamarca seeking a community that would grow organic oregano, a spice that commanded a high price in Europe and, the Norwegian insisted, could lift the poor indigenous communities out of their poverty. "Now I understand why they're poor," he concluded. "No one

---

[15]Hofstede, Hofstede, and Minkov, *Cultures and Organizations*, 191.

is willing to try anything new." There was a long pause and then Juan Luís stated without emotion, "We are grateful for your visit."

In the long silence that followed his reply, I began to think through the significance of the exchange. After we arrived in Lima, I offered to buy Juan Luís a cup of coffee at the busy Yerbateros bus stop on Lima's east side. As we talked over coffee, Juan Luís was reticent to speak too directly about the Norwegian's business proposal, but he answered my questions with a story. Many indigenous communities in Peru survived the years following the brutal Spanish conquest by doing precisely what Saqsamarca had just done: express warmth and welcome, all the while protecting their communities against foreigner-imposed change. It was these cultural traditions that kept life in Saqsamarca in balance, ensuring each segment of society got what they needed. The Norwegian's "innovation," in Saqsamarca, meant investing precious time, seed, and expensive fertilizer in a crop they had never grown. If the organic oregano experiment had succeeded according to projections, the resulting rapid rise in income for some of the community's families would have created jealousy and conflict. If the experiment had failed, all the inputs of labor, financial investment, and the leadership's prestige (and thus the community's political stability) would have been lost. The community's response—for Juan Luís—was a "no-brainer."

But my own Euro-American cultural traditions allowed me to understand the foreigner's perspective: Wasn't *anything* better than the abject poverty our eyes saw in Saqsamarca? Who could say no to the chance for additional income? Why not try oregano? Like the soccer stadium analogy, it depends on where one is socially located and the cultural assumptions one carries that influence what one sees. Because my own US White dominant cultural assumptions were closer to the Norwegian's, I could understand his frustration. How many times had I urged a Peruvian indigenous community to take action, to stand up for its rights, to dare to innovate, only to be met with a respectful silence or a pointedly lukewarm affirmation of my "brilliant" idea—what Duane Elmer calls the "relational yes,"[16] that is, an affirmative response that masks underlying doubt or refusal. I realized that on

---

[16]Duane Elmer, *Cross-Cultural Conflict: Building Relationships for Effective Ministry* (Downers Grove, IL: InterVarsity Press, 1993), 118-20.

the journey from Huancavelica I had been blessed with the chance to see more deeply into the dimension of cultural difference known as uncertainty avoidance that describes how we engage innovation and change.

Long-term versus short-term orientation. Hofstede notes that "Long-Term Orientation stands for the fostering . . . of pragmatic virtues oriented to future rewards, in particular perseverance, thrift, and adapting to changing circumstances. Its opposite pole, Short-Term Orientation, stands for the fostering in a society of virtues related to the past and the present."[17] Hofstede found a strong correlation between long-term oriented societies and saving, the perception of thrift as a desirable trait in children and a valuing of the pragmatic (which draws people to "middle road" choices) rather than more abstract principles (which can draw people to more radical, fundamentalist choices). East Asian cultural patterns in South Korea, Taiwan, Japan, and China, for Hofstede, generally illustrate this long-term orientation, such as in their concern for succeeding generations. US White dominant culture's general tendency toward instant gratification, focus on this year's "bottom line," and valuing of freedom over self-discipline illustrate countervailing tendencies.

I got an insider's look into this dimension of culture when I was the guest of a group of aboriginal Protestant leaders in Taiwan. A team of youth leaders was presenting their work plan, and I noticed how often they referenced their grandchildren as the justification for their work in Bible translation, Christian education, and environmental education. This was all the more remarkable because none of them were more than twenty-five years old: few of them even had children! But one of the leaders answered my surprised look by saying, "We will be here for but a short time. Our work needs to strengthen the church of our grandchildren." The contrast with the documented US bias toward immediate results, our decreasing rates of household savings, and our ignorance of the environmental impacts of our consumer choices was clear. I was reminded of the powerful influence our economic system, built on overproduction and the creation of need for a product, exerts on our patterns of behavior.

---

[17]Geert Hofstede, "Long- Versus Short-Term Orientation in 10 Minutes," January 2015, https://geer thofstede.com/wp-content/uploads/2016/08/Long-Short-Term-Orientation-in-10-minutes -2015-09-05.pptx.

Indirect versus direct communication. The primary goal of direct communication is "getting or giving information . . . [and] the speaker is responsible for clear communication. In indirect communication . . . the meaning is conveyed not just by the words used but by nonverbal behaviors . . . [such as] implication, understatement, and a widely shared understanding of the context of the communication. Indirect communicators seek to avoid conflict, tension and uncomfortable situations."[18]

Intercultural business consultant Eleni LoPorto describes somewhat stereotypically the contrasting behaviors of direct and indirect communicators to tease out the difference for her readers. To direct communicators,

> Meanings are explicit and on the surface. Direct Communicators are driven by a strong sense of immediacy. They are often in a hurry to get the job done. They get to the "bottom line" quickly. They don't have much patience with those who "beat around the bush." They are frequently perceived as being "brutally honest" in their interactions. They are comfortable displaying their emotions outwardly and do so routinely. They will look you in the eye and if you do not return the eye contact, they will assume that you are hiding something or that you are not to be "trusted."
>
> **Indirect communicators,** on the other hand . . . are all about respecting others and they value courtesy highly. They will always seek out the polite response. They will be hesitant to give bad news. They will find a way to avoid directly answering a question. They will change the subject. To indicate disagreement, they will say "It will be difficult." They will leave sentences unfinished. They will not admit a lack of understanding. To communicate, they will frequently tell a story and allow the listener to come to his own conclusions. Meanings are implicit and embedded. They use silence to communicate. In fact, indirect communicators believe that it is better to talk too little than too much. An indirect communicator's use of silence is a good indication of his/her power or rank in society. The "bold response" in the world of indirect communicators is a "rude response." Indirect communicators conceal their emotions.[19]

---

[18]Cynthia Joyce, "The Impact of Direct and Indirect Communication," *The Independent Voice*, November 2012, https://conflictmanagement.org.uiowa.edu/sites/conflictmanagement.org .uiowa.edu/files/2020-01/Direct%20and%20Indirect%20Communication.pdf.

[19]Eleni LoPorto, "Indirect Communication vs. Direct Communication," Cross Cultural Insights, December 21, 2010, https://crossculturalinsights.wordpress.com/2010/12/21/indirect-communication -vs-direct-communication/.

While communication styles cannot always be divided quite so neatly into categories,[20] LoPorto's observations help us distinguish some useful elements. My observations of American missionaries (short- and long-term alike) is that we consistently "over-drive our headlights"—that is, in the fog of intercultural communication, we assume we know what is going on and project our own cultural assumptions onto our mission companions. In fact, US White dominant cultures' extremely individualistic orientation, low power distance assumptions, and direct communication style can combine to create a "perfect storm" where we can be in relationship with mission companions for years and never notice we haven't actually heard the authentic voices of the community. The results can be harmful to companions and to the relationships that undergird our shared journey in God's mission. When we communicate interculturally, proceeding with caution and some intentional strategies can help us refrain from hurting people we care about.

LISTENER-ORIENTED COMMUNICATION

How I wish someone had explained these contrasting orientations of cultural difference before I went to live in DR Congo.[21] Dr. Tshihamba Mukome Luendu was the head of the Presbyterian Community of Zaire, and I worked as his administrative assistant. He had earned his bachelor's degree at Vanderbilt University and his master's and doctoral degrees in history at Howard University in Washington, DC, and had worked with many American missionaries over the years. He was extremely culturally proficient and had the heart of a patient teacher. It was Dr. Tshihamba who pointed out that there were different ways of communicating: how to speak with silence, to respond with one's eyes, to defer by merely looking downward. In our frequent conversations, I would unload pent-up feelings in a long monologue about a particular frustration or what I perceived to be an inconsistency in Congolese Christian culture. Dr. Tshihamba would listen patiently (in this region of Congo, only a child would be immature enough to air their feelings to a social superior as I did). He would often tell

---

[20]LoPorto adopts a critical view of her own cultural tradition's direct communication style and an open and appreciate attitude toward the more indirect style of communication she has learned to navigate.

[21]Then called the Republic of Zaire.

a story of a foreigner who had learned to engage effectively in indirect communication and sometimes would quote the French proverb "Toute vérité n'est pas bonne à dire" ("Every truth need not be said").

Under his tutelage, I began to see that, while communication often entails specific content and can respond to precise contexts, intercultural communication is built on the principle of listener-oriented communication—the recognition that the receivers of communication sort, decode, and make sense of a received message using the lens of their own cultural assumptions. I began to cultivate the spiritual discipline of engaging in listener-oriented communication, speaking in terms my listener could best understand. In his book on working with Hui Muslims in northwest China,[22] missiologist Enoch Jinsik Kim illustrates the application of this concept that he calls "receptor-oriented communication": no matter how eloquent your presentation, it will not be understood as you intend if the receivers cannot "map" your message onto their existing cultural categories. Listener-oriented communication invites us to be fully present with the culturally "other," watching them carefully, listening to them deeply, responding as often with a question for clarification as with an answer. I continue to work on this discipline of mirroring my conversation partner's style of communication: when a South Asian student comes to my office and I perceive him to be speaking to me from a high power distance context (thus giving me more respect than I'm accustomed to!), my feelings say to hurriedly "level the playing field" to communicate warmth and acceptance in my own low power distance terms (which would reduce my anxiety but confuse the student). But I'm learning to try to accept, at least temporarily, the status he assigns me and respond to the best of my ability on his terms: I try to speak less, to listen more attentively, to offer advice sparingly. The reactions I have observed among students and other conversation partners—of a sense of acceptance and the joy of being known by someone of a different cultural background—have led to both clearer communication and deeper relationships.

In the incarnation, God embodies the spiritual discipline of listener-oriented communication, being fully present with us, by taking on human

[22]Enoch Jinsik Kim, *Receptor-Oriented Communication for Hui Muslims in China with Special Reference to Church Planting*, American Society of Missiology monograph series, no. 37 (Eugene, OR: Wipf & Stock, 2018).

form—"tabernacling" among us in the person of Jesus of Nazareth (Jn 1:14). Jesus the Son of Man was a perfect, culturally understandable way of communicating God's deep yearning to be in relationship with humanity in first-century Palestine. The incarnation itself reveals the Holy One's desire to communicate incomprehensible love, power, and tenderness in terms we could understand. Because listener-oriented communication insists it doesn't matter how eloquent the message the speaker intends, what matters is the message the listener perceives.

In the same way, the apostle Paul practiced this spiritual discipline in his intercultural ministry with both Aramaic-speaking Jews and Greek-speaking Gentiles, as seen in 1 Corinthians 9:19-23:

> For though I am free with respect to all, I have made myself a slave to all, so that I might win more of them. To the Jews I became as a Jew, in order to win Jews. To those under the law I became as one under the law (though I myself am not under the law) so that I might win those under the law. To those outside the law I became as one outside the law (though I am not free from God's law but am under Christ's law) so that I might win those outside the law. To the weak I became weak, so that I might win the weak. I have become all things to all people, that I might by all means save some. I do it all for the sake of the gospel, so that I may share in its blessings.

Paul intentionally adapts the posture of a servant and engages in listener-oriented communication so that his communication style will not impede his hearers' understanding of God's unconditional love. As I reflect historically, I wonder how the world's perception of Christian mission would be different today had we engaged in this kind of biblical, listener-oriented communication. This communication style requires an intentional process of learning: a cycle of intercultural encounter/action and subsequent reflection on the encounter.

Culture learning is iterative: each encounter can generate a new discovery that deepens our awareness of the different mental maps, or logics, that guide our responses and decision-making in relationship to the host community. Because intercultural learnings bring together information, feelings, and our own beliefs (engaging intellectual, affective, and moral modes of learning), they tend to penetrate us deeply and stay with us.

When your church members return from volunteering a night at the local homeless shelter and process with you their feelings of being transformed, you can be sure they are experiencing the "deep learning" of the intercultural, experiential encounter. We'll discuss in chapter eight how you can invite your own church's mission leaders—or even your youth group or a Sunday school class—into intercultural, experiential learning encounters at a local homeless shelter to create a space of deep, transformative learning. To suggest how mission leaders can develop the skills to communicate effectively across cultural difference, we now turn to the concept of cultural proficiency.

CULTURAL PROFICIENCY

Anthropologists, business leaders, educators, health professionals—it seems like everyone today is talking about cultural proficiency. In a world of increasing cultural difference, cultural proficiency can be simply understood as the ability to navigate—perceiving, listening, understanding, communicating, and acting—across cultural differences. This concept is also known as cultural intelligence or cultural competence, but I will use the term *cultural proficiency* for two reasons: (1) to avoid the association of cultural intelligence (Livermore's "CQ"[23]) with the better-known intelligence quotient ("IQ"), which cannot be increased during one's lifetime, and (2) to avoid the connotation of competence as an all-or-nothing condition (as in one's mental competence that can be certified by a court). In contrast, proficiency suggests a range of capacities (beginner's proficiency, highly proficient, etc.) that seems more appropriate to the developmental stages of intercultural communication.

In our 2017 survey of Catholic, mainline Protestant, and evangelical congregational mission leaders, a large number expressed the need for concrete tools to develop their own cultural proficiency and that of other mission leaders in their congregation. In response, we reference the important work being done by the Intercultural Development Inventory® (IDI®), a scientifically valid online assessment to measure and develop

---

[23]David Livermore, *Cultural Intelligence: Improving Your CQ to Engage Our Multicultural World* (Grand Rapids: Baker, 2009).

cultural proficiency in business, universities, and the nonprofit world.[24] IDI describes cultural proficiency as

> a set of knowledge/attitude/skill sets or orientations toward cultural difference and commonality that are arrayed along a continuum from the more monocultural mindsets of Denial and Polarization through the transitional orientation of Minimization to the intercultural or global mindsets of Acceptance and Adaptation. The capability of deeply shifting cultural perspective and bridging behavior across cultural differences is most fully achieved when one maintains an Adaptation perspective.[25]

Originally developed by Milton Bennett as the Development Model of Intercultural Sensitivity, the IDI understands cultural proficiency as a developmental continuum that moves from monocultural to intercultural mindsets as illustrated in figure 4.1.

Intercultural Development Continuum (IDC™)

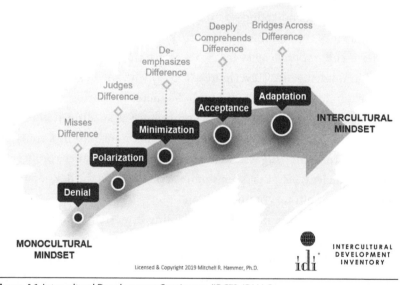

Figure 4.1. Intercultural Development Continuum (IDC™), IDI LLC

---

[24]"The Roadmap to Intercultural Competence Using the IDI," Intercultural Development Inventory, https://idiinventory.com/. I was trained by the IDI as a qualified administrator and will reference in this chapter information from IDI's website and published materials as well as my experiences using the IDI with students and faculty at Pittsburgh Theological Seminary.
[25]"Roadmap to Intercultural Competence."

IDI's research hypothesized the five orientations of cultural proficiency in the Intercultural Development Continuum (IDC™) that invites participants to work their way up the continuum of cultural proficiency:[26]

1. Denial: This consists of a disinterest in other cultures and a more active avoidance of cultural difference. Individuals with a denial orientation often do not see differences in perceptions and behavior as "cultural."

2. Polarization: "Polarization is an evaluative mindset that views cultural differences from an 'us versus them' perspective. Polarization can take the form of Defense ('My cultural practices are superior to other cultural practices') or Reversal ('Other cultures are better than mine')."

3. Minimization: "Minimization highlights commonalities in both human similarity (basic needs) and universalism (universal values and principles) that can mask a deeper understanding of cultural differences." In my own experience administering the IDI, I have found that, because minimization coincides with strongly held Christian beliefs ("All people are created in God's image"; "We are all the same in God's sight"), Christians are particularly likely to get stuck in this orientation on the journey toward greater cultural proficiency. Unfortunately, our belief that all people are equal can mask the equally true affirmation that each person is unique and that God loves them in their difference.[27]

4. Acceptance: With an acceptance orientation, individuals recognize and appreciate patterns of cultural difference and commonality in their own and other cultures.

5. Adaptation: Adaptation enables deep cultural bridging across diverse communities using an increased repertoire of cultural frameworks and practices in navigating cultural commonalities and differences.

---

[26] All information concerning the Intercultural Development Inventory (IDI) is used with permission. See "The Intercultural Development Continuum," Intercultural Development Inventory, https://idiinventory.com/generalinformation/the-intercultural-development-continuum-idc/.

[27] Jesus' differentiated approach in each human encounter (tender compassion with children, affirmation and guidance with the Samaritan woman at the well, and harsh rebukes for the hypocritical religious leaders) and Paul's missionary strategy of sensitively meeting people where they were (as in his affirming approach to the Athenians on Mars Hill in Acts 17) provided a powerful model for a long list of outstanding missionaries through history—such as the Italian Jesuit Matteo Ricci in China, Mary Slessor of Scotland in Nigeria, and Daniels Ekarte of Nigeria, who served as a missionary to Liverpool, England—whose efforts at inculturating the gospel are noteworthy.

Understood thus, cultural proficiency is not a mysterious quality that one either possesses or lacks: it is like a muscle that can be strengthened through use. Through years of careful, peer-reviewed scholarship, IDI has demonstrated that individuals can actually increase their cultural proficiency several levels by engaging in specific learning activities, as described in the individualized Intercultural Development Plan® (IDP®), provided to each person who takes the online IDI assessment. This developmental approach should be very encouraging for US mission leaders interested in increasing their cultural proficiency. North Park Theological Seminary (Chicago), the United Methodist Church, Evangelical Covenant Church, Pittsburgh Theological Seminary, and many other churches and seminaries use the IDI with seminary students and congregational mission leaders who seek to increase their cultural proficiency.[28]

One concrete strategy to place cultural proficiency on the agenda for reflection and the commitment of your congregation's mission leaders is to have them take the online IDI assessment and work through the accompanying Intercultural Development Plan (IDP) together to help them grow in cultural proficiency. By adopting a common language about responses to cultural difference, congregational leaders can make a measurable difference in the way they approach mission discernment, strategize, prioritize, communicate, and evaluate, all of which are activities strongly shaped by our cultural assumptions. When a congregation's mission leaders make a commitment to developing their cultural proficiency, they impact their congregation's local and global mission relationships and work in powerful ways because each human encounter, communication, and decision can communicate to partners honor, respect, and love. I strongly recommend the IDI for congregational mission leaders seeking to improve their cultural proficiency.

What do missional Christians operating at the "adaptation" level look like?

- A youth leader notices that her South Sudanese youth group members tended to be much more group-oriented and more deferential to older group members. When a sudden conflict arises between a South Sudanese and a Euro-American young man, she separates the

---

[28]"Who Uses the IDI," Intercultural Development Inventory, https://idiinventory.com/generalin formation/who-uses-the-idi/.

two and invites an older South Sudanese group member to "huddle" with her and the South Sudanese young man to help her listen and respond appropriately.

- A Latinx college professor is exploring with an international student from East Asia the topic the student will select for a major project. When the teacher senses the student is suggesting topics of interest to the teacher, but probably not to the student, the teacher shifts the conversation: "Write down three research topics that you think would be interesting to Simon (a student from the same country)." By engaging in indirect communication, the exercise creates a space for the student to imagine and express new possibilities.

- An African American pastor perceives that the Ghanaian seminary students his short-term mission team is visiting are reticent to voice their individual opinions in a group debrief. At a break in the program, he works with his group leaders and hosts to revamp the interaction: they allow for both groups to "caucus" separately to work on their responses to several discussion questions and then come back together to discuss their responses. By giving the Ghanaian students the chance "to get a sense of the group" first, the resulting conversation is richer and more authentic.

CULTURAL HUMILITY

I remember to this day a most unsettling conversation I had with a pastor at my church as I was about to travel to Democratic Republic of Congo to serve as a one-year mission volunteer with the Presbyterian Church. Over lunch, he asked me why I wanted to go to Africa. My response sounded like a line out of the White Savior Barbie parody. I replied, "I feel like God has given me lots of gifts that I'm to share with people there." His response caught me off-guard: he smiled, looked at me, and said, "God will use your short-comings and failings more than your gifts." I was stunned and assumed he just didn't understand how qualified I was (smile)! Up to this point, we have been discussing the mechanics of cultural proficiency—that is, the skills and knowledge that enable us to communicate effectively across cultural difference. But merely possessing a high degree of cultural proficiency in a postmodern world where mission relationships have been so deeply tarnished by colonial-era abuses is simply not enough. From everything we see in the model of Jesus' engagement in mission, I would argue that what we desperately need is cultural humility.

Tervalon and Murray-García originated the concept of cultural humility for physicians' relationships with their patients of different cultural traditions and suggest several definitional elements that are applicable to postcolonial mission encounters:

> This training outcome, perhaps better described as cultural humility versus cultural competence [proficiency] . . . is a process that requires humility as individuals continually engage in a process of self-reflection and self-critique as life-long learners and reflective practitioners. It is a process that requires humility in how physicians bring into check the power imbalances that exist in the dynamics of physician-patient communication by using patient-focused interviewing and care.[29]

Three elements of this definition merit our attention as we consider a posture of cultural humility for ourselves and for our congregation's leaders in our relationship with local and global companions. First, "a commitment and active engagement in a lifelong process"[30] suggests that the challenge of learning to navigate across cultural difference is a never-ending one and requires an ongoing commitment. The authors wrote this article because they saw physicians treat a completed "cultural competence" training module as synonymous with cultural proficiency. Nothing could be further from the truth: as soon as I believe I have mastered cultural competence, my capacity to communicate across cultural difference actually decreases because I close myself off from depending on others to teach me their understandings and hidden assumptions.

This leads to Tervalon and Murray-García's second element: this lifelong process requires regular self-reflection and self-critique, adopting the posture suggested to us in chapter three—the posture of learner.

---

[29]Melanie Tervalon and Jann Murray-García, "Cultural Humility Versus Cultural Competence: A Critical Distinction in Defining Physician Training Outcomes in Multicultural Settings," *Journal of Healthcare of the Poor and Underserved* 9, no. 2 (May 1998): 118.

[30]Tervalon and Murray-García, "Cultural Humility Versus Cultural Competence," 118.

Tervalon and Murray-García's third element brings to light the power imbalances that flourish in the physician-patient relationship because of the former's superior knowledge of many aspects of human disease and because of their role as dispensers of healing to patients. These differences cause physicians to operate with substantial power relative to their patients. The authors insist that relatively powerful physicians must check their power through patient-focused interviewing and care; that is, they must adopt a posture of learner and interview the patient to better understand the patient's worldview, feelings, symptomology, and hopes. The learner's attitude allows physicians to engage the patient in the healing process, admitting they cannot heal without the patient's active engagement in that process. If medical educators are taking steps to train physicians toward cultural humility, what should be the position of mission leaders who seek to help their people acquire the skills and heart-attitudes of cultural humility? The implications for our intercultural, missional engagement with local and global partners are powerful.

It's important to note what cultural humility is *not*: cultural humility is not a lower view of oneself, just a more accurate one. Christian psychologist Carissa Dwiwardani's research shows that "instead of being synonymous with self-deprecation, humility has been found to be positively related to self-esteem."[31] True cultural humility takes "the ability to recognize and appreciate patterns of cultural difference and commonality in their own and other cultures" (as described in the IDI[32]) and adds to it the heart of a learner.

In summary, Tervalon and Murray-García's "commitment and active engagement in a lifelong process" of learning cultural humility coincides with our call to engage in mission as learners. In Mark 10:13-16, Jesus praises children's qualities of openness and nonjudgmentalness, their willingness to risk making mistakes, their capacity to enter into the world of the other, and their capacity to respond to the mystery of the world with a sense of wonder.

When we moved from the United States to Lima, Peru, with our three young children, they spoke no Spanish. Our then nine-year-old daughter,

---

[31]Carissa Dwiwardani, "Humility and Self-Esteem: Exploring the Relationship and Issues of Measurements," *Dissertation Abstracts International, Section B: The Sciences and Engineering*, 73(2-B), 1303.
[32]"Intercultural Development Continuum."

Ndaya, in particular, had the capacity to imagine herself speaking fluent Spanish: from her first day of school in Spanish, she would work to shape her mouth to be able to pronounce the new sounds of the Spanish language with its wide-open vowels, trilled double Rs, and staccato consonants. At first, she seemed to be the only one who believed she was speaking actual Spanish, but in her imagination, she could speak it fluently. Her imagination enabled her to learn to speak fluent Spanish with the beautiful coastal Peruvian accent in a few months' time! When adults claim it is impossible to learn a foreign language at their age, could it be that what they really lack is the ability to imagine themselves speaking the new language?

In Mark's Gospel, the children's attitude of openness to receive from God is contrasted by the following text of the rich young ruler, whose inability to imagine God's provision for him (if he were to sell all his goods and give to the poor) keeps him from receiving God's realm. God's realm is, in fact, the space of the *missio Dei*: the space where God reaches out, extending perfect love and enfolding all of us in that movement. Entering into God's realm and the *missio Dei* requires us to "become like a child," armed only with our hopeful imagination of the world God intends. Could it be that we are unable to end war and hunger in our world because we lack the imagination to see ourselves treating each other with dignity and respect?

As congregational mission leaders work to lead their congregation into opportunities for intercultural learning and service, they open the door to the opportunity for the deep change that the *missio Dei* creates. As leaders help their congregations grow in cultural proficiency from denial and polarization to minimization, acceptance, and even adaptation (to use the IDI continuum), the quality and depth of our intercultural relationships and work will be greatly enhanced, resulting in more effective and faithful relationships and work. Moreover, we will find that observing our hosts' cultural lenses in operation begins to shift and deepen our own reading of Scripture, our worship and fellowship, and our engagement in God's mission. Global worship and theological reflections and statements developed ecumenically with the contributions of global Christians are richer because they are formulated in an intercultural space rather than remaining captive to our peculiar cultural assumptions.

Nothing is more frustrating than the feeling of awkward incompetence and confusion we feel in intercultural understandings. Even the local children "get it," but we're clueless. Yet I am convinced that the confusing and sometimes frustrating cultural differences we stumble over are the learnings that allow us to see ourselves and our world with new eyes. New immigrants and international students tend to see the context they live in with more critical eyes—with a broader perspective. The acclaimed Indian-British novelist Sir Salman Rushdie summarized it beautifully: "The only people who see the whole picture . . . are the ones who step out of the frame."[33] The irritations we feel as we err in intercultural communication are, in fact, the feeling when "iron sharpens iron, and one person sharpens the wits of another" (Prov 27:17). Our relationship with a person from a different cultural background, when we act with cultural humility, can be a space of learning and transformation. What began as a formidable perceived barrier to God's mission has become for us an invitation to adopt a posture of cultural humility to embrace and then to leverage the space of uncertainty (that "I have no idea what's going on right now" moment) to slow our pace, open all our senses, and establish deep and lasting bonds with the very people who can shine new light on our own limited understanding of what it means to live in Christ.

In this chapter, we have added to a theology of companionship by proposing cultural humility as a way to free us to love our neighbor across lines of difference. After the questions for reflection at the end of the chapter, you'll find Tool 2, an exercise you can use with your congregation's mission leaders (pastoral staff, lay leaders, youth and women's leaders) to build their awareness of cultural differences and whet their appetite to grow in cultural proficiency. In chapter five, we will add the third and final stone to our hearth by looking at how communities change, and we will propose the concept of co-development to help us see the mutually transformative power of the *missio Dei*.

FOR REFLECTION

1. Learning about a different culture is a journey that never ends; there's no going back. What have you learned about different cultures that surprised you and changed your perception about that place?

---

[33]Salman Rushdie, *The Ground Beneath Her Feet* (New York: Picador, 1999), 43.

2. Please describe either one positive or one negative intercultural experience you've had and what made it go well or not.

3. *"The only people who see the whole picture . . . are the ones who step out of the frame."* Can you remember a time when an intercultural experience (travel, an intercultural conversation, a short-term mission trip) caused you to see your own context differently?

4. In which of the different dimensions of cultures discussed (individualistic-collectivistic, power distance, uncertainty avoidance, direct versus indirect communication, short-term versus long-term orientation) has your congregation encountered the most misunderstandings or conflicts? According to the chapter, what are ways you can develop cultural proficiency in these areas?

5. We often think of US cultures as strongly influenced by Judeo-Christian principles. Either from your own experiences or from the book's examples, describe a situation when another culture's insights/values have been more in line with gospel values than our own US cultural values.

SEEING INTO OUR BLIND SPOTS

Anticipating and Addressing Cultural Differences

BACKGROUND

It's a truism that "we can't know what we don't know." This is painfully true of intercultural communication. As you drive your car down the highway, you simply aren't aware of the large truck just now passing you on your right because it's located in your blind spot. Though it's no one's fault, your relative positions make you an accident waiting to happen. But your car's side mirrors enable you to see into your blind spot and avoid unnecessary accidents.

When communicating with mission companions who have cultural backgrounds different from ours, we will almost certainly miscommunicate. Our cultures have shaped and oriented us to see and understand the world differently. Therefore, it is essential we learn to anticipate the areas where we tend to miscommunicate.

NOTE: Each person is a unique individual and conforms with cultural descriptions to varying degrees. It is very important to be cautious and not to generalize these tendencies into stereotypes or caricatures of others. Also, each country has various cultural groups and an individual's identity and social location (race/ethnicity, gender identity, economic position, etc.) will shape the ways they conform or vary from their context's general patterns—no one can be as easily categorized as the diagram demonstrates. Even so, developing our sensitivity to general *patterns of cultural difference* serve as "side mirrors" and help us to see into our blind spots, anticipating areas of common disagreement or difference.

OBJECTIVE: To improve cultural proficiency by anticipating areas of common misunderstanding and taking steps to address them.

DIMENSIONS OF CULTURE[1]

Culture has multiple dimensions: time orientation, personal space, the role of the individual, and so on. Please read the section "Five Dimensions of Cultural Difference" (pp. 85–92) for a full description of these aspects. Below is a description of how five specific dimensions of cultural difference can be anticipated and addressed.

1. Collectivist versus individualist orientation.

Figure T2.1

When engaging with people from a more collectivist orientation (sub-Saharan Africa, Latin America, Middle East):

- Decisions may require significantly more time due to the need for community consultation. Being patient is key in decision-making.

- You expose an individual to potential criticism when you ask him/her directly for their opinion. Asking more open-ended questions (e.g., "What would be the advantages of this idea? Disadvantages?") allows mission companions more space to add contextual details (voice tone, use of silence, nonverbal cues, etc.) to communicate with clarity without dishonoring anyone or threatening group harmony.

- A gift or public honor that singles out an individual or a community can create a sense of shame in that person as it makes them "stand

---

[1]The categories and data sets used to develop these cultural comparisons are taken from Geert Hofstede, Gert Hofstede, and Michael Minkov, *Cultures and Organizations: Software of the Mind* (New York: McGraw-Hill, 2010). For Hofstede's other dimensions of culture and research methodology, see Hofstede Insights, www.hofstede-insights.com/.

above" their peers. Being "singled out" for praise or even being considered "outstanding" are less desirable.

When engaging with people from a more individualistic orientation (USA, Western Europe, Israel):

- Decision-making is more likely to occur among only a few individuals and consequently can occur more quickly than when full community input is needed.

- You honor an individual when you ask them directly what they think.

- People value taking the initiative on their own: consensus—or even consultation—can be less valued than individual decisiveness and quick decision-making.

2. Power distance orientation.

Figure T2.2

When engaging with people from a higher power distance orientation (Latin America, Asia, East Africa):

- The acknowledgment of local leaders is an important first step: begin by going to the leaders for advice. The approval of leaders is essential to work on most projects.

- From the beginning, ask people first how they would like to be addressed. Don't assume you can use first names or nicknames without permission. Titles may be more important than you assume.

- An enduring legacy of the colonial era is that in many Majority World contexts, Westerners are often perceived as having more power and privilege than others.

When engaging with people from a lower power distance orientation (USA, Western Europe, Israel):

- Immediate use of first names is more common and not generally seen as a sign of disrespect.

- It is acceptable to ask questions respectfully of those in authority and those in partner organizations.

- Your partner is more likely to expect direct, explicit feedback from you. State positive feedback as succinctly as possible; frame negative feedback as questions (e.g., "I wonder what the long-term implications of this decision might be?" "I am curious how church neighbors might feel about this decision").

3. Risk avoidance orientation.

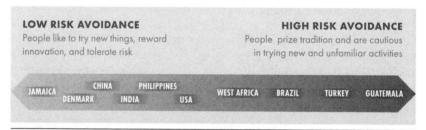

LOW RISK AVOIDANCE
People like to try new things, reward innovation, and tolerate risk

HIGH RISK AVOIDANCE
People prize tradition and are cautious in trying new and unfamiliar activities

JAMAICA   CHINA   PHILIPPINES   WEST AFRICA   BRAZIL   TURKEY   GUATEMALA
        DENMARK   INDIA   USA

Figure T2.3

When engaging with people from a higher risk avoidance orientation (Latin America, Middle East, West Africa):

- Change is slow but often deep. New ideas or projects might be more acceptable when built on or connected with existing traditions and values. Continuity with the past is essential, and innovations are often evaluated based on their consistency with traditional values.

- Often there are norms and customs that restrict people from taking risks that might negatively impact the community.

- Every community has innovators. Identify who the innovators are in the community and assess their willingness to try new ideas on a small, limited scale.

When engaging with people from a lower risk avoidance orientation (USA, Western Europe, Asia):

- Generally, people are willing to try out new ideas or projects.

- Often, people are less afraid of failure because they know that there is always a possibility of significant change. When wealth or resources are abundant, risk is easier.

- Appreciate the mobility and flexibility of the culture while also expressing your own concern when things seem to be moving too fast. The downside of a willingness to try new things is that consistency/perseverance over time is sometimes lost.

4. Long-term versus short-term orientation.

SHORT-TERM ORIENTATION
People prefer benefits in the present over saving for tomorrow

LONG-TERM ORIENTATION
People value thrift, saving for tomorrow

GHANA COLOMBIA   PERU USA   EAST AFRICA   VIETNAM   ITALY SWITZERLAND   TAIWAN SOUTH KOREA

Figure T2.4

When engaging with people from a long-term orientation (Asia, Eastern and Northern Europe):

- Longer-term orientation tends to be focused on the future. In this way people are more willing to compromise knowing that there's something better in the future.[2]

- People are more likely to place a high value on ensuring that a gift or project to the community will last and thus are more interested in investing in physical structures because of their lasting quality.

- People tend to think in a longer-term time frame (such as ten years from now) and do not expect immediate results.[3]

When engaging with people from a short-term orientation (USA, Latin America, and North Africa):

---

[2] "Long Term Orientation Versus Short Term Orientation (LTO)," CQFluency, February 22, 2017, www.cqfluency.com/blog/long-term-orientation-versus-short-term-orientation/.
[3] Ron Christian Antonczyk, Wolfgang Breuer, and Astrid Juliane Salzmann, "Long-Term Orientation and Relationship Lending: A Cross-Cultural Study on the Effect of Time Preferences on the Choice of Corporate Debt," *MIR: Management International Review* 54, no. 3 (2014): 387-88, www.jstor.org/stable/24570560.

- People are focused on the past and present: how we did things in the past and how we will do things now. Therefore, people are less likely to compromise because that can be seen as a sign of weakness and also because they highly value ideas and principles over longer-term change.[4]

- In short-term orientation, people are more willing to invest time and money into present leisure activities and interests rather than spending time planning for saving money for the future.

- People are more willing to put their time, effort, and resources into receiving an immediate result.

5. Direct versus indirect communication orientation.[5]

INDIRECT COMMUNICATION
People value group loyalty and speak figuratively to avoid direct confrontation and public embarrassment

DIRECT COMMUNICATION
People value literal truthfulness and say what they think with less hesitation

CHINA   INDIA   EAST AFRICA   GUATEMALA   USA

Figure T2.5

When engaging with people who communicate more indirectly:

- Silence or not speaking out does not necessarily mean a person has no opinion or questions. People from this cultural orientation may need more time to think through how their words could impact others. Pressing for a quick decision may lead to embarrassment for companions and frustration for you.

- Slow down and make sure to clarify if needed: Use language such as "What I think I heard . . ." and then wait and listen how your companions

---

[4]"Long Term Orientation Versus Short Term Orientation (LTO)."
[5]This is not part of Hofstede's dimensions of culture. Edward T. Hall's work on high- and low-context cultures shed light on direct and indirect communication styles. But we've located the above countries on the continuum based on how the majority of people from these countries tend to communicate with others. "Direct Communication vs. Indirect Communication," *Watershed Associates*, www.watershedassociates.com/learning-center-item/direct-communication-vs-indirect-communication.html.

correct your understanding. Pay attention to body language, gesture, and voice tone.

- Convey your disagreements in a polite and respectful manner, using questions rather than declarations.

When engaging with people who communicate more directly:

- People are likely to give you very direct feedback that may offend you.

- People from these cultural orientations generally prefer to be clear and direct (say what they think) rather than polite and discreet (anticipate how the listener will react).

- Typically, direct communicators feel anxious or impatient with long, indirect messages.

Again, although these cultural dimensions, norms, and practices are helpful to know as you navigate through cultural differences, it is very important to be cautious and not to generalize these patterns to everyone in the entire community or cultural background. While these descriptions help locate your cultural blind spots, in truth, cultural patterns are built from the "bottom up"—that is, you learn about the larger patterns by getting to know individuals and noticing the patterns in their behaviors. Don't allow cultural generalizations to become prescriptive.

FIVE

THE THIRD STONE

The Power of Co-development

*You cannot develop people. You must allow
people to develop themselves.*

JULIUS NYERERE, FIRST PRESIDENT OF TANZANIA

I'm standing in the middle of Peru's coastal desert, a million miles from
anything, wondering what in the heck I'm doing here. Miles and miles of
sand and broken rock frame the horizon. "It's just ahead, brother. Can you
see it yet?"

"Definitely not," I think to myself.

A U.S. Christian development agency had asked me to visit the Haya de la
Torre Association, a group of landless farmers who had been working together
once a week for sixteen years in an attempt to cut a 1.4-mile-long irrigation
canal out of solid rock. The canal would irrigate 2,700 acres of parched land
and provide the farmers with land for themselves and their children after
them. With only 124 yards left to go, they had requested funds to rent the
heavy machinery necessary to cut and cart away the rock. I took one look at
the granite mountain in front of us and chuckled to myself. It looked like pure
foolishness. But I guess I'd never really seen faith move mountains before.

A charter member of the association, sixty-eight-year-old Alicia Moraga,
showed me the 1.3-mile ditch already cut and carefully lined with rock. Using
ancient technology that dated back to the Inca Empire, the community had
coaxed water out of the Huara River, high above the arid lands, and brought
it within reach of their goal. I looked at Alicia, perplexed. "Sixteen years?
What kept you going, Señora?" I asked.

Now it was Alicia's turn to be perplexed. "But you should know about hope, pastor! We want our children to have a better life than we've had, and they'll need land for that." Alicia said the association had bet that if they could bring water to the arid, unclaimed land overlooking the town of Humaya, they could obtain land—approximately 40 acres per family. All along Peru's bone-dry Pacific coast, the equation is simple:

$$\text{land} + \text{water} = \text{life}$$

I stopped in my tracks. The thought of dirt-poor peasants working for 16 years with picks and shovels to access water for their children made my definition of hope look pretty wimpy. They had already raised money for the hydrological study and had successfully battled both a mining company and the government to retain title to the arid land (once it became clear that the irrigation project might, in fact, succeed, you'd be amazed at who became interested in the land).

I would hesitate to send an absurd little project like this to most international development organizations—on paper, the whole thing just looks impossible. There is nothing "feasible" about this project, except that it is a community-developed response to a critical problem as defined by the community: a desperate need for arable land. I smiled as I suddenly realized our God's remarkable sense of humor. This is precisely where the church works best: sharing modest funding with poor and oppressed communities through community-initiated, community-managed projects. This is mission "with," not "for."

And so in Humaya, Alicia Moraga and her small band of poor, landless farmers are opening up a small piece of God's Reign to provide hope and an inheritance for their children. And I'm thankful to Alicia and her community because they have shared with me a faith that moves mountains.

As of this writing, the association members are still battling the local powers-that-be for control of the land that they worked so many years for. But my money's on Alicia and her team because the God whose hand is on the arc of history continues to bend it toward justice.[1]

Even in some of the poorest, most oppressed communities in the world, we encounter a power whose intensity may surprise us: moms and dads endure difficult and even dangerous conditions to provide for their children.

---

[1] B. Hunter Farrell, "July 2016: 'Can You See It Yet?,'" Presbyterian Mission Agency, www.presbyterian mission.org/wp-content/uploads/Hunter-July2016.pdf. Used with permission.

Underpaid teachers work overtime so their students can learn their way to a better life. Pastors preach grace, cast vision, and inspire their communities—despite the odds. Like Alicia Moraga of the dusty Peruvian town of Humaya, these are people with whom you want to partner.

Across the significant differences that divide America's Catholics, evangelicals, and mainline Protestants—doctrine, worship style, politics—our research among congregational mission leaders suggests that we agree on this: a major part of God's mission is helping people around the world to access the abundant life Jesus Christ promised (Jn 10:10). A 2019 study noted that more than half of the 670 US congregational mission leaders surveyed affirmed that the primary purpose of mission is "to improve the quality of life by reducing poverty, disease and human suffering," "reconciliation," "social justice," or "eco-justice."[2] Addressing these needs is clearly high on the priority list of many US Christian congregations and parishes. Many Christian congregations affirm that mission in the way of Jesus Christ requires us to address the quality of life of the poor and oppressed. The challenge to many congregations is how to do this.

DECOLONIZING DEVELOPMENT

Most of our congregations earnestly seek ways to lend a helping hand to their neighbors near and far. But many congregational mission leaders report feeling stuck in an inadequate understanding of how they can help another community. They observe suffering or what appear to be fixable problems in another community and their response is an authentic desire to help. But our tendency to underestimate the depth and complexity of the process of human development—and our rush to see quick results—push us to help in often counterproductive ways. The publication of books like *When Helping Hurts*, *Toxic Charity*, and *Doing Good, Says Who?* have named this challenge. We give generously but, like overwatering a growing plant, we can easily overwhelm a resource-challenged community. Despite our best intentions, we can create unhealthy dependencies, impossible expectations, and even "commodify" the human relationships with our companions that are precisely the point of our mission work. Many US mission leaders

---

[2]World Mission Initiative, survey of 670 US Catholic, evangelical, and mainline Protestant mission leaders, conducted April 2019.

have met gifted and committed leaders like Alicia Moraga and have sought ways to support the movements such leaders have founded and grown. But it is clear that development studies—that area of study that harnesses the learnings of a range of academic disciplines (economics, anthropology, political science, sociology, etc.) to reduce human suffering by enabling communities to provide for their own basic needs—has not been in the toolkit of US congregations who annually fund millions of dollars' worth of development projects in communities near and far. Let's begin by recalling the place of the poor and oppressed in our theology of companionship. We affirmed our understanding that mission is God's—not ours—and that it is God who calls us to walk together with others as companions, sharing bread in a spirit of vulnerability, and holding space for God so that our focus stays on God's intentions rather than our agenda. We also saw that walking as a companion in God's mission requires us to look for and support the leadership of people living in poverty or oppression.

Yet many middle- and upper-income readers will attest to the fact there are strong cultural narratives separating us from the people we want to help: class, power, and often race/ethnicity. The colonial legacy of both Christian mission and secular development can cause a more resourced foreigner to assume she or he is superior to these leaders and believe if they could just be more like the developed West, they could attain the sought-after Western lifestyle. Though we may not have considered the connections, these cultural assumptions echo the European colonial thinking we discussed in chapter two that was so problematic:

- *Europeans know what is best for the colonized*: like my experience with the village soccer field effort, we assume we know best because of our "superior" education and culture.

- *Europeans should control the process of development*: our control of the development process, we assume, ensures success (and its corollary: local communities cannot be trusted to manage their own development).

- *Development is a function of European benevolence to colonized peoples*: we're doing it for their own good, even if they don't immediately appreciate our efforts.

Corbett and Fikkert call this implicit sense of superiority of the relatively wealthy "the god-complex" in their book *When Helping Hurts: Alleviating Poverty Without Hurting the Poor . . . or Yourself*: "A subtle and unconscious sense of superiority in which [the economically rich] believe that they have achieved their wealth through their own efforts and that they have been anointed to decide what is best for low-income people, whom they view as inferior to themselves."[3] These are hard words, I know. Perhaps, like me, you are a leader who has become aware of these unspoken assumptions and you find yourself in a struggle with something larger, trying to recognize and "unlearn" the assumptions and patterns with which we were raised. By naming and disrupting its power that can reduce gifted and called mission companions into the passive recipients of our benevolence, we take an important first step in *decolonizing* our false understanding of development.

WHY I CAN'T "DEVELOP" YOU

"What you do for us without us is not for us."

On a wall of Agape Christian Academy in Mukono, Uganda[4]

Is there a way to understand the development of human beings and their communities differently—in a postcolonial way—stripped of the paternalistic assumptions of "*I* develop *them*"? Can we recognize the image of God in each person and understand that it is impossible for me to develop any other human being—that each person and community is responsible before God for developing themselves to the best of their ability? In a very real sense, the verb *develop* cannot take an object: I cannot *develop* you. But perhaps, by God's grace, I can contribute to the conditions that allow you to develop yourself by removing barriers and offering tools. The end result of this kind of co-development is the abundant life Jesus promised in John 10:10 for all: poor and rich, marginalized and powerful. Co-development is holistic: body and soul, spiritual and physical together. It is neither a sterile, otherworldly spirituality devoid of life's physical necessities nor guaranteed "health and wealth" and the crass materialism the prosperity gospel can generate. Rather,

---

[3]Steve Corbett and Brian Fikkert, *When Helping Hurts: How to Alleviate Poverty Without Hurting the Poor . . . or Yourself* (Chicago: Moody Press, 2012), 61.

[4]Quoted in Ashley Purcelle Goad, "Mind the Gap: Navigating the Pitfalls of Cross-Cultural Partnership," (2016), http://digitalcommons.georgefox.edu/dmin/129, 85.

as Wheaton College professor and missions leader Ed Stetzer reflects, abundant life is better measured by what we give than what we have:

> At the end of the day, perhaps that is how we know we have an abundant life—when we have shared our life with others. When we have enough of the blessings of God (mercy, peace, love, grace, wisdom, etc.) to share with our others, and then actually do it; that's when we truly have abundant life.[5]

The power of co-development is in its radical mutuality. It rejects the implicit sense of power and control "givers" assumed they possessed. Co-development insists that, as companions walk together with God, there is no "giver" and "receiver": there are only human beings desperately in need of God's grace in Christ. Thus, co-development is a radically mutual process that invites all to bring to the circle the gifts God has given them to offer to their mission companions. In doing so, all will be changed. Perhaps you've heard a missionary, after a lifetime of sacrificial giving in communities of material poverty, sum up their entire missionary career with the surprising words, "I received so much more than I gave." What is it these servants understand about life in God's realm that many in the church have missed?

I remember driving across metropolitan Lima, Peru, late one night in July to pick up a short-term mission group. Flights from the United States generally arrive at Lima's Jorge Chavez International Airport after midnight, and I stood in the crowd of several hundred people milling about in the large International Arrivals Hall. As each flight arrived from the United States, several hundred passengers would enter the hall, and I was surprised by the large number of groups wearing matching colored T-shirts, the locally recognized symbol of Christian mission groups. As I stood behind a group of teenagers, I overheard one of them comment to his friends,

"*¿Por qué quieren cambiarnos?*"—"Why do they want to change us?" Rather than perceiving our short-term mission groups as Christians seeking their friendship, we are often perceived as traveling long distances to change the people we encounter.

I don't know about you, but even in the most important relationships in my life—my wife, my friends, my siblings—my efforts to "develop" them

---

[5] Ed Stetzer, "What Does It Mean to Have an Abundant Life? Some Thoughts on Prosperity," *Christianity Today*, March 18, 2015, www.christianitytoday.com/edstetzer/2015/march/what-does -it-mean-to-have-abundant-life.html.

have been notorious failures. These loved ones would (with good reason!) question and even resent my efforts to *change* them. But they have generally welcomed my willingness to walk with them in their efforts to improve their own lives—if I enter that space with some humility, empathy, and compassion and if I'm willing to open my life to *their* companionship. Without that sense of reciprocity, human relationship becomes casework or a task list: it's my job to improve you. If you've ever spent time with a couple who has not discovered this truth, you know how painful it can be—one seeks to change their partner into a "better" person. The process is as sad as it is condescending. When we strip away our own ego needs from our good intentions to develop "communities of need," we see we can only pray and work for co-development, that is, to walk with our companions in God's mission by offering tools and removing barriers to their development.

Now we're moving from a flawed understanding of development onto a more solid, biblical footing as we think about how individuals and communities change. The apostle Paul was an educated, multilingual, Roman citizen, and a pious Jew of the Pharisee tradition. Yet his humility is noteworthy as he points past himself to the true agent of change:

> What then is Apollos? What is Paul? Servants through whom you came to believe, as the Lord assigned to each. I planted, Apollos watered, but God gave the growth. So neither the one who plants nor the one who waters is anything, but only God who gives the growth. (1 Cor 3:5-7)

In other words, *it's not all about us*: it's all about the God who unconditionally loves and desires blessing for all God's children. Corbett and Fikkert allude to the profound mutuality of the development process: "Until we embrace our mutual brokenness, our work with low-income people is likely to do far more harm than good."[6] These words probably don't surprise you, because each one of us has at some time experienced this kind of mature, unconditional love that doesn't "do *for* us" so that we become mere photocopies of our helper, whether parent or spouse or friend, but rather loves us for who we are. From this place of belovedness, we are free to choose the direction of our life. This is the genesis of true development, both personal and communal. As we walk as companions in God's mission, it is critically

---

[6]Corbett and Fikkert, *When Helping Hurts*, 61.

important that we walk in the freedom of unconditional love, freeing the other to be the person God intended them to be and not what we would desire them to become. This prevents us from treating the people God invites us to accompany as the *objects of our mission* and safeguards their place as *subjects* in the mission of God. Honestly examining our plans and actions against a commitment to relate to our companions as the primary subjects of God's mission in their community can free us from old, colonial patterns in ways that can upend hierarchical mission relationships and open a space for a closer, more authentic companionship in mission. I am convinced there are few actions we can take that so profoundly improve our mission relationships and enhance the changes our companions and we seek.

So how can we outsiders help—even as outsiders in a complex context of which we understand little? A Congolese proverb shows the value of local knowledge: "The foreigner doesn't recognize the *mpotshi* palm tree"; that is, when an outsider arrives in a village of Congo's Kasai region, she only sees many varieties of palm trees and can't identify the *mpotshi* variety that yields the sap that makes the best palm wine. Yet every child in the village knows which are the *mpotshi* palm trees since they know where the men gather daily to tap the best quality sap. We enter every community as an outsider. How, then, can we remove barriers and provide tools for our companions' development— and open ourselves up to their contributions to our development?

Our first inclination, of course, is to give—generously. In fact, the average American annually gives to charity twice as much as the average Canadian and seven times more than the average European![7] Moreover, in the United States, "charitable (giving) correlates strongly with the frequency with which a person attends religious services"; that is, the more often we worship, the more we tend to give to both religious and secular causes.[8] This is a beautiful facet of our shared American religious culture given to us by our ancestors. Our challenge is how to channel this natural generosity into actions that make sense in the long run—not just my knee-jerk reaction of putting some coins in the hand of a person I perceive as needy. While a quick response may serve to quiet my anxiety that the person's apparent need generates in

---

[7] "Who Gives Most to Charity?," Philanthropy Roundtable, accessed May 28, 2021, www.philanthropy roundtable.org/almanac/statistics/who-gives.
[8] "Who Gives Most to Charity?"

me, we cannot apply this "quick fix" approach to mission relationships or to any process of co-development. French Reformed pastor and theologian Jacques Ellul wrote, "Almsgiving is Mammon's perversion of giving. It affirms the superiority of the giver, binds the recipient, demands gratitude, humiliates him and reduces him to a lower state than he had been before."[9]

In summary, what had been a hierarchical and paternalistic approach ("I will develop your community") can give way to a mutual journey of two or more companions who, like the wisdom saying of Proverbs 27:17 ("iron sharpens iron"), bring out the best in each other. Now that we have stripped away the colonial varnish that often clouds our understanding of how we can impact communities—and how they impact us—let's clarify our understanding of what co-development really is.

THE CRITICAL INGREDIENT OF AGENCY

Traditionally, development has been understood in primarily materialistic terms: increases in income and improvements in education, nutrition, and health, for example. In 1999, Indian economist Amartya Sen broadened the understanding of development by relating it to freedom; that is, development consists in increasing an individual's capacity to make choices that benefit their life.[10]

The Evangelical Lutheran Church in America (ELCA) offers this definition of development: "a process that leads to improving the quality of life of people. It ensures their cultural, social, political, spiritual and economic well-being through a participatory and integrated process of empowerment, self-reliance, regeneration, and the removal of obstacles to this process."[11] The Lutherans understand development to be a person-centered process that involves all aspects of life. Despite the American Lutherans' location in a context of rising secularism, they maintain a space for the very real spiritual aspects of development. Secular development agencies generally ignore this vital aspect—religious beliefs serve to organize other disparate cultural elements and provide a community with the values, shared stories, images, and

---

[9]Jacques Ellul, *Money and Power*, trans. LaVonne Neff (Downers Grove, IL: InterVarsity Press, 1984).

[10]Amartya Sen, *Development as Freedom* (New York: Random House, 2000), 112.

[11]"A Social Statement on: Sufficient, Sustainable, Livelihood for All," Evangelical Lutheran Church in America, August 1999, Denver, Colorado, https://download.elca.org/ELCA%20Resource%20 Repository/Economic_LifeSS.pdf?_ga=2.250391041.648112418.1592083222-2823516.1592083222.

language with which to make sense of both their situation and what "freedom" (or "development") looks like. The Lutherans are clearly aware of the colonial background of mission efforts in development and stress empowerment and self-reliance. For the ELCA, it is important that community members lead as the protagonist of the story—after all, it is the story of *their* community—and that their efforts support, accompany, and empower.

This question of agency—who is responsible for the direction a church or community takes to develop within its context—echoes one of the most impactful missiological principles developed during Protestant mission history. We can understand agency as the capacity of individuals to act independently—to make their own choices. In everyday language, we call this "skin in the game" or "sweat equity"—the concept we associate with Habitat for Humanity that works only with clients committed to helping themselves. While a disaster situation operates under very different rules, agency is an essential ingredient in the process of development. Let's look at two stories from mission history that illustrate the importance of agency: a negative, recent example and a historical, more positive one.

"WHO'S IN CHARGE?" TWO LESSONS IN AGENCY

In the 1990s, I boarded a boat to travel west across the ten-mile-wide Lake Volta of central Ghana (West Africa) to visit four communities on the Afram Plains. Much of the population of this dry, rocky region had migrated there from more fertile parts of Ghana when the building of the Akosombo Dam had caused the massive Volta River to flood their lands. Household income, nutrition, and infant mortality for the people of the region were major concerns for the churches. Upon arriving in each of the five towns, people quickly gathered around my travel companion and me and asked, "When are you going to fix your well?" I had no idea what they were talking about. Evidently, a little more than one year before my trip, a Christian development organization had sunk more than two dozen wells across the plains to provide clean drinking water. But water wells in Afram Plains' sandy soil, if not maintained, quickly become "silted in," and the townspeople, accustomed to free, clean water, were frustrated with me, whom they perceived to be a representative of the development agency. In each of the communities, people believed the wells belonged to the foreign agency and were waiting for the agency to send technicians to repair "the agency's wells." The agency saw its task as completed and had no plans to maintain the wells—it had already done its part and expected the local community to service its wells.

I can't in good conscience criticize this profound "disconnect" between a local population's and a foreign group's sense of who is responsible for a project because this sad scenario has been repeated in hundreds of communities around the world. I know I've committed this error more times than I can count! Perhaps your church has struggled with how to cultivate a sense of ownership for a joint project among mission partners or realized that, after embarking on a project that seemed to require outside funding, you had felt embarrassed to raise the question of how much of the total cost the local community would cover. As a result, the community looked to you with a degree of complete dependency that made you uncomfortable. Deep in our hearts, we recognize that a "free ride" like this denies the community's agency.

Traditional wisdom in many Latin American communities reminds us that everyone can bring their *granito de arena*, their "grain of sand," to add to the community's building project. Everyone—no matter how poor—has something they can contribute to the shared effort. To say or act otherwise is to deny that member's agency and even their personhood. That small, sometimes sacrificial, local contribution is of sacramental importance: it signals companionship rather than patronage. One of the greatest errors our churches commit is the all-too-easy assumption that they should cover all the expenses of a project, when this is almost never the case. Cultivating a local sense of ownership when one side is footing the bill is a fool's errand. Ironically, one of the most common questions I receive from churches engaged in mission is how they can transfer the sense of ownership for a project from their shoulders to the local community. The sad truth is that they can't—*it's already too late*. The patterns of dependency have already been set, and any local leader who proposes that her/his community "step up" and begin to contribute financially would almost certainly be laughed off the stage—criticized for offering scarce community resources for something for which eager outsiders have been willing to pay. But mission history can help us learn a different way forward in recognizing the God-given sense of agency of our mission partners present in the Lutherans' definition of development.

The positive lesson from mission history begins in the late nineteenth century when Protestant missiology at its best recognized the critically important element of agency in the development of the church. Some missionaries understood their mission efforts as planting and building up the church overseas into a healthy, "indigenous" church by applying the "three-self principles." John Livingston Nevius, an American missionary to China, developed the earlier thinking of the Church Missionary Society's Henry Venn and the American Board of Commissioners for Foreign Missions' Rufus Anderson into what historians later called "The Nevius Plan," whose goal was a "self-supporting, self-governing and self-propagating indigenous church" (Mennonite missiologist Paul Hiebert would helpfully later add "self-theologizing" to refer to the work of indigenous churches to reflect on Scripture for their own context[12]). At the invitation of the American Mission in Korea, Nevius traveled from China to Korea in 1891 on a two-week trip to give a series of lectures to Presbyterian missionaries in that country. These missionaries in Korea adopted and applied these principles with remarkable success. The local churches planted grew into resilient, independent, locally supported units that, in turn, reached out to their communities. Today there are more than ten million Presbyterians in Korea, and Korean Presbyterian churches send out thousands of missionaries around the world. While there are many missiological, historical, and cultural reasons for the vitality of the Presbyterian churches in Korea, an important one is the attention given, from the earliest days, to nurturing the growth of a truly *indigenous* church with its own sense of agency. Nevius and the early Presbyterian missionaries in Korea saw the critical importance of allowing the Korean churches to be *Korean*, not merely American cultural offshoots planted in Korean soil. This meant it was the Korean Presbyterians who selected and financially supported their own pastors and chose the direction of their outreach and mission work and felt primary responsibility for reaching out to their neighbors with the good news. The foreign missionaries, to be sure, still made numerous decisions for the Koreans, and the transfer of power from American to Korean hands was hardly smooth, but the application of the

---

[12]Rochelle Scheuerman, "Self-Theology, Global Theology and Missional Theology in the Writings of Paul Hiebert," *Trinity Journal* 30NS (2009): 209-21, www.academia.edu/16081942/Self_Theology_Global_Theology_and_Missional_Theology_in_the_Writings_of_Paul_Hiebert.

Nevius principles nurtured a sense of agency ("who's in charge?") among the indigenous Korean leadership before unhealthy patterns could develop. It meant that, from very early in the history of their church, the Korean Presbyterians sensed it was their church and that they were responsible for its direction and its growth. They had "skin in the game." They possessed a sense of agency which ensured that, even when the missionaries were absent (as happened during the Japanese Occupation in the 1930s and 1940s and when many of the missionaries returned to the States in the 1970s), the Korean church continued to lead.[13]

BEYOND CHARITY

The Lutherans' definition of development also refers to "the removal of obstacles" to permit full human development. In our globalized, interconnected world, when relatively richer, more powerful Christians like ourselves walk together with people with less money and power, one of the things we steward is our power. Sometimes our global Christian partners will tell us that a particular cause of their poverty is located not in their community but in Washington or a US corporate headquarters. For example, while every trade treaty is the result of complex negotiations and necessarily creates some economic "winners" and "losers," the North American Free Trade Agreement (NAFTA), signed in 1994, lowered tariffs that had previously kept US corn out of the Mexican market. In the United States, corn is highly subsidized by the federal government to the tune of $10.2 billion per year.[14] Mexico does not subsidize its corn farmers, so when NAFTA was signed, tariffs were dissolved, cheap US corn flooded the Mexican market, and the price of corn in Mexico fell precipitously. Farmers simply couldn't make a living—in fact, one in four Mexican corn farmers abandoned their farms in Mexico and migrated to the United States in the first seven years of the treaty.[15] The result was the separation of thousands of Mexican families,

---

[13] I am grateful to my former colleague, the Reverend Dr. Insik Kim, for his insights on the historical factors contributing to the growth of the church in Korea.

[14] "Dumping Without Borders: How US Agricultural Policies Are Destroying the Livelihoods of Mexican Corn Farmers," Oxfam Briefing Paper #50, August 2003, 2, https://oxfamilibrary .openrepository.com/bitstream/handle/10546/114471/bp50-dumping-without-borders-010803 -en.pdf?sequence=1&isAllowed=y.

[15] "Dumping Without Borders," 6.

forced by plummeting commodity prices to send a father or a brother across the border. It is possible that, if we are walking with Mexican companions, they may ask us to help them remove a barrier to their development.

When God calls us to work with global partners that we might experience abundant life together, how do we respond if the barrier to their abundant life are laws or policies that enhance *our* lifestyle?

If I'm benefiting from "unbelievably low prices" at my favorite clothing store, could it be that my purchases support unbelievably dangerous working conditions in a sweatshop like the one I visited in Dacca, Bangladesh, soon after a 2012 fire killed more than 110 workers who had been locked inside by the company to keep them working longer? If my financial investments in certain companies generate a higher dividend for me precisely because the company cuts costs by mistreating its workers or polluting impoverished communities, I need to ask myself if I am privileging my own economic gain over my neighbor's safety, rights, and development. The lordship of Jesus Christ redeems and transforms all dimensions of our life: spiritual, social, political, and economic. In the same way, engaging in Christ's mission must be every bit as holistic and all-encompassing: it extends to the purchases I make with the money God has entrusted to me (buying fair trade products, avoiding clothing produced in sweatshops, asking questions about supplier compliance with fair trade and worker safety standards, ensuring my money is invested in socially responsible companies, etc.). More than mere charity, God's love, as expressed in mission, requires justice.

For myself, there was a day in the 1980s when I realized with painful clarity that a portion of my tax dollars as a US citizen was used to pay the salaries of the security police of Congolese dictator Mobutu Sese Seko, who had rounded up and tortured a college student in my Congolese Presbyterian youth group, simply because he advocated for democracy at the teachers training college in our city. Though I understood myself to be wholly dedicated to serving the people of the Congo, I realized that I had been ignoring painful contradictions out of my own privilege—at the peril of the people I was called to love. Thus, building on the Lutheran concerns for the holistic nature of development and the central importance of agency, we would understand co-development to be "a participatory process that leads to the holistic improvement of the quality of life whereby diverse communities provide each other with the needed tools and remove barriers from each other's path."

The trips and projects that occupy much of our attention as mission leaders are not an end in themselves but rather a means to tune our hearts with the Spirit's work of bringing our earthly reality in line with God's realm—"on earth as it is in heaven," as we so frequently pray. This journey into God's realm that leads all of us to "abundant life" clearly doesn't happen in a day—or in the space of a short-term trip or project. In the proper conditions, what our companions and we offer to God's mission grows and can, like the mustard seed, produce abundant fruit in sustainable ways. How to align our mission relationships and work with God's mission to produce sustainable fruit is the subject of our next reflection. Let's start with a biblical text that shines challenging and hopeful light on our predicament.

ZACCHAEUS AS MODEL FOR THE CHURCH OF THE ONE PERCENT

The eighteenth and nineteenth chapters of the Gospel of Luke provide the evangelist's account of two contrasting models of how the rich respond to Jesus Christ. In chapter eighteen, Jesus directly challenges the pious, law-abiding man known as the "rich young ruler": "There is still one thing lacking. Sell all that you own and distribute the money to the poor, and you will have treasure in heaven; then come, follow me" (v. 22). But the potential Christ-follower becomes sad "because he was very rich." We are left with the unsettling possibility that the rich cannot enter the kingdom.

By the time Luke introduces us to the wealthy chief tax collector, Zacchaeus, he has our full attention. Of course, very few of us think of ourselves as rich. Yet economically, "the U.S. stands head and shoulders above the rest of the world. More than half (56%) of Americans were high income by the global standard, living on more than $50 per day in 2011 . . . in other words, almost nine-in-ten Americans had a standard of living that was above the global middle-income standard."[16] Most of us feel like we struggle just to get by in an age of rising prices and relatively stagnant wages. We often feel insecure about a volatile global economy and worry if we'll have enough for

---

[16]Rakesh Kochhar, "How Americans Compare with the Global Middle Class," Pew Research Center, July 9, 2015, www.pewresearch.org/fact-tank/2015/07/09/how-americans-compare-with -the-global-middle-class/.

retirement. Yet the surprising truth is that, compared with the rest of the world's Christians, including where the majority of Christians live (the Global South)—countries like Myanmar, Ghana, Lebanon, Brazil, and China—we are, in fact, among the very wealthiest: the average annual household income for US Christians is $47,000,[17] while global Christian annual household income is $19,460[18] (a figure that includes the Christian population of higher-income nations). Thus, US Christians represent the Church of the One Percent; that is, on average, we are among the top one percent of Christians worldwide in wealth accumulation.

Earlier in the Gospel, Luke lifted up Jesus' teaching to the disciples: "To whom much has been given, much will be required" (Lk 12:48). By the time Zacchaeus enters the stage in chapter 19, we have the uncomfortable feeling that Luke is talking to *us*. Let's examine Luke's presentation of Zacchaeus's conversion—the model of *metanoia* ("repentance" or "turnaround" in Koine Greek)—the Jesus-initiated "about-face" that leads the chief tax collector into a new relationship with God, the poor, and with the victims of his unjust actions.

Zacchaeus appears to serve as a powerful counterpoint to the rich young ruler. In contrast to the ruler, he responds to his encounter with Jesus from the sycamore tree with contrition and resolve. Before he met Jesus, Zacchaeus's relationship with God was clouded by what many Bible scholars believe was a sinful, exploitative lifestyle. A careful reading of the text suggests that it is difficult to say that "Zacchaeus accepted Christ"; it is Christ's surprising, open-hearted acceptance of the sinful Zacchaeus that motivates the latter's immediate response: Jesus' forgiveness actually precedes Zacchaeus's confession. His encounter with Jesus opened his heart and changed his relationship with God and the poor. Christ restores him to the family of God from which he was separated, and Zacchaeus proclaims that he will "make right" his relationships with the poor and all those he has hurt. He voluntarily turns away from that which has held his heart captive for so long—Mammon—and offers to pay reparations to all the victims of his

---

[17]"Wealth and Religion," Wikipedia, https://en.wikipedia.org/wiki/Wealth_and_religion#:~:text=According%20to%20the%20study%2C%20the,the,the%20dataset%20was%2048%2C200%20USD.
[18]"Status of Global Christianity, 2020, in the Context of 1900–2050," Center for the Study of Global Christianity, Gordon Conwell Seminary, www.gordonconwell.edu/center-for-global-christianity/wp-content/uploads/sites/13/2020/01/Status-of-Global-Christianity-2020.pdf.

sinful gain. Zacchaeus's encounter with Jesus Christ transforms his spiritual life, to be sure, but also his lifestyle—what he does with his money—because Jesus Christ is Lord of every aspect of our lives.

Jesus warned, "It is easier for a camel to go through the eye of a needle than for someone who is rich to enter the kingdom of God." Yet Jesus responds to the disciples' astonished question ("Then who can be saved?") with hope: "For mortals it is impossible, but not for God; for God all things are possible" (Mk 10:25-27). Zacchaeus's response to his encounter with Jesus Christ inspires us. Deep change is possible, even for congregations that by global standards are part of the Church of the One Percent. The only alternative we see in Luke's Gospel is that of the rich young ruler: "But when he heard this, he became sad; for he was very rich" (18:23). Zacchaeus's turnaround to follow Jesus sheds light on how those of us who are relatively rich can live in relation to the poor and oppressed in our own country and globally.

In the 1980s, urban missionary Viv Griggs and Fuller Theological Seminary mission professor Dr. Elizabeth Susan Brewster promoted the Zacchaeus Pledge, a simple challenge to US Christians to consider the potential impact of every decision they made on people struggling with poverty. Individuals and churches would adopt the pledge, and church councils and mission committees would reflect on decisions they were called to make from the perspective of the decision's impact on the poor. The pledge echoes mission companionship's "mission from the margins" principle—that in God's upside-down realm, those whose voices have been excluded by poverty and injustice should have the first and the last word in the congregation's engagement in mission and we would challenge parish councils, vestries, sessions, and mission committees to take the Zacchaeus Pledge to govern how they relate to others in mission.

The related application of the Zacchaeus Pledge to a congregation's mission projects (see Tool 3 at the end of this chapter) is designed for congregations to assess their plans in relation to the work of co-development with mission companions—to help structure the needed, regular times of reflection on the dynamics that naturally arise between mission companions. Disciplined self-examination, attending to the priority of the marginalized in the dialogue, and working sustainably can help reduce the natural tendency toward power imbalance that is often present in our mission relationships. When a congregation enters a local or global community and begins work by covering 100 percent of the costs or without having in mind an "exit strategy" ("When will outside support end?"), it can set itself and mission companions up for unrealistic expectations and disappointment. We are not suggesting congregations enter a mission relationship with a fixed endpoint already in mind ("We'll be your friends for three years and then evaluate our work"). This kind of "limited mission partnership" would be unnatural and presumptuous. Rather, we are suggesting that companions should not begin an intervention (contributing funding, technology, labor, or expertise) without reflecting together on the time parameters of the outside intervention—for how long can they count on the intervention. While this can be a difficult conversation between mission companions, the alternative can be toxic in mission relationships: if you build the well, you will be expected to maintain it forever. If you begin to subsidize health workers', teachers', or pastors' salaries, you create expectations that you will do so for the foreseeable future. If you pay full costs for the Vacation Bible School the first year of your relationship, you will probably be expected to cover all the costs of every joint activity. In many communities, even your promise to "go back home and seek funds for the project" is understood to mean, "count on us—we will cover these costs." Your promise could actually thwart a local leader struggling to lead her or his community toward greater self-reliance.

Speaking honestly from the beginning about co-development as a shared desire and the commitment to avoid dependencies that demean and dehumanize can help mission companions avoid false expectations and disappointments. Again, while these honest conversations are difficult (and sometimes third-party facilitation with a bicultural "bridge person" renders the task easier and more effective), the alternative is sobering: the natural progression of intercultural mission relationships puts our engagement in God's mission on the steep and slippery slope of power asymmetry, financial dependency, unmet expectations, mutual resentment, and decreased engagement on both sides of the relationship. The many aborted and broken mission relationships around the world are testimony to the need to think ahead and bring the principles of co-development to our mission conversations of dreaming, discernment, planning, and evaluation. Tool 3 identifies a specific process by which leaders can help their congregations engage in planning for co-development.

Even so, sometimes by God's grace, unreflective missional relationships characterized by traditional power imbalances of "donors" and "recipients" can be interrupted by the generosity of oppressed people. My wife, Ruth, worked for years with artisans in Peru, where in 2014 more than 60 percent of the people lived in poverty or in "a vulnerable situation," according to the World Bank.[19] In one women's group of knitters, the members had worked for several years to painstakingly grow their businesses to increase their monthly income to better feed their families. In the fall of 2005, one church in the United States sold knitted products created by these artisans and had generated a profit. The church asked the artisans what they needed most (equipment, a loan fund, or training, for example) so the church could send them a designated "donation." But before the artisans could respond, television images of the utter destruction of Hurricane Katrina and the suffering it caused were beamed throughout the world. The artisans watched in horror as New Orleans families struggled to climb to safety from the quickly rising waters. The level of human suffering touched them deeply and, even though the artisans were "living in poverty," they asked the church to donate the excess profits generated from the sale of their products to the victims of Hurricane Katrina instead. One of the artisans, stated, "We know what it is like to be victims. We see the pictures on television and . . . it gives us joy to be able to help our brothers and sisters in the USA through the sale of our products. Never in my life did I think that I would be able to give money to help an American."[20]

How many US Christians haven't been humbled by the generous hospitality of their mission companions, who sometimes live on the edge of food insecurity themselves? How many times have we been the recipient of a meal served to us by a community that quietly offers its own scarce resources to welcome us?

In retrospect, my sense of surprise at the generosity of the poor serves as a painful indicator of the fact that, even after decades of mission experience, I am still very much a "work in progress." These feelings reveal my own

---

[19]"Peru—Systematic Country Diagnostic," World Bank, February 1, 2017, p. 34, https://documents .worldbank.org/en/publication/documents-reports/documentdetail/919181490109288624/peru -systematic-country-diagnostic.

[20]Judy Hoffhine and Ruth Farrell, "Fair Trade: A Bible Study" (St. Louis, MO: Partners for Just Trade, 2008), 26-27.

assumptions of my cultural superiority, my own benevolence, my own starring role in God's mission, often in ways that threaten to eclipse the desires, sacrifices, and love demonstrated by communities I used to consider "poor." In *Transforming Mission: Paradigm Shifts in Theology of Mission*, South African missiologist David Bosch notes the mutual transformation that God's mission initiates: mission transforms both the receiving community and the ones sent in mission, even as it transforms their understanding of what God's mission is.[21] By avoiding our natural, colonial tendency to "develop" others, we open up the mission encounter to the mutual transformation that co-development makes possible. By incorporating into the rhythm of our mission relationship questions of mutuality and sustainability—by insisting on mutuality of relationship despite vastly differing economic situations—we help ensure that what is occurring between us is not "our mission" but the *missio Dei*. This movement of God's Spirit doesn't divide people into "givers" and "takers" or "donors" and "project beneficiaries" but draws us together in God's mission on the road where all are transformed.

In summary, throughout our history, Christians have been characterized as a generous people. We seek to give of ourselves to make the lives of others better in all ways. Yet many of us have struggled with how to help impoverished communities change. Zacchaeus provides us with a clear biblical example of the importance of beginning our engagement in God's mission with self-examination in a spirit of cultural humility. By prioritizing the voice of the companions who have been marginalized—even over our congregation's desire for a meaningful mission experience—we force ourselves to anticipate and acknowledge the impact of our words and actions in the host community. By committing to work sustainably, we show respect to mission companions by acknowledging that the process of development in their community is theirs and that, while we anticipate a long and close relationship, our resources are limited and temporary and intended to build the host community's capacity to provide for its own needs. We have provided Tool 3 for you to use with your mission committee or leaders as you consider engaging in projects designed to enhance the quality of life in another community.

---

[21]David Bosch, *Transforming Mission: Paradigm Shifts in Theology of Mission* (Maryknoll, NY: Orbis, 1991).

In the first five chapters of this book, we sought to carefully place three foundational stones around which we gather with mission companions to enjoy the sustaining shared meal that is God's mission. In proposing a theology of companionship in chapters two and three, we sought to deconstruct elements of colonial and "selfie" mission and articulate our calling as companions in God's mission. In chapter four, we suggested a foundation of cultural humility to help US Christians better navigate a world of increasing cultural diversity. In the present chapter, we have challenged congregational mission leaders to tap into the learnings of development studies to ensure that our good intentions do not result in negative impacts such as dependency, paternalism, and the unfulfilled expectations of unsustainable interventions.

In the second section of this book, we will apply these foundational concepts to three specific areas that our research suggests are pressing concerns for congregational mission leaders:

- Rather than discard short-term mission trips that are often criticized as wasteful and ineffective, how can we re-engineer these trips to become a powerful space of mutual transformation that can actually change the world? (chapter six)

- Many children in US rural and urban contexts and in communities around the globe struggle with getting enough to eat and getting access to basic education and health care. How can congregations care for God's children in healthy and sustainable ways? (chapter seven)

- In the emerging landscape of mission, leadership requires different skills and insights than it did before. Most of our congregations assign a committee to *manage* the church's mission rather than understanding mission as the entire church's reason for being. What are ways to help our congregations see themselves as a missionary order—each member, a missionary, called to offer to God's mission everything they have? (chapter eight)

FOR REFLECTION

1. What is your initial reaction to the story at the beginning of the chapter about the author's visit to the Haya de la Torre Association in

Peru's coastal desert? Would you or your church have contributed to this project? Why or why not?

2. Consider the saying seen in a school in Uganda, "What you do for us without us is not for us." What would your church need to change in its ways of interacting with mission companions for them to know that you are committed to collaborate with them?

3. Out of all the statements of mission practices listed in Tool 3, which would be the easiest for you to implement and why? Which is the most important for you to implement and why?

4. Given the power and the long-term impact that co-development can bring to the community you partner with, what concrete steps might your church take in order to cultivate a sense of agency/ownership in your mission companions?

CO-DEVELOPMENT EVALUATION TOOL

A Self-Check to Help Leaders Evaluate the Implications of Their Actions in Development Projects

BACKGROUND

Co-development is a mutual process whereby two communities accompany each other toward a more abundant life economically, socially, and spiritually by providing tools and removing barriers to their companions' growth (see chapter five). In our desire to show compassion to our mission companions, sometimes we forget to think critically and carefully on how our actions may affect the communities we seek to help.

OBJECTIVES: To provide mission leaders and their churches (from a more individualist, low power distance cultural perspective) a tool to evaluate their joint mission activities with their mission companions (whether this is short-term mission trip, campaign for justice, development project, jointly planned event, etc.) from the lens of co-development.

INSTRUCTIONS

As mission leaders and individuals who are responsible for mission engagement in your church, please rate on a scale of 1 to 5 how your congregation's involvement with your neighbors near and far has been in the past with regard to the following mission practice statements. For this activity, have each person rate individually and then go through each statement as a group to create an average. Be honest with your responses. Tally your total at the end of each step. Based on how you respond to each of the following statements, these statements or principles should guide you as you move forward to improve your mission projects with your mission companions. Also, please use the questions after the matrix to further discern how you can better implement these practices in your mission engagement.

NOTE: For an enriching experience you can have both sides (e.g., US and Guatemalan) participating in the evaluation exercise, yet practically it is challenging because of logistics and cultural dynamics. Even if your mission companions can't participate, it is still vital for your group to reflect on your mission engagement.

Step 1: Disciplined Self-Examination

Disagree ◄———————► Agree

Mission practices: In the evaluated activity . . .

1. We invited mission companions to review with us our actions or projects from the perspective of cultural humility (the ability to listen, relate, and respect those from a different cultural background), realizing that we have much to learn from others.

① ② ③ ④ ⑤

2. Because mission companions often perceive us as relatively wealthy and powerful, we intentionally chose to remain silent at times so we could listen more attentively to our companions' voices.

① ② ③ ④ ⑤

3. We sought to develop skills in active listening, soliciting our partners' opinions and identifying their initiatives.

① ② ③ ④ ⑤

4. I believe our mission companions would say that we treated them with respect during our work together.

① ② ③ ④ ⑤

Total Score _____

Step 2: Prioritizing People Who Have Been Marginalized

Disagree ◄———————► Agree

Mission practices: In the evaluated activity . . .

1. We first studied the context of the community in which we were engaged in mission: its history, its people, their hopes and dreams, and *their* analysis or understanding of the causes of their challenges.

① ② ③ ④ ⑤

2. We disciplined ourselves to recognize that it was our mission companions' community and that we are their guests, invited into a process of co-development with them.

① ② ③ ④ ⑤

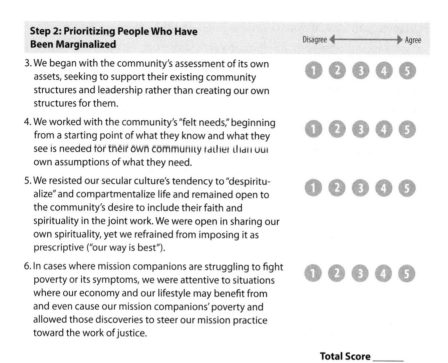

Step 2: Prioritizing People Who Have Been Marginalized

Disagree ◄————————► Agree

3. We began with the community's assessment of its own assets, seeking to support their existing community structures and leadership rather than creating our own structures for them.

4. We worked with the community's "felt needs," beginning from a starting point of what they know and what they see is needed for their own community rather than our own assumptions of what they need.

5. We resisted our secular culture's tendency to "despiritu-alize" and compartmentalize life and remained open to the community's desire to include their faith and spirituality in the joint work. We were open in sharing our own spirituality, yet we refrained from imposing it as prescriptive ("our way is best").

6. In cases where mission companions are struggling to fight poverty or its symptoms, we were attentive to situations where our economy and our lifestyle may benefit from and even cause our mission companions' poverty and allowed those discoveries to steer our mission practice toward the work of justice.

Total Score _____

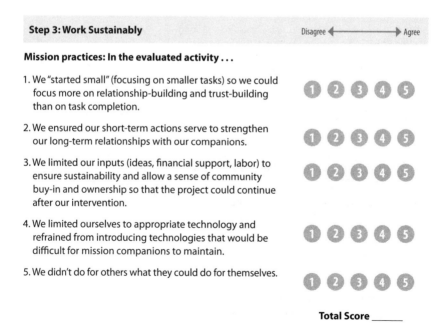

Step 3: Work Sustainably

Disagree ◄————————► Agree

Mission practices: In the evaluated activity . . .

1. We "started small" (focusing on smaller tasks) so we could focus more on relationship-building and trust-building than on task completion.

2. We ensured our short-term actions serve to strengthen our long-term relationships with our companions.

3. We limited our inputs (ideas, financial support, labor) to ensure sustainability and allow a sense of community buy-in and ownership so that the project could continue after our intervention.

4. We limited ourselves to appropriate technology and refrained from introducing technologies that would be difficult for mission companions to maintain.

5. We didn't do for others what they could do for themselves.

Total Score _____

Next Steps: If your total score from the three steps is 45 or above, please continue your good work in implementing these practices in your mission engagement. If your score is less than 45, we strongly encourage you as a team to use the following discussion questions to discern ways you can implement these principles or practices of co-development in your mission engagement.

1. **If you're struggling with mission practices 1.1, 1.2, 1.3, 2.4, 2.5, 3.3, consider this question:**

   What are some of the barriers you could address as a church along with your mission companion(s) so you can receive clearer input on the joint work?

   _____

   _____

   _____

   _____

   _____

   _____

   _____

2. **If you're struggling with mission practices 1.2, 1.4, consider this question:**

   What are some ways you could consider helping you and your team balance out the power and privilege you have over your mission companion(s)?

   _____

   _____

   _____

   _____

   _____

   _____

   _____

3. If you're struggling with mission practices 1.4, 2.2, 2.3, consider this question:

What measures could you consider to be able to treat your mission companion(s) as equal companions in your planning and decision making about the joint work?

_____

_____

_____

_____

_____

4. If you're struggling with mission practices 2.1, 2.6, consider this question:

Why do you think understanding the context of the community you are serving would be important? What kind of things do you need to be aware of and educated about before moving forward with new projects?

_____

_____

_____

_____

_____

5. If you're struggling with mission practices 2.3, 2.4, consider this question:

What are some strategies you could use to get a sense of the felt needs of the community? And what kind of assets or resources are available within the community that might contribute to the community's ability to solve their own challenges?

_____

_____

_____

_____

6. If you're struggling with mission practices 3.1, 3.2, consider this question:

What kind of project/activity are you planning to implement within the community (locally and globally) in the future? How could you ensure that this project will foster relationship-building with your companion(s)?

\
\
\
\
\
\

7. If you're struggling with mission practices 3.2, 3.3, consider this question:

What kind of long-term impact would you like to see your project play in the lives of your community members and the companion community you work with?

\
\
\
\
\
\

8. If you're struggling with mission practices 3.2, 3.3, consider this question:

How can you and your companion organization(s) work together to ensure the sustainability of new projects?

9. If you're struggling with mission practice 3.4, consider this question:

What kinds of technology are available and you can use that are both effective and easily accessible for your companion(s) that can help advance new projects?

_____

_____

_____

_____

_____

10. If you're struggling with mission practice 3.5, consider this question:

Specifically, what tasks/services did your group provide in the past that could have been provided by your mission companions? In the future, how can you ensure that you as a team don't overstep or do things that your companion(s) can do for themselves?

_____

_____

_____

_____

_____

SECTION TWO

USING THE
THREE STONES

SIX

REDEEMING SHORT-TERM MISSION

NEW KID ON THE BLOCK

Though it hardly existed fifty years ago, short-term missions (STM)—groups of Christians who travel locally, nationally, or internationally for four to fourteen days to engage in mission in another community—has grown to become one of the mission activities to which US congregations give the most time and money. Today, it is estimated that US Christians and their local churches spend between 3.5 and 5 billion dollars annually to send more than 1.6 million participants on these trips.[1] Seventy percent of the 670 US Catholic, evangelical, and mainline Protestant mission leaders we surveyed in 2019 indicated that their congregations participated in STM as a congregational mission strategy.[2]

Many STM participants experience what they describe as a transformative experience and feel motivated to take another trip or engage in other forms of congregational mission. Hundreds of new organizations have sprung up to organize STM trips for congregations. It's important to acknowledge how new and utterly revolutionary this understanding of mission is. In reviewing the last half century, I am convinced that short-term mission is by far the biggest and most profound innovation in the way American congregations participate in God's mission. Curiously, despite the rapid growth and current massive scope of the STM phenomenon, only recently have mission scholars begun to study it.

---

[1]Robert Lupton, "Colonialism or Partnership?," Focused Community Strategies, January 22, 2014, www.fcsministries.org/fcs-ministries/blog/colonialism-or-partnership.

[2]World Mission Initiative, Survey of 670 US Catholic, evangelical, and mainline Protestant mission leaders, conducted April 2019.

Perhaps it was simply because of the deep level of innovation that the shift to short-term mission represents—the move from the traditional "centralized mission agency" paradigm to the newer "congregationally led mission" paradigm—that mission scholars were slow to perceive the importance of this "new kid on the block." While there had been a few earlier studies on STM, evangelical missiologists Robert Priest and Brian Howell did much to shine the light of research on STM's impacts on both short-term travelers and the communities visited. Robert Priest's *Effective Engagement in Short-Term Missions* (2008) gathered contributions from twenty-two other scholars on short-term mission, and he challenged others to deepen their understanding of the phenomenon. Brian Howell's ethnography of short-term mission (2012) helped stimulate a broad range of mission scholars to begin to consider STM as a grassroots movement worthy of serious study. In a similar way for the Catholic Church, a 2015 article by Robert Schreiter of Chicago's Catholic Theological Union noted the shift from the traditional, centralized, top-down mission structures (such as Catholic missionary orders, Protestant denominations, independent missions) to what he termed the "Third Wave of Mission,"[3] which includes short-term mission trips, parish twinning relationships and activities, and other mission work initiated and led primarily by local parishes. Today, a growing group of scholar-practitioners is researching Third Wave mission activities and sharing their results in books, scholarly journals, and useful training videos on a YouTube channel.[4] While some missiologists' initial impressions of STM were quite negative—among them Ralph Winter, who called STM "the re-amateurization of missions"[5]—for the most part, the academy followed Priest, Howell, and Schreiter in their approach of meeting the growing movement where it was and bringing missiological research to strengthen STM practices.

---

[3]Robert Schreiter, "Third Wave Mission: Cultural, Missiological, and Theological Dimensions," *Missiology* 43, no. 1 (2015): 5-16. Schreiter explains the term by pointing to the third period of globalization (from the 1980s and continuing today) and the technological advances in transportation and digital communication. In the Catholic Church, Third Wave mission includes short-term mission, parish twinning work, and other activities led primarily by local parishes rather than the more specialized missionary orders.
[4]Third Wave of Mission, www.youtube.com/channel/UC65d6v5kpcm6mz-rjNy0XnQ.
[5]Ralph Winter, "The Greatest Danger: The Re-amateurization of Mission," *Missions Frontier Bulletin* 5 (March–April 1996).

This tectonic shift in the landscape of mission as practiced in the United States is all about the central question of *agency*—that is, who will lead, participate in, and financially support these new forms of mission. The Catholic Church's pre–Vatican II mission structures and Protestant denominational mission boards and missionary sending organizations were structured hierarchically, led by professionals who sent qualified specialists (Bible translators, doctors, preachers, educators, etc.) into mission for long periods of time. But the depth of the changes in the US mission landscape is revealed in the trend toward decreasing numbers of long-term missionaries and increasing numbers of short-term missionaries.[6]

Today, authors from across the American churches have noted the positive impacts of mobilizing many Christians to meet, get to know, and work together with mission partners, people who are often from different cultural backgrounds and live in places sometimes quite distant from the STM participants. The STM phenomenon has generated a new identity (the short-term missionary) in a way that has encouraged many US Christians to reclaim a missionary identity as they travel to a host community, even if only for a matter of days. While Pope Francis and many missional thinkers are working to help the church reimagine itself as a missionary society, the STM movement has made a singular contribution to the emergence of this new and needed identity. But this massive phenomenon has not been without its critics.

ACKNOWLEDGING THE CRITICISM

A growing wave of criticism of the STM movement has focused on the inherent inefficiencies of STM, the pervading lack of cultural awareness, the negative impacts on local Christian witness or social services, and the superficial nature of the "transformation" of both missioners and host communities that has emerged as a primary objective of STM. Critics point out that funds which could have gone to support long-term missionaries are being used by congregations to support their own short-term mission teams, and mission agency staff are increasingly allocating their time to facilitate US Christians' experience of STM.[7] To take one example, in many

---

[6]A. Scott Moreau, "Short-Term Missions in the Context of Missions, Inc.," in *Effective Engagement in Short-Term Missions: Doing It Right!*, ed. Robert Priest (Pasadena, CA: William Carey, 2008), 9.
[7]Moreau, "Short-Term Missions," 9-20.

Guatemalan communities, where there are skilled, but unemployed, carpenters and a lack of funding for construction projects, we can understand that transporting fifteen US volunteers—none of whom has ever built a building—to build a school in rural Guatemala is inefficient and could be perceived as disrespectful of local capacities. If our overarching goal is to follow Jesus' model of developing deep relationships with mission companions, what key messages are we communicating to them and their community by arriving en masse in an effort that does *for* rather than *with* them? This is the most obvious challenge in the way we have structured short-term mission that can damage our shared witness.

Other scholars have noted the common problems associated with medical STM teams: while cleft palate surgery, for example, represents a one-time, life-changing intervention, the vast majority of medical and surgical interventions require follow-up consultations and care that are not possible in the short-term time frame of STM. Evangelical medical anthropologist Laura Montgomery's early study revealed the troubling underside of STM medical teams: short-term medical mission teams produce "insignificant and even negative consequences"; patients experience an "erosion of health" as they wait for the free health care offered by foreign medical teams rather than seeking local medical attention; free, foreigner-provided medical care may actually put local medical practitioners out of business because they cannot make a living competing with free care; and the short-term design of the projects emphasizes the role of "cut and fix" surgeons over public health workers, who could address longer-term causes of poor health in preventive and more sustainable ways.[8]

Due to STM's short-term time frame, travelers default to strategies of charity work—important and valid as a response to human need—because they don't have time to identify and address the root causes of much suffering. Thus evangelism (which requires a depth of relationship) and justice work (which requires a deep knowledge of a community and the causes of its poverty or oppression and relationships of trust between allies) are often not possible as STM activities. "Giving a fish" is important in disaster and post-disaster situations, but "teaching others to fish" (education, equipping

---

[8]Laura Montgomery, "Short-Term Medical Missions: Enhancing or Eroding Health?," *Missiology: An International Review* 21, no. 3 (1993): 333-41.

and training activities) builds the capacity of the local community to provide for its own needs in a sustainable way. But STM teams are often limited to giving fish: the short-term scope of trips makes it difficult to provide appropriate training.

Finally, a growing number of mission scholars are raising pointed questions about the effectiveness of STM in both the visited community and the STM mission group members themselves. A 2008 article by Calvin University professor Kurt ver Beek summarized thirteen quantitative studies that together suggested there was little evidence of lasting change in STM participants—precisely the opposite of what mission leaders desire.[9] At its worst, STM can create unhealthy dependency between mission companions and foreground the "White Savior complex" in graphic and demeaning ways.

Rob Haynes's *Consuming Mission* notes the way our consumer culture has shaped the role and scope of STM in American church life: "Cultural influences are significantly influencing STM participants as they use their time, money, sacrifice, and service, applied in the name of mission, to purchase a personal growth experience commonly sought by pilgrims."[10] Haynes notes that in his own Methodist tradition, STM is often devoid of any biblical grounding and sufficient orientation and training. He describes STM as a product US Christians purchase, even as they would purchase a cruise, an entertainment package, or a tour of the Holy Land. This understanding of STM as the *commodification* of mission—the reduction of the *missio Dei* to a product available for purchase by Christians with ample disposable income—could help explain STM's growing popularity in the United States despite its lack of effectiveness. If STM domesticates the missional encounter, replacing the possibility of authentic mission companionship with a shiny, mission-flavored "treat" available for purchase, as Haynes asserts, are we in danger of replacing our sovereign God's mission—the dynamic movement of the triune God, leading all creation toward a deep knowledge of God's unconditional love and a world of justice and peace—with "consumer sovereignty," where the desires and needs of consumers determine the output of mission product producers and thus the shape of the mission marketplace?

---

[9]Kurt A. ver Beek, "Lessons from the Sapling: Review of Quantitative Research on Short-Term Mission," in Priest, *Effective Engagement in Short-Term Missions*, 480-88.
[10]Robert Haynes, *Consuming Mission: Toward a Theology of Short-Term Mission and Pilgrimage* (Eugene, OR: Wipf & Stock, 2018), 1.

Ebralie Mwizerwa, a Rwandan-born Christian leader and former project coordinator of the Nashville-based Outreach Foundation, explained:

> The U.S. church does short-term missions because it feels good. It is dangerous for the church in the U.S. to only use STM to help itself. Looking at the continued decline of the church here [in America], we must ask the question: What transformation has there been for the U.S. church as it participates in STM? The movement is good, but where is the key to transforming this movement for good? The number one thing I tell STM groups is . . . don't look for problems or other people's needs. Building relationship is key—this should be your attitude: "Let us go see our cousins whom we've never met!" . . . U.S. Christians use relationships to get to projects, rather than allowing your work in projects to bring you into relationship with others.[11]

Mwizerwa's challenge ("Let us go and see our cousins whom we've never met!") forces us to grapple with a troubling question: Is our fascination with STM rooted in the troubling theme of "donor satisfaction"? In a postmodern world where images of poverty and violence are transmitted onto our computer screens and televisions every day and many of our people struggle with finding purpose in life, an STM trip that helps us engage in benevolent activities surely provides a sense of meaning. But can STM become a particularly dangerous form of "selfie mission," whose often one-way directionality primarily benefits *me* and not my neighbor? Whatever our feelings about STM, we have to grapple with these sobering assessments that have come from across our ecclesial families. Despite the numerous criticisms, I am convinced that, if certain conditions are met, STM can establish and nurture relationships, trust, and collaboration in profound ways that open the door to the robust solidarity consistent with our calling as differently gifted members of the body of Christ. Let's look carefully at what it is about STM that makes it worth saving.

STM'S SAVING GRACE

Despite the criticisms of STM, I have been amazed at the intensity of the "pushback" from many when questions are raised about STM. How can we understand this intense sense of connection between so many US Christians

---

[11]Personal interview, September 5, 2020.

and STM? Particularly given our culture's high valuation of the efficient use of resources, this surprisingly countercultural strategy points to something deeper. Having reflected on mission companionship, cultural humility, and co-development in the first part of this book, let's apply what we've learned to this oft-criticized but potentially powerful way to join God in the transformation of our mission companions, our congregations, and the world.

When critical questions are raised about STM, most of us react defensively because we have experienced the transformational power of STM. I have seen US Christians' lives changed when they have had an authentic experience of God working powerfully in a different cultural context. By stepping out of their own everyday reality, STM participants open themselves to the possibility of encountering Christ in a new place—and this profound experience can give them "new eyes" to see their own context in new ways. Many of us have experienced that STM, when done well, can provide this "outside the frame" experience that so challenges and changes our perspective that our lifestyle and ministry can be transformed as well. I have met dozens of individuals who point to their STM experience as *the* experience that enabled them to hear their call. Rick Delaney experienced his first mission trip in 2006 and his testimony for what STM has done for him, his family, and his congregation is compelling:

> I was a guest in my own church: Broad Street Presbyterian Church (BSPC) in Columbus, Ohio. Sure, I poked my head in when I felt inspired but I kept the ministry and fellowship at arm's length. Though volunteering was a part of our family's life, it was not specifically anchored at BSPC.
>
> In 2004, some of BSPC's long-term mission partners in DR Congo, the Haningers, were speaking at BSPC and my daughter Sean (then, age 14) and I decided to learn more about their work and the obstacles surrounding clean water, nutrition . . . domestic violence and the importance of ministry and partnerships both in Congo and back in the States. The clarity in their message . . . inspired us both that chilled winter night and we gave each other "high five's" as we imagined ourselves participating in the work. We talked for weeks: what's next?
>
> As a family, we agreed the two of us would submit our application as volunteers with the BSPC Peru Crew 2004 team. We were accepted and found ourselves immersed in orientation meetings, local volunteer opportunities,

cross-cultural education, emotional & spiritual preparation and reviewing the covenant prepared by team members as a guidepost and expectation. . . . For our family, the trip to Peru was transformative. Our worldview changed . . . the work of listening and partnership. Advocacy and the encouragement to empower those being served. This experience moved us to engage further: work in education, environment, social justice and reconciliation for two decades in Peru; health services in Haiti; ongoing protected shallow wells and medical fistula surgery [Rick's wife, Carol, is an obstetrician-gynecologist] and education in Africa. Sean returned to Peru for a year's service as a Young Adult Volunteer in the slums supporting women and children suffering from domestic violence. Ultimately, she earned her Master of Social Work with a career today guiding youth in impoverished and underprivileged communities. Her younger sister, Anna, also participated in BSPC's STM activities and is now earning her degree in Human Rights and Political Science. . . . All of this percolated through our family's life: STM mission changed the trajectory of our family's life.[12]

Many of us have heard similar testimonies of STM creating a space of deep, personal transformation that changed the trajectory of an individual's life. Another member of Broad Street Church's "Peru Crew" noted the impact on her vocational choices that sent her to seminary and on to ordained ministry: "I had to travel to one of the most polluted places on earth, at 14,000 feet altitude, to hear God whisper in my ear . . . and crack wide my heart to hear Jesus ask me to follow him into ministry."[13] The anecdotal evidence suggests that STM's saving grace is that it can be a powerful tool in human transformation—at least under certain conditions. To ascertain what is needed to tap into the transformative qualities of STM, we will examine the STM experience through two lenses: the lens of the liminal experience of religious pilgrimage and the lens of social capital.

STM AS A LIMINAL SPACE

Haynes, Howell, Katongole, Priest, Richter, and others have compared STM to the kind of "liminal" or threshold experience of a religious pilgrimage.

---

[12]Personal note sent October 28, 2019.

[13]Shana Vernon, personal communication, July 6, 2009. Shana graduated from McCormick Theological Seminary in 2011 and, after leading a major food bank in Columbus, Ohio, for several years, currently serves as a chaplain at Barnes Jewish Hospital in St. Louis, Missouri.

"Liminality" (from the Latin, *līmen*, "a threshold") was described by nineteenth-century Belgian ethnologist Arnold van Gennep and, later, by British social anthropologists Victor and Edith Turner as a space of "in-betweenness," such as twilight, a couple's engagement period, or the "rites of passage" (for example, the initiation rites that mark the passage from youth into adulthood).[14] Religious pilgrimages like the Roman Catholic pilgrimages to Lourdes or Santiago de Compostela, the Muslim *hajj* to Mecca, or the many Hindu pilgrimages in India create the three spaces theorized by Van Gennep: separation, liminality, and reintegration. Richter describes pilgrimage thus:

> A pilgrimage, like the life of faith, involves transformation. The pilgrim first separates from the known world. Donning distinctive clothing and carrying special provisions, the pilgrim enters the *liminal*, or threshold, space while on the road. Think of this as "betwixt-and-between space," such as the space where a bride and groom find themselves during a wedding ceremony. Life-defining change often occurs during this liminal phase, when the pilgrim is literally in transition and reality seems in flux. The pilgrim finally returns home and is reincorporated, just as a married couple is introduced to guests as a new entity after the ceremony. The rite of passage is complete.[15]

Anthropologists have noted that during the liminal stage of a pilgrimage, social hierarchies are flattened: wealthy merchants and beggars walk the road and eat together in an egalitarian, countercultural social space where each takes care that the other has enough to eat. This time of inverted values serves as an implicit critique of society's ordinary, hierarchical values. Victor Turner described this inverted space where the sacred and the profane come together as *communitas* and noted the intense bonds that form between group members who experience them. But in most pilgrimages, when the pilgrims complete their journey, they reincorporate themselves into their ordinary, hierarchical relationships. STM's structure, embedded in a web of relationships in ongoing congregational life, provides an extraordinary opportunity to adapt the qualities of the liminal period into congregational life after the trip ends.

[14]Van Gennep's original 1909 work was, in fact, titled "Rites of Passage." Reprinted as Arnold van Gennep, *The Rites of Passage* (London: Routledge and Kegan Paul, 1960).
[15]Don Richter, *Mission Trips That Matter: Embodied Faith for the Sake of the World* (Nashville: Upper Room, 2008), 34-35.

STM's three-part structure parallels that of a spiritual pilgrimage: *separation* from family, friends, and everyday behaviors; the *liminal period* in which STMers and mission companions exist in a space of mission and experience inverted values and intensified relationships with each other; and *reintegration* as they return to their ordinary activities and relationships yet are somehow changed. We would argue that STM's structural similarities with religious pilgrimage are in part responsible for its widespread popularity and for the widely held perception that it generates personal transformation. The intense experience of "bonding" with other STM travelers, the change in perspective that enables the traveler to see with new eyes, and the deeper questions travelers ask regarding their own identity and purpose when present in the liminal space can generate personal transformation. As is true for religious pilgrimages, STM's structure creates an unusual space of deep learning and personal transformation and generates a powerful form of connection that, we believe, can change the world precisely because it opens up a space where companions of varied levels of power and privilege can connect deeply in a foretaste of God's realm.

STM-GENERATED SOCIAL CAPITAL

In order to redeem STM, we need to recognize an understudied impact: its capacity to create, extend, and strengthen what sociologists call "social capital"—what we can define as "the potential of individuals to secure benefits and invent solutions to problems through membership in social networks."[16] We can think of social capital as the mortar that binds bricks together, enabling the bricks to do together what they cannot do individually. In his work on social capital, Princeton sociologist Robert Putnam has noted that the development of strong communities requires relationships of mutual trust that over time develop into reciprocal acts of service or assistance.[17]

Kersten Priest's concept of the "globalization of empathy"[18] helpfully focuses our attention on a powerful, initial impact of STM: it gives travelers

---

[16]Margarita Poteyeva, "Social capital," Encyclopedia Britannica, www.britannica.com/topic/social
-capital.

[17]Robert Putnam, *Bowling Alone: The Collapse and Revival of American Community* (New York: Simon & Schuster, 2000).

[18]Kersten B. Priest, "Women as Resource Brokers: STM Trips, Social and Organizational Ties, and Mutual Resource Benefits," in Priest, *Effective Engagement in Short-Term Missions*, 254.

and hosts the opportunity to see the world from the perspective of their mission companions—to *empathize* with them and prepare them to take up a posture of Christian solidarity. These seeds of empathy, often expressed as the surprising discovery to STM participants that they have much in common with their mission companions, can open the door to the development of trust, reciprocal acts of service, and a shared agenda across lines of cultural difference, status, prestige, and power. STM can serve as a powerful antidote to the colonial script of racial superiority by grounding STM participants in a solid experience of the "other" as companion. Let's look more closely at the three kinds of social capital that can be tapped in the STM experience.

BONDING SOCIAL CAPITAL: "I NEVER FELT SO MUCH A PART OF THIS CHURCH"

In the US cultural context of loneliness and alienation described by Putnam in *Bowling Alone*, STM affords participants the rare opportunity to develop extraordinary *bonding social capital*—the deep ties with their fellow travelers ("people who are like me") that ordinary church activities often don't provide. Rick Delaney and the Broad Street Presbyterian Church's STM experiences in Peru showed that the "Peru Crew"—the alumni of the church's regular Peru STM experiences who continued to meet regularly for years after their STM experience—served as an unusually powerful (and large!) "small group" in the context of a large downtown church. Together, they journeyed on a pilgrimage outside their comfort zone, crossed lines of cultural difference, took risks, and returned home with new eyes that saw lines of race, class, and power differently than when they ventured forth—and differently from how other church members who hadn't gone on this STM experience. They had become a part of something larger than themselves. Their STM trip served as a powerful bonding experience that years of weekly worship, Sunday school, or small group work couldn't reproduce.

A particularly powerful feature of this church's STM practice in Peru and elsewhere has been their reliance on intergenerational STM. The church consistently selects and sends groups composed of equal numbers of adults and teenagers. Teens who might struggle to communicate with their own parent find that the liminal space of STM bonds them with new "aunts and uncles" in countercultural relationships, many of which have proven to be enduring.

At Pittsburgh Theological Seminary, one commuter student attended classes for two years before participating in a seminary-sponsored STM trip to Cuba. The trip provided her with a bonding experience with her classmates that she had not experienced with them before: "I'm grateful the trip gave me the chance to develop relationships at seminary."[19] STM's "on the road together" liminal dynamic creates the possibility of generating bonding social capital, giving participants a sense of belonging and trust with their fellow travelers. The importance of this tangible result of STM cannot be overstated for churches struggling to gather people and minister in an American society characterized by fragmentation, isolation, and loneliness.

BRIDGING SOCIAL CAPITAL: "WE HAVE SO MUCH IN COMMON"

Second, STM's structure carries with it another powerful capacity: in a global context perceived by many Americans to be complex and confusing, STM provides the possibility to meet and develop relationships with culturally distant people on the other side of town or across the globe ("people different from us"). US Christians often return from STM experiences and express delighted surprise at the fact that their mission companions "are just like us!" They aren't, of course. But the STM experience creates bridging social capital: their STM experience causes them to become aware of the ties that bind them together with disparate parts of the human family. They return feeling that they have been with family, not strangers. It is no longer "those people over there": they have become our mission companions. This insight can serve to ground future collaboration in fulfillment of God's mission—even if that collaboration calls for greater risk or sacrifice. Bonding and bridging social capital can provide the "carrots" that draw an individual into greater risk-taking and deeper relationship, all because the initial, liminal experience created the elements of mission companionship: the experience connected the travelers with each other, with a community of difference, and with something greater than themselves.

Let's reflect for a moment on these first two kinds of social capital: bonding (enhanced connection and trust with one's fellow church members) and bridging social capital (enhanced connection and trust with culturally

---

[19]Jill Croushare, course evaluation for MI-310, January 2019.

different mission companions). What factors contribute to this intra- and intergroup cohesion, and how can it be strengthened and made more durable? Based on my experience with dozens of STM groups over the years, my hypothesis is that the strength of this connection across lines of difference is directly related to the intensity of the experience during the STM trip. If you have ever played the "Trust Game" in a group (a blindfolded participant falls backward into the arms of a waiting fellow player), you know that trust is built most quickly when the consequences of mistaken trust are highest. Because members of both groups—STM visitors and hosts alike—are venturing into "unknown territory," engaging in atypical activities, often using underdeveloped skills, and being forced to trust God and each other for the results, powerful connections can result.

Perhaps the most intense example of this kind of social capital I observed between an STM group and their hosts occurred when I was accompanying a small STM group from St. Louis churches that were meeting their mission companions in Peru for the first time. In a local context of political tension produced by an ongoing environmental conflict, the city's mayor invited our group to be interviewed on live municipal radio. The company responsible for the local smelter's emissions—fearful of public, negative comments—allegedly contacted the city's police department, and, suddenly, the police arrived in the radio studio and closed down the interview. Our STM group of US and Peruvian Christians was detained in police custody and our passports were confiscated. As we neared the police station, we paused and prayed together in earnest, scared out of our wits and utterly dependent on God's provision. The mayor quickly corrected the error and we were soon set free and our passports returned. But the intensity of that experience forged strong bonds of trust between Peruvian and American group members that I hadn't seen before. This powerful connection, created in a moment during that initial STM pilgrimage when none of us knew what would happen, served as the foundation of bridging social capital on which a remarkably effective mission companionship was built—now twenty years old and counting.

When STM leaders intentionally break down the traditional, binary, "donor/ recipient" dynamic and include not only the worship, work projects, and fellowship typical of STM trips but also opportunities for STM participants and mission companions to engage in "collaborative risk" (activities where both groups are required to step out of their "comfort zone" in ways that cause them to depend on God and on each other), they can strengthen bridging social capital. Specifically:

- **Subverting the donor/recipient dynamic:** Rather than framing the STM experience as one well-resourced congregation taking needed labor, supplies, and ideas to help a resource-poor group in ways that divide groups into "givers" and "receivers," consider the model piloted by Mercy Street in Dallas, Texas (www.mercystreetdallas.org/): Sunday school classes and individual volunteers from African American and White churches in Dallas come together around the fourth and fifth graders and their families of a particular elementary school. Mercy Street provides the screening, training, and support for these volunteer mentors who make multiyear commitments to accompany the children and their families. Children's test scores in school—and the average length of volunteer commitment—have increased substantially and a space is created for racially diverse Christians to come together in mission.

- **Joint learning:** A mixed group of "city-dwelling" students from a Filipino and a US seminary was sent to a rural Filipino community without electricity or running water for a "homestay" of several days with the assignment of interviewing community members to better understand the rural context. The shared anxiety of this new experience provided the seminarians—none of whom had ever lived without electricity, water, or cellphones—with a powerful experience of bridging social capital across national lines.

- **Joint service:** Teams from an urban and a suburban church in your town can be tasked to work together to organize a health drive or evangelistic outreach evening and to invite community members through a door-to-door campaign in ways that will increase the outreach and social capital of the urban congregation.

- **Joint advocacy:** Mission companions can be invited from different contexts (in a domestic or global mission companionship relation) to organize an advocacy campaign based on the host community's needs and proposals for change and to lobby decision-makers (city council members or state or national legislators) together.

In all these examples, culturally different groups generate strong bridging social capital by stepping into a place of modest risk as they collaborate together as mission companions. By disrupting traditional "giver/receiver" models of mission and aligning mission companions in a shared pilgrimage, mission leaders can create bridging social capital in early STM experiences that will pay big dividends in deepened relationships and enhanced witness across differences that quickly become part of the spreading circle of love that is the *missio Dei*.

LINKING SOCIAL CAPITAL: A FULCRUM FOR WORLD CHANGE

Wuthnow noted a third form of social capital that later writers called "linking social capital,"[20] by which they mean "individuals with less influence are enabled to acquire influence and other resources through their connections with persons of higher status."[21] Linking social capital offers the chance for participants and hosts to continue to live out the inverted social and economic relationships that they experienced in the liminal STM space and point to the realm of God where "the last will be first, and the first will be last" (Mt 20:16). A carefully designed and implemented STM experience can transform the relationships between participants and hosts into linking social capital that serves as a fulcrum to leverage influence, power, and prestige for marginalized mission companions lacking access to power. Moving beyond Wuthnow's definition, STM also leverages the power of authenticity when local community members share their first-person accounts, local knowledge, and their community's history. When we engage in God's mission across economic, racial, or cultural lines, our mission companions may have significantly fewer economic resources: many suffer forms of oppression unimaginable to us and may be unable to access the power that our social

---

[20]Wuthnow's original term is *status-bridging social capital*. To distinguish it from *bridging social capital*, other scholars use the term *linking social capital*, and we will follow them. Tristan Claridge provides a helpful overview and bibliography on social capital. See "What Is Linking Social Capital?," Social Capital Research and Training, January 7, 2018, www.socialcapitalresearch.com/what-is-linking-social-capital/.

[21]Robert Wuthnow, "Religious Involvement and Status-Bridging Social Capital," *The Journal for the Social Scientific Study of Religion* 41 (2002): 670.

location and relative privilege give us. In chapter five we saw that one important way US Christians can work with mission companions toward co-development is to help them remove the barriers that prevent their families from flourishing. STM can serve as an important strategy to do this very thing.

STM, then, is a God-given opportunity that mission leaders must steward well. Many mission leaders are deeply sensitive to this truth: to travel across distances to worship, work, and fellowship with materially challenged mission companions and *not* address the issues that keep them from participating in the abundant life that Jesus evokes in John 10:10 is something less than the mission of God. Our challenge is how to take advantage of STM's powerful potential to bond their group members together into a missional unit (through bonding social capital), connect their group members deeply with their mission companions (with bridging social capital), and to link more powerful and disempowered mission companions in relationships that leverage status, power, legitimacy, professional contacts, authenticity, and local knowledge, enabling under-resourced companions to remove the barriers that poverty and injustice have placed in the way of their community (linking social capital).

In each of these examples, STM allows for people of different economic, racial, linguistic, or cultural groups to walk together through the shared, liminal experience in the pilgrimage of God's mission. STM provides an important space where US Christians can, for a few days, take some steps toward experientially bridging the US and global wealth gaps and experience the *communitas* described by Luke in the Acts of the Apostles: "All who believed were together and had all things in common; they would sell their possessions and goods and distribute the proceeds to all, as any had need" (Acts 2:44-45).

REDEEMING STM: A CASE STUDY

But what does this kind of companionship-based STM look like in real life? What would it look like for the transformative power of STM to be applied to the leaders and emerging leaders among both your global companions and your congregation? One highly effective use of STM was a network of Peruvian and US Catholic and Presbyterian local churches, nongovernmental organizations (NGOs), and an American Jesuit university that together used

STM as a tool to create enough social capital to actually fight injustice and protect the health of many children and their families.

The story involves a local group of parents, teachers, health workers, and children in the Peruvian city of La Oroya (population 35,000, including about 8,000 children). La Oroya's air and land were so contaminated by the toxic emissions of the US-owned metal smelter located there, compounding previous years of pollution, that in 2006 the Blacksmith Institute ranked the city one of the ten most polluted places on the planet.[22] According to a study conducted by the Centers for Disease Control and the St. Louis University School of Public Health in 2005, more than 97 percent of La Oroya's children under age six suffered from lead poisoning.[23] In numerous cases, the lead levels were so high that the children would have been hospitalized immediately had they lived in the United States. One US environmental health scientist noted that lead levels as high as those registered in La Oroya could reduce a child's intelligence by one to three IQ points for each year lived in the city.[24]

Many of La Oroya's parents, teachers, and health workers became concerned as they observed increased headaches, aggressiveness, learning disabilities, and even cognitive impairment among their children. Each day the smelter operated, it released more than one million pounds of toxic contamination into the atmosphere over the city: sulfur dioxide, lead, cadmium, arsenic, and other heavy metals. Living in a "company town" where the largest employer was the company responsible for most of the pollution, local leaders began to despair that they would ever know the truth of what was hurting their children or be able to press the company to reduce the pollution. They turned to the Joining Hands Against Poverty Network of Peru (*Red Uniendo Manos contra la Pobreza*), a network of fourteen churches and faith-based NGOs organized by the Presbyterian Hunger Program to identify the root causes of poverty and injustice and to address them with the linking social capital that STM experiences generate. This social capital

---

[22]"World's Worst Polluted Places," Blacksmith Institute, June 6, 2009, https://content.sph.harvard.edu/mining/files/article_-_The_Blacksmith_Institute_f_MJB.pdf.

[23]Barbara Fraser, "La Oroya's Legacy of Lead," *Environmental Science and Technology* 43 (2009): 5555-57, https://pubs.acs.org/doi/pdf/10.1021/es901734g.

[24]Mark Chernaik, "Predicted Health Impact of Exposure to Pollutants Levels Resulting from Doe Run's Failure to Capture SO2 Emissions with a Sulfuric Acid Plant," unpublished paper, May 2006.

empowered Peruvian mission companions in their struggle for justice *and* provided US Christians with the opportunity to align their actions and life-styles with God's mission as they learned that some of the solutions to La Oroya's concerns lay in the United States. The results were gospel-inspired solidarity that gathered God's people in mission with the children's families.

The original request was made in 2002 to the Joining Hands Network by the parents and teachers loosely organized by the local Catholic parish and three local nonprofit organizations into the Movement for Health of La Oroya (MOSAO). They asked for two specific kinds of help: (1) to provide accurate, independent, scientific information on the levels of pollution present in La Oroya and their impact on children's health and (2) to enable the children's parents to share their stories with the Peruvian and US media, as they believed that by publicizing the situation, MOSAO could generate pressure on the government of Peru to enforce the legal commitments the US-owned Doe Run Company had made to lower its pollution levels when it purchased the smelter in 1997 but had not fulfilled.

As dozens of STM groups traveled from the United States and the Peruvian cities of Lima and Huancayo to the polluted city beginning in 2002, relationships between Peruvian and US Christians formed, trust deepened, and social capital was created: first bonding social capital within the STM groups themselves, then, bridging social capital cementing US and Peruvian companions across considerable economic, language, and cultural difference. Finally, linking social capital was formed, allowing the gifts of diverse companions to be brought to the table:

- A preliminary blood lead study, led by Broad Street Presbyterian Church (Columbus, Ohio) STM participant Patty Nussle, found that nearly all the children studied had lead poisoning, giving scientific legitimacy to local parents' fears. As a pharmacist in the Central Ohio Poison Center at Columbus's Children's Hospital, Nussle's professional expertise and contacts allowed her to strengthen local companions with essential preliminary data. She would publish her startling findings in the *Journal of Toxicology*, grabbing the attention of medical professionals and journalists.[25]

---

[25]"Abstracts of the 2003 North American Congress of Clinical Toxicology Annual Meeting," *Journal of Toxicology: Clinical Toxicology* 41, no. 5 (2003): 739-40.

- The Roman Catholic archbishop of Huancayo, Peru (La Oroya's archdiocese), Msgr. Pedro Barreto, a Jesuit, and St. Louis Presbyterians leveraged their connections with St. Louis University (SLU) School of Public Health—a Jesuit institution—which resulted in the university providing the desperately needed environmental health study valued at more than $400,000 free of charge![26] That study, led by SLU professor Fernando Serrano, allowed La Oroya parents and community leaders to substantiate their claims of measurable levels of toxicity and the resulting impacts on their children's health and respond accordingly.

- One of Joining Hands–St. Louis's leaders, the Rev. Ellie Stock, quickly perceived the potential of linking social capital in a globalized world. She arranged to send two key witnesses to testify at hearings in Peru's Congress in April 2003: Leslie Warden, a local mother from Herculaneum, Missouri, whose family had been adversely affected by another Doe Run Company smelter's pollution in their Missouri community, and a dedicated legal professional, Lisa Martino-Taylor. The results sent shockwaves throughout Peru: "Warden's voice wavered as she addressed the session, but her mere presence made the Doe Run executives in the room flip open their cell phones and begin dialing frantically. "I came here," she said, "to share some of what Herculaneum has learned and experienced over the last few years. . . . Our children should not continue to be the price the world pays for lead."[27] As Joining Hands–Peru leader Esther Hinostroza commented later, "We'd been fighting the same battle for years—we just hadn't met!"[28] Linking social capital became the glue that bound together a growing global solidarity and lent the power of authenticity to local voices, both Peruvian and North American.

- Martino-Taylor, after returning from testifying in Peru's Congress, began legal and financial research that resulted in the discovery that the company, seeking to justify its failure to comply with its environmental

---

[26]Fernando Serrano, personal communication, April 7, 2021.
[27]Sara Shipley Hiles and Marina Walker Guevara, "Lead Astray," *Mother Jones*, November/December 2006, www.motherjones.com/politics/2006/10/lead-astray/.
[28]Personal interview, October 17, 2006, Lima, Peru.

commitments, had hidden profits from the Peruvian government. This discovery resulted in the Peruvian government cracking down on the company with a fine and increased enforcement.

* Linking social capital gave the suppressed voices of local mission companions access to the international press, generating significant power to the local testimonies. The news raised concerns in the United States, especially in the company's hometown, St. Louis. A local CBS-TV affiliate investigative reporter, Craig Cheatham—a Baptist layman whose faith, he later said, kept him working on the story despite its challenges—made two trips to Peru to bring to light the hometown company's legacy of abuse. He later won industry awards for his coverage. The story spread quickly to more than five hundred US newspapers and *Vanity Fair* and *Mother Jones* magazines and was broadcast on National Public Radio, CNN's *Planet in Peril*, and the St. Louis CBS-TV affiliate. The US coverage, in turn, pressured Peruvian media to cover the story in ways that strengthened the local advocates' legitimacy and power.

Over the years, thanks to the perseverance of Peruvian and US mission leaders, a powerful web of solidarity was woven, binding together US and Peruvian Christians, church members and environmental and human rights activists, and pastors and environmental scientists. The specific forms of linking social capital generated through STM in the form of legitimacy, prestige, moral authority, power, and access to the press, scientific information, and a network of professional services and consultants resulted in a significant shift in awareness of the potential impacts of the toxic emissions. Peru's Supreme Court ordered the Ministry of Health to step up enforcement of existing legislation, and the government of Peru moved to suspend Doe Run's operations temporarily and then proceeded to legally take the smelter from the company to sell it to another owner. Toxic emissions have decreased and numerous families sent their children away from the polluted city. Now the churches' focus is on providing treatment and compensation for the affected children.[29]

---

[29] At least one collective action lawsuit against the company and a case before the Inter-American Human Rights Commission against the Government of Peru are, as of this writing, still pending.

These clear and tangible results surprised even the most hopeful observers. While the local conditions in La Oroya make this example an extreme one, there are innumerable situations of injustice and oppression in the United States and around the world that can be impacted by the powerful linking social capital generated through the churches' strategic use of STM. A methodology called collective impact, proposed several years after the churches' experience in La Oroya, was described in the *Stanford Review of Social Innovation* and provides a helpful theoretical framework for churches seeking to accompany local communities' search for justice.[30]

But linking social capital through STM was not merely a benevolent gesture from the "powerful" lending their status, prestige, and power to the "weaker" mission companions. In fact, the churches' solidarity created a space where each companion—local, national, and international—could bring to the table that which God had given it:

- Local: La Oroya's local churches and community organizations welcomed the outsiders, provided essential local knowledge, and contributed their eyewitness accounts of how the pollution had hurt their children. The authenticity and moral authority that these local voices lent to the campaign—since it was their lives that were affected—was uniquely powerful. Without these courageous, "insider" testimonies, the campaign would have failed as a blatant attempt of outsiders to "meddle" in local affairs. MOSAO leader, Rosa Amaro commented, "I believe the most important contribution of the [Joining Hands] Network was that I was able to tell my story of what the Company was doing here and foreigners actually did something about it!"[31]

- National: Peruvian Christians from Lima and Huancayo volunteered, provided pastoral care, prayed, and wrote letters. They sent environmental, legal, health, and communications experts from the capital city to offer technical expertise. Archbishop Pedro Barreto's invaluable leadership brought significant legitimacy, national media connections, and the resources of the powerful Catholic Church, including the global Jesuit network.

[30]John Kania and Mark Kramer, "Collective Impact," *Stanford Social Innovation Review*, Winter 2011, https://ssir.org/articles/entry/collective_impact.
[31]Rosa Amaro, personal interview, March 11, 2007.

- Global: Across the years, US STM participants learned first about the community and its campaign for children's health before traveling and then were assigned specific tasks by Peruvian mission companions based on the travelers' professional expertise. Rev. Ellie Stock gathered together the US churches and organizations to coordinate continuing prayer and advocacy efforts as the "Friends of La Oroya," which grew to include fourteen groups, including US Catholic religious orders, Protestant denominations, and environmental and human rights organizations and generated eighteen thousand advocacy letters that were presented to the Peruvian government for the February 2006 Prayer Vigil.[32]

Together, the Peruvian and American Christians offered each other what their companions were lacking and created a formidable coalition, bound together by powerful linking social capital—a structure of Christian solidarity that literally changed the destiny of thousands of children and their families—and transformed several hundred STM participants.[33] Pastor Kirk Miller of Allen Park, Michigan, took his church's high school group to La Oroya and described his own transformation:

> The aspect of our short term mission project in La Oroya that changed me the most [was] being on the ground, seeing and experiencing firsthand the abuse and injustices that are so far removed from my daily existence—except for my culpability in them as a member of the consumer society from which they are generated in the first place. The images of the mountains that had been ravaged by pollution for generations and the courage of the young people calling for a new future, I will never forget.[34]

---

[32]The "Friends of La Oroya" includes Catholic groups (Catholic Relief Services/Baltimore, Missouri Jesuits, Springfield (IL) Dominican Sisters, Peru Solidarity Forum (Jefferson City, MO), and the Diocese of Jefferson City, MO); Protestant groups, including the Presbyterian Church (USA) Joining Hands Peru Network (composed of nineteen local congregations) and the Evangelical Lutheran Church Office on Corporate Social Responsibility; and nonprofit, scientific, and academic organizations, including Oxfam-America, Earthjustice/AIDA, OK International, E-Law, Sierra Club (Ozark Chapter, Mining Section), Alliance for a Lead-Free America, and the St. Louis University School of Public Health.
[33]Evidence of the impact on the STM participants themselves, in terms of the consequent faith commitments and vocational choices, is detailed in my "From Short-Term Mission to Global Discipleship," *Missiology: An International Review* 46, no. 1 (2018): 37-49.
[34]Rev. Kirk Miller, personal correspondence, July 2009.

US STM travelers returned home to continue companionship work: prayer, advocacy, hosting Peruvians in their homes, and recruiting and orienting others with the skills required for particular needs. Two decades of mission companionship trained US Christians in mission companionship, cultural humility, and co-development in profound ways and served as a call to seminary and ordained ministry for numerous STM participants. Broad Street Presbyterian's pastor, Rev. Amy Miracle, summarized the impact on her church thus:

> Broad Street's twenty-year history in La Oroya has profoundly shaped those who directly experienced that work in ways deep and broad, influencing their vocational decisions and how they live out those vocations. Just as profound has been the way in which this relationship has shaped the congregation as a whole. So much of who we are as a church and how we relate to the surrounding community is connected to what we learned and experienced in Peru.

STM AS CATALYST

At its worst, STM can be a commodity purchased by relatively comfortable US Christians that brings the pleasurable experiences of Christian tourism and a troubling kind of "poverty voyeurism" in which participants gaze through tour bus windows onto the suffering of the world. But the examples of a growing number of congregational mission leaders' efforts to redeem STM prove its powerful potential: when STM is understood and lived out as *pilgrimage*, it can become the embodiment of a theology of companionship, cultural humility, and co-development in which differently gifted mission companions offer what God has provided to them—for the common good.

But mission companionship, while intimate and personal, is not private. In fact, mission activities that do not lead us into deeper solidarity with our local or global neighbor may simply be distractions that keep us from experiencing mission in the way of Jesus. Christian solidarity doesn't admit to "givers" and "receivers" but insists on a roundtable where all contribute what they have been given. La Oroya's children helped Herculaneum mother Leslie Warden and hundreds of US Christians understand the reality of environmental racism on a global scale: as US companies increasingly "offshored" their pollution, sending it to poorer and more vulnerable communities, it is, in fact, the children of oppressed communities who have become the price the world pays for lead, gold, silver, and other metals.

This transformation—from being a church that provides STM experiences to "mission tourists" to one that uses STM as a "seedbed" to grow and nurture mission companionship and transformed leaders—does not happen by itself. Every congregational mission leader must ask which kind of experience they are offering their church members and recognize that addressing a congregational culture of mission tourism requires prayerful discernment and an intentional strategy for change—beginning with the education of the congregation's other mission leaders. Through a shift in the "framing" of the experience, joint trip planning with mission companions, group orientation, community-building, on-site daily processing, reflection and post-trip reflection, integration, and accountability work, STM can become an effective tool for the transformation of your congregation's members. But most of our congregations can't do this work alone; we need dedicated teachers and companions for the journey.

Almost without exception, your STM work will be both more faithful and fruitful if you partner with a bicultural bridge person to help you navigate linguistic and cultural difference: a local professional who has studied in the United States, a missionary familiar with the language and cultural ways of your mission companions, an organization which specializes in bridging the gaps that separate mission companions. There are a host of community-based, culturally proficient Christian organizations ready to partner with you to help you transform your short-term mission experience from "voluntourism" to companionship, to engage in a deeper analysis of the issues a community faces and connect you with local Christians who seek to walk with you as mission companions. For thirty years, Guatemala's CEDEPCA (the Central American Center for Pastoral Studies) has pioneered connecting American Christians with indigenous communities in what we would describe as *mission companionship* through their Intercultural Encounters program (www.cedepca.org). Amos Health & Hope was founded by a Nicaraguan Baptist physician and, as part of its work, provides US Christians with opportunities to experience health work in Nicaraguan rural and urban contexts (www.amoshealth.org/). Just Haiti (www.justhaiti.org) and Frontera de Cristo (http://fronteradecristo.org/), located in Agua Prieta, Mexico/Douglas, Arizona, partner with coffee farmers in those two nations to build mission companionship and solidarity and offer STM experiences around fair-trade coffee. The formative, liminal experiences that these and many other organizations can provide through STM invites our members to establish deep and lasting bonds with the very companions who can give us the gift of seeing what it means to follow Christ in a globalizing world.

Two of the most urgent requests we receive from congregational mission leaders are for a multisession STM orientation curriculum and for a daily reflection guide for STM groups to engage in the action/reflection model that can be so transformative. Using the six-session STM orientation curriculum (Tool 4, "Preparing for the Journey") and the STM Daily Reflection Guide (Tool 5), you can missionally transform a small group of mission leaders from your congregation—deacons, mission committee members, youth workers—as they engage in STM with a mission companion (local or global companions). We should note that it is not our mission companions' responsibility to train us nor should mission travel be exclusively "one-way." At the same time, walking together in long-term relationships will necessarily include leader formation on both sides of the relationship. Our work with congregational mission leaders suggests that this kind of intercultural, experiential, and postcolonial learning can be a powerful tool for forming mission leaders.[35] We will develop this strategy of mission leader formation in chapter eight.

Without a prayerful, intentional commitment to use the power of STM to establish relationships and nurture leaders, STM will remain an experience of selfie mission that can increase ethnocentrism and make us feel better about ourselves. But this chapter has shown that a reframed and redirected STM experience can be the crucible where prayer, hope, courage, some risk—and the essential ingredients of companionship, cultural humility, and co-development—are forged together to change the world. The choice is yours to make.

---

[35]Kimberly Gonxhe and B. Hunter Farrell, "Intercultural, Postcolonial, Experiential: A Case Study in Forming Congregational Mission Leaders in Seminaries," *Missiology: An International Review* 48, no. 2 (April 2020): 192-206, https://doi.org/10.1177%2F0091829620909097.

FOR REFLECTION

1. Describe a positive and a negative experience you've had with STM trips. After reading this chapter, what negative and positive qualities of STM would you identify in a presentation to your congregation's mission leaders?

2. *"There was little evidence of lasting change in STM participants—precisely the opposite of what mission leaders desire! At its worst, STM can create unhealthy dependency between mission companions and foreground the 'White Savior complex' in graphic and demeaning ways."* Against the criticisms of STM, why do you think it is important to hold on to STM as a valid mission strategy, if in a re-engineered form? How have you seen STM powerfully impact you or someone you know?

3. Three kinds of social capital are described: bonding social capital (bonding among "like" individuals), bridging social capital (connecting team members with their mission companions who are different from them), and linking social capital (linking relatively powerful and disempowered mission companions). How have you seen these three kinds of social capital at work in your congregation's mission relationships?

4. Identify three to four concrete steps that your congregation could take to increase the impact of the STM trip so that it will be a transformative experience for both your mission companions and your church participants.

PREPARING FOR THE JOURNEY

Short-Term Mission Orientation Curriculum

BACKGROUND

Pre-STM trip orientation is one of the most powerful ways to enhance the impact of your group's experience. This comprehensive pre-trip orientation is vital for trip participants to be fully ready and will also help create a transformative experience for both participants and hosts. This is a six-session program that can be used for in-person or online learning. The first five sessions are approximately one hour long and the last session is ninety minutes long. Participants should expect to read an article or book chapter or watch a video before each session.

AUDIENCE: Short-term mission trip leaders and participants.

ANTICIPATED CHALLENGES: Though these sessions are designed to be held within one hour, depending on the group dynamic you may extend beyond the hour. Also, it helps to create a space where everyone feels valued and their voice is heard by using "mutual invitation,"[1] where each participant can share and then invite someone else to speak.

---

[1] Mutual invitation is a method develop by Eric Law and is taken from his book *The Wolf Shall Dwell with the Lamb: A Spirituality for Leadership in a Multicultural Community* (Chalice Press, 1993). In this method a leader or facilitator invites an individual to share his or her opinion, and if that person is not ready or even not willing to share, he or she can pass and has the power to invite others to share, and this continues until everyone gets the chance to share and invite others.

SESSION 1: BIBLICAL BASIS AND THEOLOGY OF MISSION

OBJECTIVES/GOALS: Participants will understand that mission is at the core of God's message throughout the entire Bible. God is the source and the beginning of mission. We are just participating in what God is already doing in this world.

Checklist before the session

A week before you gather:

▶ Send out to participants the outline and topic for the session.

▶ Choose a participant and send the Scripture (Jn 20:19-23) to read at the beginning of the session.

▶ Send this video by iGo Global, "Biblical Basis of Mission—Ancient Work for Limelight" (https://vimeo.com/97239141) to watch during the session.

▶ Invite participants to think of a Scripture that comes to mind when they hear the word *mission*.

▶ For your presentation, you can use a PowerPoint or not, but you will still need a computer and an internet connection to watch the video during the session.

Total time: 1 hour

1. Set the stage—10 minutes

• Purpose: Center everyone and the conversation in God's Word and prayer.

• Let the chosen participant read the Scripture: John 20:19-23.

• Then one of the leaders can share this suggested short reflection: Jesus appeared among his disciples who were living behind closed doors due to their fear of the Jewish leaders. Jesus came to encourage and to commission them to go out into the world. Jesus informs them that they serve a missional God, a God who not only sent him into this world but who also sends them out by the power of the Holy Spirit into a world that desperately needs God's love. So, mission begins with God, and we are called by Jesus to participate in it.

- If time permits, you can discuss this question; otherwise, you can just post the question for people to reflect on throughout the session: *If mission belongs to God, why do you think God still desires us to be a part of God's mission?*

- Finish with a prayer.

2. Sharing Scripture that comes to mind about "mission"—10 minutes

- Purpose: To get an idea of which Scripture passages shape the way participants understand mission.

- Using mutual invitation, ask participants to share what Scripture comes to mind when they hear the word *mission.*

If a PowerPoint presentation is used, have an image of the Bible with the question on the screen.

3. Biblical presentation about mission—15 minutes

- Purpose: To demonstrate that mission begins with God and that God's active work continues.

- Present on the biblical texts that show God is all about mission from Genesis to Revelation. God called, chose, and blessed Abraham so he could be a blessing to all nations (Gen 12:1-3). God called God's people to seek righteousness and justice (Is 58:6-9). God through Jesus Christ dwells among us and commissioned us to proclaim the good news to all people (Mt 28:18-20). God through the power of the Holy Spirit anoints and empowers us to be a witness to the ends of the earth (Acts 1:8). God's ultimate goal is to gather all of God's children from all nations, tribes, languages, culture, and so on (Rev 7:9-10).

4. Open discussion or questions on the presentation—5 minutes

- First, ask participants if they have any questions or comments on the presentation. Otherwise, use this time to ask the question, *Are there any other Scriptures that speak to you of the God who is in mission?*

5. Clarify that not everyone has the same understanding of mission— 5 minutes

- Purpose: To acknowledge and explore tensions that might occur due to different understandings of Scripture and mission among participants.

Some understand mission in terms of evangelism, while others see mission as social activism.

- Take the time here to stress the importance of understanding one another throughout this whole process. Just because you disagree with someone does not mean you cannot learn from one another.

6. Watch a video on the biblical basis of mission—3 minutes

- Purpose: To reiterate that God is already at work even before we go.

- You will need a computer and a projector for this.

- Watch the video "Biblical Basis of Mission" together (https://vimeo .com/97239141).

7. Reflection on the video—8 minutes

- Use these suggested questions: *What are things that you heard from the video that reaffirm your beliefs? What did you hear that is new to you or that challenges your understanding of a God who goes before us and leads us to participate in God's mission?*

8. Our role in God's mission—3 minutes

- Purpose: To help learners realize that we are just followers and participators in God's mission.

- Reiterate the concept from the video of a God who goes before us, which limits our role in God's mission by using the following information.

- Historical church leaders Martin Luther, John Calvin, and Karl Barth all believed that God's mission and salvation do not rely on the church's ability to proclaim because God is already at work and reveals Godself through Scripture and Jesus Christ. Therefore, as Christians and as a church, we need to realize that

  - *Mission does not belong to us or our church but to God.*

  - *We don't start a mission; we just respond to God's call.*

  - *We are not the sender of mission, but it is God who sends us.*

  - *We are not the one who decides who is worthy or not of God's salvation; we are just called to proclaim and extend God's love and grace to everyone.*

9. Closing prayer—1 minute

SESSION 2: MISSION IN THE WAY OF JESUS AND ITS BARRIERS

OBJECTIVES/GOALS: Participants will explore the consequences of the historical fact that the "Great Century of Mission" (1815–1914) coincided with the European colonial period. Learners will be able to distinguish between "mission in the way of Jesus" and "mission from power" or "top-down mission."

Checklist before the session

A week before you gather:

▶ Send participants the outline and topic for the session and invite them to think of a time when they have been offered help or if they have helped someone and how each situation feels.

▶ Choose a participant and send the Scripture (Lk 4:18-19) to be read during the session.

▶ Ask participants to read chapter two of *Freeing Congregational Mission,* "Unchecked Baggage," to learn about the history of mission and also this excerpt of Pope Nicholas's papal bull from the fifteenth century that initiates the Doctrine of Discovery (https://doctrineofdiscovery.org/dum-diversas/).

▶ Send the excerpted story from *Toxic Charity* (pp. 32-33) by Robert Lupton about a father who felt embarrassed that his children received gifts from strangers that he could not provide himself, and encourage participants to read it before you meet.

▶ You may want to create your own PowerPoint presentation to share the material you present, and you will need a computer and an internet connection to share the Pope Nicholas V papal bull if you wish to.

Total time: 1 hour

1. Set the stage—10 minutes

- Purpose: Center everyone and the conversation in God's Word and prayer.
- Before reading Scripture, ask the participants to listen for how Jesus engaged in mission.
- Let the chosen participant read the Scripture: Luke 4:18-19.

- Then one of the leaders can share this short reflection: Jesus inaugurated his ministry by reading a scroll of Scripture from Isaiah that predicts Jesus' mission in this world. Jesus' mission is indeed good news to the poor, liberty for the prisoners, sight for the blind, and freedom for the oppressed because Jesus always stood alongside the poor, the marginalized in his society, and sought what was right and just for those he encountered. Jesus not only had compassion and healed the sick and needy but also sat and dined with sinners and tax collectors, listened to their stories, and even liberated them (for example, lepers, Zacchaeus, and the woman caught in adultery) from the unjust system that oppressed them and ultimately gave up his own life for the sake of others.

- After sharing you can ask participants to name the ways Jesus engaged in mission.

- If time permits you can discuss this question; otherwise, you can just post the question for people to reflect on throughout the session: *How is Jesus' way of doing mission similar and different from that of our church?*

- Finish with a prayer.

2. Share the story of an unintended consequence of giving from the book *Toxic Charity* and your reaction to receiving help if this has ever happened to you—10 minutes

- Purpose: Demonstrate how our actions, although with good intentions, can hurt those we help. Also, help participants realize how it feels when others help them when they do not want help.

- Retell the story from *Toxic Charity* briefly to help everyone remember what they read.

- Then ask the group to share if something like this has happened to them or how they would feel and what they would do if they were ever on the receiving end of this kind of help. Ask how they would provide help differently if they were the one who was wanting to help others.

3. Presentation on the history of mission—20 minutes

- Purpose: To help participants be aware that the church hasn't always been faithful in following the way of Jesus in its mission involvement throughout the centuries.

- Give a warning to the group that the information shared here can be uncomfortable for some but that we need to understand and confront the wrong that has been done in the name of mission.

- Using insights from both chapter two of *Freeing Congregational Mission* and the excerpt of Pope Nicholas's papal bull, you can present the history of mission from the persecution and migration era (32–313 CE to the 1960s). You can divide this history into three stages: Christian mission through persecution and migration (32–313 CE); mission through the European monarchs beginning with the conversion of Emperor Constantine (313–1492); mission through colonialism, slavery, and conquest (1492–1960). Look at both the positive impacts like education and social reform and the negative impacts like colonialism, the conquest of lands, and the imposition of Western cultures and how they were advanced along with the spread of the gospel.

4. Open discussion on the presentation—10 minutes

- This history of mission might be something new to many participants, including the leaders. Therefore, it is good to take the time to discuss and clarify with one another any questions that might come to mind.

- First, ask participants if they have any questions or comments on the presentation. Otherwise, use the questions below to discuss the topic with your group.

  - *What differences did you see in the church's mission efforts throughout history compared to that of Jesus' mission?*

  - *What is one thing that encourages or discourages you the most about the history of Christian mission?*

  - *Is there anything you learned that you would not want to see in how your church does mission these days?*

5. Mission in the way of Jesus—8 minutes

- Purpose: Illustrate the contrast between the mission history of the Christian church and how Jesus dealt with others in his life and ministry. Jesus' methods can serve as a model on how we approach engaging in God's mission with others.

- Use examples from Jesus' ministry to show how he identified with everyone through his life, pain, suffering, and death, experienced as a human being (Jn 11:32-33; Phil 2:5-11) and how Jesus never imposed on someone and generally healed or performed miracles after receiving a request and listening to people's stories (Mk 7:24-30; Lk 19:1-10). Note especially his humble attitude and self-giving for the sake of others (Jn 13:1-17).

6. Closing prayer—2 minutes

SESSION 3: GOSPEL AND CULTURE
The Invitation to Build Cultural Competence to Enhance Crosscultural Communication and Decrease Conflict

OBJECTIVES/GOALS: Participants will learn about the concept of culture and its critical importance in the mission of God and will understand four dimensions of cultural difference so they can appropriately communicate with others from different cultures.

Checklist before the session
A week before you gather:

▶ Send out to participants the outline and topic for the session.

▶ Choose a participant and send the Scripture (Lk 15:11-20) to read during the session.

▶ Send also the reflection by Mark Allan Powell on the prodigal son mentioned in the section "Intercultural Bible Study" in chapter eight of *Freeing Congregational Mission*, to be used for the "set the stage" activity.

▶ Send all these videos from Third Wave of Mission: Culture Module: "Understanding Culture" (https://youtu.be/BAFt9hxVP2s), "My Culture" (https://youtu.be/Qd_F0affDck), "Crossing Cultures" (https://youtu.be/9JMjBWDSZ30), and "How Cultures Differ" (https://youtu.be/Sw RpeVzbWJg). Ask participants to watch them before you meet.

▶ Also, invite participants to read chapter four, "An Invitation to Cultural Humility," and Tool 2 of *Freeing Congregational Mission* to learn more about cultural dimensions and how to engage with people from different cultural backgrounds.

▶ For your presentation, you will need a computer and an internet connection if you plan to watch any of the videos during the session.

Total time: 1 hour

1. Set the stage—10 minutes

- Purpose: Center everyone and the conversation in God's Word and prayer.

- Let the chosen participant read the Scripture: Luke 15:11-20.

- Then a leader can either read the reflection by Mark Powell on this parable (see chapter eight, "Unbinding Mission Leadership," of *Freeing Congregational Mission*) or briefly review the concepts presented in it.

- You can use these questions for discussion or you can just post the questions for people to reflect on:

  ▪ *What surprises you the most about how culture shapes the way we see and understand what happens in life differently?*

  ▪ *What do these different perspectives on the parable of the prodigal son teach us about culture?*

- Finish with a prayer thanking God for the ways cultural difference enriches our understanding of God and God's mission.

2. Presentation on culture and its concept—15 minutes

- Purpose: To help participants realize how much our life and daily engagement are shaped by culture.

- Provide a presentation on culture and its concept, focusing on the definition of culture and how it shapes the way we understand and interpret Scripture and how we engage in God's mission by using input from the Third Wave of Mission videos: "Understanding Culture," "My Culture," and "Crossing Cultures."

3. Open discussion on the presentation—5 minutes

- First, ask participants if they have any questions or comments on the presentation. Otherwise, ask participants to take a few minutes to think of any cultural values or assumptions they are aware of that have shaped their understanding of themselves, others, and their relationship with others and God.

4. Presentation on dimensions of cultural difference—20 minutes

- Purpose: Help participants to understand the difference in our cultures so they know how to engage with people from other cultures whom they might encounter in their upcoming trip.

- Using insights from chapter four of *Freeing Congregational Mission*, the video "How Cultures Differ," and Tool 2, you can provide a presentation on the dimensions of cultural difference: individualism versus collectivism, low versus high power distance, low versus high risk avoidance, short- versus long-term orientation, direct versus indirect communication, and also differences within cultures due to ethnicity and gender, with special emphasis on the cultures of the country you will be visiting.

5. Questions and reflections on the presentation—8 minutes

- Allow participants to raise questions or provide comments. You can also use the following questions to further the conversation:

  ▪ *Can you think of a crosscultural misunderstanding caused by differences in one or more of these dimensions?*

  ▪ *How do you think knowing about these cultural dimensions will help you and your church engage with people from a different culture?*

6. Closing prayer—2 minutes

SESSION 4: SHIFTS IN CHRISTIANITY AND GOD'S MISSION

OBJECTIVES/GOALS: To understand current trends in God's mission and the fact that God is already at work in different parts of the world. To engage with greater respect in God's mission with others.

Checklist before the session

A week before you gather:

▶ Send participants the outline and topic for the session.

▶ Select a participant and send the Scripture (1 Cor 3:4-6) to read during the session.

▶ Send the *Washington Post* article—"Think Christianity Is Dying? No, Christianity Is Shifting Dramatically" (www.washingtonpost.com/news /acts-of-faith/wp/2015/05/20/think-christianity-is-dying-no-christianity -is-shifting-dramatically/) and the ABWE International article "World Christianity Is Undergoing a Seismic Shift" (www.abwe.org/blog/world -christianity-undergoing-seismic-shift).

▶ Send Jehu Hanciles's video "Christian Unity and Witness in a New Age of Migration" (www.youtube.com/watch?v=ATyCCrXfm7M), and encourage participants to review these materials before you meet.

▶ For your presentation, you can use a PowerPoint or not, but you will still need a computer and an internet connection if you want to watch the video during the session.

Total time: 1 hour

1. Set the stage—10 minutes

• Purpose: Center everyone and the conversation in God's Word and prayer.

• Let the chosen participant read the Scripture: 1 Corinthians 3:4-6.

• Then a leader can share this short reflection: Paul wrote these words to the Corinthian Christians, who were divided in their allegiance toward their past and present leaders Paul and Apollos. The older Christians who learned about the gospel through Paul's teaching saw him as their leader, while new Christians who heard the gospel through Apollos saw him as their true leader. Paul admonished the Corinthians to center their beliefs on God and no one else. For Paul, he and Apollos were merely servants through whom God proclaimed the good news in different times and with different roles. He shared that God works differently through both of them; therefore, the Corinthians should not see that one is better than the other but rather that each is complementing the other.

• If time permits you can discuss this question; otherwise, you can just post the question for people to reflect on throughout the session: *How does the understanding that God works differently in a different context or through different people help you understand God's mission?*

- Finish with a prayer.

2. Sharing thoughts, comments, or surprises about the shift of world Christianity based on the provided article—10 minutes

- Purpose: To help participants think through these significant changes.

- During the session ask participants for comments or surprises in the article they read, "Think Christianity Is Dying? No, Christianity Is Shifting Dramatically." You can ask these questions for discussion:

  - *What gives you hope about these changes?*

  - *What does it teach us about whose mission we are engaged in?*

- If you create a PowerPoint presentation, find an image of a person in an empty church that speaks to what the article is about or just display the two questions mentioned above.

3. Presentation on the great shift in Christianity—15 minutes

- Purpose: To help participants see God's movement around the world.

- Using insights from the articles—"Think Christianity Is Dying? No, Christianity Is Shifting Dramatically" and "World Christianity Is Undergoing a Seismic Shift,"—present to the group on the changing landscape of Christianity throughout the world with special emphasis on the impact of migration.

4. Open discussion or questions on the presentation—5 minutes

- Let participants raise questions or make comments.

- You can use these questions for discussion:

  - *Why do you think such a great shift in Christianity is taking place?*

  - *What would the church of Jesus Christ in the Western world be like if not for the migration of people?*

5. Present on the current trends in mission—8 minutes

- Purpose: Help participants realize that mission engagement in today's world has to be done with mutual respect, love, and learning from one another.

- Present on the current trends in mission, especially the state of the global church (for example, there are more Pentecostal or charismatic churches, church life is seen as a way of life, Christians are passionate to share the gospel or their faith with others and to even exhibit sacrificial faith, sending more missionaries all over the world, and so on). You can also refer to some of the insights from the video "Christian Unity and Witness in a New Age of Migration."

6. Question and reflection on the presentation—5 minutes

- Allow participants to raise questions or make comments. Otherwise, ask this question: *What advantages does the church in the Global South have compared to the Western church concerning church growth?*

7. Lessons to learn—5 minutes

- Before sharing the lessons that the US church can learn, first ask the following question to the participants:

  - *Giving all these dramatic shifts in Christianity and the way God is at work in our world through migration, what lessons do you think we, the Western or US church, should learn about how to engage in God's mission?*

- After a few responses, you can share your response using insight from this article by Ed Stetzer: "4 Ways Immigration Impacts the Church Mission" (https://churchleaders.com/outreach-missions/outreach-missions-articles/177025-ed-stetzer-ways-im-migration-impacts-the-mission-of-the-church.html).

8. Closing prayer—2 minutes

SESSION 5: SHORT-TERM MISSIONS
Deep Challenges and God-Given Potential

OBJECTIVES/GOALS: Participants will be able to explore the challenges and potential of short-term mission trips.

Checklist before the session
A week before you gather:

▶ Send participants the outline and topic for the session.

▶ Select a participant and send the Scripture (Lk 10:3-12) to read at the beginning of the session.

▶ Send all the videos—"Going on a Short-Term Mission Trip" by ACCI Missions & Relief (https://vimeo.com/236674151) and "Helping Without Hurting" by The 410 Bridge (www.youtube.com/watch?v=XThVJZcQouU) —and encourage participants to watch them before you meet.

▶ Ask participants to read chapter six, "Redeeming Short-Term Mission," of *Freeing Congregational Mission.*

▶ Also, invite participants to think about why a short-term mission trip is so popular and why we go.

▶ For your presentation, you can use a PowerPoint or not, but you will still need a computer and an internet connection if you want to watch the videos during the session.

Total time: 1 hour

1. Set the stage—10 minutes

- Purpose: Center everyone and the conversation in God's Word and prayer.

- Let the chosen participant read the Scripture: Luke 10:3-12.

- Then a leader can share this short reflection: In this text, Jesus appointed and sent seventy of his followers on a mission to uncharted territory. These are not the twelve disciples, but the others whom Jesus entrusted to go ahead of him in proclaiming the good news and healing the sick. Jesus gave two instructions here that made this text more interesting. First, he instructed them to take nothing with them on their journey but rather to trust in the hospitality of those whom they encountered for their daily needs. Second, he instructed them to eat and drink whatever was set before them. For Jesus, these two directives were key to their success in this mission. It seems as if Jesus understands very well that it would be hard for the seventy to receive hospitality, to eat what was set before them if they had already brought with them everything they needed. It is only when you realize that you don't have anything to offer that you can then open up yourself to receive graciously with your empty hands and heart the hospitality and generosity offered by others.

- If time permits, you can discuss this question; otherwise, you can just post the question for people to reflect on throughout the session: *What does it mean for us today to go or journey with empty hands?*

- Finish with a prayer.

2. Sharing on why short-term mission trips are so popular and why we go—10 minutes

- Purpose: To help participants think through the many reasons they and others have gone on a mission trip before.

- First, show a slide that depicts the growing number of participants in STM trips and the amount spent annually. For example, Steve Corbett and Brian Fikkert in their book *When Helping Hurts* reported that "in 1989, there were 120,000 American 'short-term missionaries.' This number has exploded to 2.2 million and at a cost of $1.6 billion in 2006" (p. 151).

- Then ask the participants to share their thoughts on why they think STM trips are so popular, especially with US Christians. Let participants share their thoughts first, and if time permits you can share yours or use some of these common reasons given by others—to help others, especially those who are poor and needy, to be able to witness and share the gospel with others, to deepen our faith in God, to expand our understanding of others and our worldview.

3. Presentation on some of the pitfalls and myths of short-term mission trips—5 minutes

- Purpose: To open participants' eyes to the reality of short-term mission trips.

- Get the participants' opinions first by asking this question: *Are there any shortcomings you are aware of or see with STM trips?*

- After you get a few responses, and if time permits, you can share your thoughts using insights from chapter six of *Freeing Congregational Mission,* "Redeeming Short-Term Mission."

4. Watch a video—5 minutes

- Purpose: To help participants realize that there can be some danger and harm in participating in STM trips even with our good intentions.

- Some participants might have already watched the video ahead of time, but since it's short you can also watch it during the session.

- Show the video by ACCI Missions and Relief, "Going on a Short-Term Mission Trip," that speaks to the potential danger of STM visits to children in orphanages.

5. Open discussion or questions—5 minutes

- Ask the participants these questions:

  - *What most surprises you in this video?*

  - *How would you feel if an unqualified stranger were taking care of your child or younger siblings?*

6. Presentation on how we can reconstruct STM trips—10 minutes

- Purpose: Demonstrate the great potential of STM trips if done better.

- First, ask the participants' opinions on how we can make STM trips better. After a few responses, you can share your thoughts using insights from chapter six of *Freeing Congregational Mission,* "Redeeming Short-Term Mission," and also this online tool on ethical short-term missions and volunteering by ACCI Missions & Relief (www.ethicalmissionstrips .org/ethicalframework).

7. Watch the video "Helping Without Hurting in Short-Term Missions" from The 410 Bridge (www.youtube.com/watch?v=XThVJZcQouU)—5 minutes

- Purpose: Demonstrate best practices in doing STM trips by focusing more on relationship-building.

- Some participants might already have watched the video ahead of time, but it's short so you can also watch it during the session.

8. Discussion questions and reflections—8 minutes

- Purpose: To help participants strategize on how to make STM trips better.

- You can ask the group to share their thoughts or comments on what they heard and saw in the presentation and discussion. Then you can further the discussion by using one or both of these questions:

  - *What would an STM trip be like if we go with an openness to learn, to grow, to be challenged, and to be changed?*

  - *How will you use the energy around STM for God, not "selfie mission"? What steps or measures should we take to make STM trips effective and transformative for both those who go and those who host?*

9. Closing prayer—2 minutes

SESSION 6: EVANGELISM AND DISCIPLESHIP AND SHARING THE STORY
Interpreting God's Mission

OBJECTIVES/GOALS: Participants will be able to learn how to share their own faith stories with others and also how to ethically represent or share the stories of those whom they encounter with friends and family when they return home. Since this is the last session, which includes sharing of testimony, you might want to add more time to your session.

Checklist before the session

A week before you gather:

▶ Send participants the outline and topic for the session.

▶ Select a participant and send the Scripture (Ps 96:1-4) to read in the beginning of the session.

▶ Send these materials: PCUSA World Mission, "Crafting Mission Stories" (www.presbyterianmission.org/resource/short-term-mission-trip -toolkit-crafting-respectful-mission-stories/) and Tool 1, "What's in a Picture?" from *Freeing Congregational Mission*. Encourage participants to go through both of these materials before you meet.

▶ Also, ask participants to prepare a three- to five-minute faith story to share with everyone during the session and to think about the importance of sharing faith with others. In this invitation to share their faith story, describe for participants what could be shared in a faith story, using tips from the Cru article "Tell Your Story: 10 Tips for Sharing Your Testimony

with Others" (www.cru.org/us/en/train-and-grow/share-the-gospel
/evangelism-principles/10-tips-for-sharing-your-testimony-with-others
.html).

Total time: 1 hour 30 minutes

1. Set the stage—10 minutes

- Purpose: Center everyone and the conversation in God's Word and prayer.

- Let the chosen participant read the Scripture: Psalm 96:1-9.

- Then a leader can share this short reflection: Psalm 96 is a psalm that
  calls all of God's people to praise God's name and to proclaim God's
  mighty acts to all the earth. The psalmist reminded us that it is the Lord
  God who created the heavens and earth and is the only one who is to be
  feared more than any other gods. It seems that the psalmist alludes to
  the fact that this praise is not limited to God's people in the temple but
  encompasses all of God's people throughout the nations. Furthermore,
  the psalmist emphasizes the importance of declaring God's wonderful
  acts because God is not done yet but continues working marvelous
  deeds, and God's glory appears among all peoples and nations day after
  day. God's strength and glory are manifested not only in the past but
  continue in the present and future days.

- If time permits, you can discuss this question; otherwise, you can just
  post the question for people to reflect on throughout the session: *How
  are we called today to proclaim God's marvelous deeds in our lives to the
  people we encounter?*

- Finish with a prayer.

2. The importance of sharing your faith stories—5 minutes

- Purpose: To encourage participants to recognize that they all have a
  story to share with others and it doesn't have to be elaborate.

- Ask participants, *Why is it important to share our faith stories, and why
  do we shy away from doing so?* What they share might generate enough
  conversation, but if time permits you can touch on or present ideas that
  haven't already been mentioned using the biblical mandate (Ex 10:2;

Deut 6:7, 20-23; Mk 8:38; Rom 10:14) and the general reasons why we shy away from doing so (e.g., "I don't have a dramatic testimony," "I'm not old enough," or "I don't know where to begin").

3. Provide an opportunity for participants to share their own faith stories—30-45 minutes (this time allotment depends on the number of participants)

- Purpose: To help participants practice and learn to be confident in sharing their faith stories.

- Remind everyone that we all have a story to share and that each of our stories is part of God's story. Give no longer than one minute for everyone to prepare themselves for sharing their faith journey/stories, focusing on where and how God is at work in their everyday lives. They can begin their stories through an influential person, experience, or encounter they had in their lives. Also, they can focus on what faith has informed them about themselves, the world, and their relationship with others.

- After everyone has shared their stories, you can acknowledge and thank them for their courage to share with everyone. Then transition into the next step by saying that *sharing our own story can be hard but it is even harder to share the stories about others fairly and meaningfully.*

4. Presentation on how to represent others—20 minutes

- Purpose: To help participants prepare for their post-trip testimonies— what stories to share and how to communicate them to represent the people and places they visited with respect and love for them.

- Using insights from the above resources—"Crafting Mission Stories" and the tool from *Freeing Congregational Mission* (especially the re-flection questions)—present on how to represent others and to share the stories of people they encounter on the trip (through social media posts, testimony, pictures, etc.) with special focus on ways to capture stories, steps to consider, and how to frame and tell the stories. Talk about the two ways of capturing and sharing the stories through:

    ▪ photography (using the critical questions to ask yourself before taking and selecting pictures in Tool 1 from *Freeing Congregational Mission*)

- journaling (not on what you did but how you experienced God in what you did)

• Then move on to the steps to consider how to better represent others and how to frame and tell the stories using insight from the suggested materials.

5. Discussion and reflections—3 minutes

• Ask participants this question: *If someone wants to tell your story through photography, what would you like them to know and how would you want to be portrayed?*

6. Commissioning and closing prayer—7 minutes

• You can use this time to commission your group and pray for one another as you are about to begin your journey together.

SHORT-TERM MISSION
DAILY REFLECTION GUIDE

BACKGROUND

Intercultural experiences are by their very nature *different* from what we anticipate or can easily comprehend. For example, the lack of direct eye contact from mission companions from a high power distance cultural background can make a person from a low power distance cultural background feel like their companions are being less than honest, when in fact they may be expressing respect and deference for what they perceive to be their companions' social status. We need time and help to process intercultural cues and contextual differences to help us "make sense" of our experience; otherwise, we force our observations into the old framework of our own cultural assumptions.

For this reason, it is extremely difficult for an individual to learn from and be changed by an intercultural experience without a regular, intentional process of reflection. Rather than packing in as many activities as possible each day, set expectations from the beginning to reflect on each day's experiences.

There are advantages to scheduling daily debriefing times *with* mission companions. But if it is your group's first intercultural experience with your mission companions, it's best to separate the groups in the early stages to allow for open and direct initial processing of feelings. Later in the multiday experience (or in later visits), scheduling joint reflection can deeply enrich learning for all.

INSTRUCTIONS

Communicate clearly in your first interaction with participants the expectation that the group will reflect together daily, and plan the day's activities to leave room for reflection time.[1] Begin with a time of silence and then a brief prayer. Instruct participants to bring to mind the experiences of the day. Use this simple, three-level guide to lead your group to reflect on the day's experiences. Feelings and content can be focused on throughout the intercultural experience; integration is best addressed in the final third of the experience.

1. Content. To help participants recall and reflect on key elements of what they saw/heard/experienced, use one to two questions from this list:

- "What did you see today?"

- "What did you hear our mission companions saying today?"

- "What is an image of an interaction or situation you saw today that stays with you?"

- "What did you learn today that challenged a previously held assumption?"

2. Feelings. To help participants become aware of and process their feelings, use one to two questions from this list:

- "When did you feel particularly joyful/hopeful today?" "When did you feel particularly sad/hopeless?"

- "Did anything make you feel angry today?"

- "What were your high and low points today?"

- The classic Ignatian *examen* questions ("When today did you sense God's presence/absence?")

- "What experience today challenged/intrigued/encouraged you the most?"

Note: The more challenging the day's activities (conflict, misunderstanding, anger), the more important it is to process feelings.

---

[1]With thanks to Rev. Elinor Stock for her insights on evaluating experiential learning.

3. Integration. Beginning in the final third of a multiday experience, help participants to integrate their experiences and learnings into their ministry and life using one to two questions from this list:

- "How might one learning you had today change how you engage in mission in your home context?"

- "During your intercultural experience, who is a person you met after whom you would like to model a part of your ministry and why?"

- "What is one step you can take to continue to accompany our mission companions?"

In general, the fewer questions you ask, the deeper participants will go. Break into small groups if necessary to allow everyone the chance to share. Many groups find Eric Law's "mutual invitation" particularly helpful (easy to learn, it creates a space where more people are willing to share) and we highly recommend it:

> The leader or a designated person will share first. After that person has spoken, he or she then invites another to share. Whom you invite does not need to be the person next to you. After the next person has spoken, that person is given the privilege to invite another to share. If you are not ready to share yet, say "I pass for now" and we will invite [you to share later on]. If you don't want to say anything at all, simply say "pass" and proceed to invite another to share. We will do this until everyone has been invited.[2]

FOLLOW-UP

Research suggests that the mere act of setting one or more specific, concrete, actionable goals by each participant at the conclusion of their intercultural experience, together with regular follow-up by group leadership to hold participants accountable for their public commitments, increases the transformational power of the experience.[3] Just as scattered embers are quickly extinguished, the impact of "mountaintop experiences" are often short-lived:

---

[2]Eric H. F. Law, *The Wolf Shall Dwell with the Lamb*, quoted in Kaleidoscope Institute, "KI Toolbox," https://static1.squarespace.com/static/5c3631609772ae2563852818/t/5d2780613d10f200016344d8/1562869859015/KI+Toolbox+-+English+PDF.pdf.

[3]Kurt A. ver Beek, "Lessons from the Sapling: Review of Quantitative Research on Short-Term Missions," in *Effective Engagement in Short-Term Missions: Doing It Right!*, ed. Robert Priest (Pasadena, CA: William Carey, 2008), 493-94.

participants return to their workaday world and may be tempted to file away their experience in the category of "exotic vacation" experiences. Gathering participants together monthly or bi-monthly for the year following (to reconnect, share memories, catch up on news from mission companions, pray together, and share "one action I have taken" to fulfill commitments made) can markedly increase the transformational power of short-term mission trips.

SEVEN

CARING FOR VULNERABLE
CHILDREN AND FAMILIES

CARING FOR VULNERABLE CHILDREN lies very close to the heart of God's mission precisely because children are so close to the heart of God. Psalm 68:5 describes God in powerful language: "Father of orphans and protector of widows is God in his holy habitation." In a seminal text in Deuteronomy 10:17-18, the essence of the law is grounded in the very nature of the God, who has a particular concern for the marginalized who have no one else to help them: "For the LORD your God is God of gods and Lord of lords, the great God, mighty and awesome, who is not partial and takes no bribe, who executes justice for the orphan and the widow, and who loves the strangers, providing them food and clothing."

In biblical times, widows, orphans, and foreigners (also translated as "resident aliens") lived in a context where hunger and violence made provision and protection absolute necessities. In the patriarchal society of Bible times, these three social categories were linked by their utter vulnerability: the widow lacked a husband, the orphan lacked a father, and the foreigner lacked legal status. Without a male protector or legal status, these three social groups were condemned to a life of permanent insecurity, poverty, and injustice: the widow, orphan, and foreigner were perpetually taken advantage of. As we saw in chapter two, from its earliest recorded texts, Scripture doggedly insists that God's very nature reveals a peculiar, unquenchable love for those who otherwise would have no hope: the poor, the marginalized, and the oppressed. Given the weight of the biblical witness, it is impossible to imagine God's mission excluding vulnerable children.

God shows this concern for children not only through prescriptives of
Deuteronomy and the poetry of the Psalms but also through the stories of
God's people. When Pharaoh seeks to kill all Hebrew male babies at their
birth (Ex 1), the midwives, Shiphrah and Puah, intervene to protect children
despite the danger to them and despite the illegality of their actions. The
midwives "cleverly circumvent the order of infanticide, and ensure the survival of Hebrew boys (verses 17-19). A conspiracy of love to preserve children
equates to faithfulness to God."[1] Jesus shows God's standard of cherishing
children: he teaches the disciples to welcome and receive children, and to
do so in his name. He even goes further to say that in doing this, they are
also welcoming him and the God who sent him (Lk 9:46-48). In a society
where children were marginalized and had no voice, Jesus' numerous, grace-
filled encounters with children point to their inherent worth and their countercultural inclusion in the *missio Dei*: "Let the little children come to me,
and do not stop them; for it is to such as these that the kingdom of God
belongs. Truly I tell you, whoever does not receive the kingdom of God as a
little child will never enter it" (Lk 18:16-17). While the world minimizes,
commodifies, and exploits the humanity of children—seeing them as "less
than" adults—Jesus lifts them up as models of what it means to follow him.

It's not difficult for most American Christians to sense the importance
of prioritizing vulnerable children in their engagement in God's mission.
Nothing moves generosity of spirit like seeing a child in need. In a 2014
study of more than seven hundred Presbyterian congregational mission
leaders, almost half (46.08%) personally sponsored a child through a
child-sponsorship program. More than a third (33.44%) of those surveyed
reported that their congregation financially supported an international
orphanage. Forty percent of Presbyterian congregations surveyed participate regularly in meal-packaging programs for global or local
communities,[2] an activity widely understood to benefit hungry children.
More broadly, in a 2019 survey of 649 evangelical, Catholic, and mainline
Protestant mission leaders, large numbers affirmed their congregations

---

[1] These insights from Scripture on the inherent worth of children come from the "Final Report of the Independent Abuse Review Panel, Presbyterian Church (USA)," October 2010, www.pcusa.org/site_media/media/uploads/iarp/pdfs/iarp_final_report.pdf, p. 10.
[2] B. Hunter Farrell, "Congregational Mission Leaders Survey," a survey of 729 Presbyterian Church (USA) congregational mission leaders, May 2014.

had supported in the past year meal-packaging programs (51%), child sponsorship (42%), or orphanages (32%).[3]

This major emphasis on caring for vulnerable children explains, then, the impressive array of options that confront congregational mission leaders. Any local church can find a multitude of ways to care for children: they can be fed, housed, educated, sponsored, evangelized, or discipled, depending on the church's values and objectives. Short-term mission trips are frequently organized around caring for kids at an orphanage, teaching them at a Vacation Bible School, or feeding them in post-disaster recovery situations.

SERVING THOSE WITH GREATER VULNERABILITY REQUIRES GREATER ACCOUNTABILITY

In the world of philanthropic giving, children serve as a kind of "magnet," attracting interest, concern, and financial giving: "Children serve the international humanitarian community as embodiments of a basic goodness and as symbols of world harmony; as sufferers; as seers of the truth, as ambassadors of peace, and as embodiments of the future."[4] A curious facet of our congregations' engagement in God's mission is that in the hypercompetitive marketplace of mission products and services, the inclusion of children in any mission project generally enhances its attractiveness and makes fundraising for the project a much easier task.

Thus children draw attention to a need—whether simple or complex, local or global—and inspire people to give because children are perceived by adults to embody human goodness and we Christians often respond generously to them. More importantly, children are understood to be without fault and innocent. While some church members may question why the same men are still relying on a homeless shelter's services after several years of the church's support, children are in a decidedly different category. Few members will raise questions about children's "worthiness" or related issues of dependency as they might with a program that involves adults. This is due to our perceptions of the causes of poverty. A Kaiser Family Foundation / *Washington Post*

---

[3]S. Balajiedlang Khyllep and B. Hunter Farrell, "Survey of Local Church Mission Leaders," a survey of 649 evangelical, Catholic, and mainline Protestant congregational mission leaders, May 2019.

[4]Erica Bornstein, "Child Sponsorship, Evangelism and Belonging in the World of World Vision Zimbabwe," *American Ethnologist* 28, no. 3 (2001): 597.

2017 poll found US Christians are almost twice as likely to blame a person's poverty on his or her own lack of effort: "46 percent of all Christians said that a lack of effort is generally to blame for a person's poverty, compared with 29 percent of all non-Christians."[5]

Children embody innocence and consequently motivate generous giving by side-stepping donor concerns about the "worthiness" of beneficiaries. Many orphanages, child-sponsorship programs, child feeding, and other programs have framed their mission around the needs of children and have tapped into this wellspring of financial giving. It is important to note this connection, lest we be drawn into an emotional appeal for support without considering what we have learned about mission as companionship—about recognizing children and their families as our companions in God's mission and not the *objects* of *our* mission. This is because children, who suffer from a legally and culturally imposed inability to speak for themselves, are in an extremely vulnerable position. Unlike adults, who in principle have voice and can represent themselves in a court of law, express their needs, and freely consent to participate in any activity they choose,[6] children can generally do none of these things: even a child's expression of need must be approved by adults to be considered valid. This lack of voice can easily lead to the victimization of children.

In societies around the world, including our own, children are disproportionately the victims of many forms of human trafficking, such as child labor, sweatshops, child pornography, prostitution, and organ trafficking. Of the estimated 40 million victims of human trafficking today, more than a quarter are children.[7] Just as the God of Scripture has a peculiar and abiding love for

---

[5]Julie Zauzmer, "Christians Are More Than Twice as Likely to Blame a Person's Poverty on Lack of Effort," *Washington Post*, August 3, 2017, www.washingtonpost.com/news/acts-of-faith /wp/2017/08/03/christians-are-more-than-twice-as-likely-to-blame-a-persons-poverty-on-lack -of-effort/. The report continues, "The gulf widens further among specific Christian groups: 53 percent of white evangelical Protestants blamed lack of effort while 41 percent blamed circumstances, and 50 percent of Catholics blamed lack of effort while 45 percent blamed circumstances. In contrast, by more than 2 to 1, Americans who are atheist, agnostic or have no particular affiliation said difficult circumstances are more to blame when a person is poor than lack of effort (65 percent to 31 percent)."

[6]Obviously, hunger, poverty, fear of violence, and culturally constructed constraints like sexism and racism can keep some adults from freely expressing themselves and exercising their own agency, thus, the importance of walking with mission companions to understand realities that more privileged Christians may never have experienced.

[7]"27% of Trafficking Victims Are Children," World's Children, www.worldschildren.org/child -trafficking-statistics/.

the poor and oppressed who would otherwise have no hope, God exhibits that same love to vulnerable children who do not have the voice, agency, or power to protect themselves from a dangerous world and calls us to do the same.

Our earlier biblical reflections remind us why caring for vulnerable children is so important to our congregations: because it is so important to God. For this reason, it is important to ensure that our mission efforts to love God's children reflect God's ways of caring for them with all their particular needs. We understand the need for clear boundaries when we work with our community's children in our congregation's daycare program or Vacation Bible School. We need to ensure each adult has been screened and trained and does not represent a threat to the safety of these children. We readily accept that we will need to refrain from embracing or touching children in ways that could be upsetting to them. In the same way, we will need to carefully examine the strategies we choose to work with resource-challenged communities to support them as they strive to improve their children's quality of life.

We understand that requiring a hungry adult to attend a Bible study as a precondition to receive a hot meal violates that adult's personhood: a person's hunger should not negate their right to decide if they wish to attend the study or not. If we're not working in partnership with a child's parents, to require that child to attend a Bible study in order to receive a meal is a more serious ethical violation because it does more harm: a child doesn't exercise the same level of agency that an adult can. It is for these reasons that congregations need to consider carefully how they work with vulnerable children. Can we imagine working with children and their parents as companions in God's mission in a spirit of cultural humility, engaging in the intimate work of co-development so that they and we grow into all God has created us to be?

According to our research, three of US congregations' most popular mission strategies to care for children—meal packaging, child sponsorship, and support of orphanages—enjoy widespread support from mainline Protestants, evangelicals, and Catholics alike, despite the significant questions being raised about each of these strategies. In the next part of the chapter, we will apply what we learned in the first section of the book about companionship, cultural humility, and co-development to these three mission strategies. We will assess their potential benefits, harm, and costs; consider alternatives; and identify questions that mission leaders can use with their congregations as they evaluate their work.

MEAL-PACKAGING PROGRAMS

Prepared meal–packaging projects have exploded in popularity as a mission activity among US Christians, especially among mission conference attendees and youth or college groups, as demonstrated by the growth in both the number of institutions providing this service and the volume of their operations.[8] In 2018, the nine largest meal-packaging organizations distributed a total of 549.9 million meals.[9] Since its founding in 1987, Feed My Starving Children has packaged and delivered more than 2.4 billion meals in more than 102 countries.[10] By prepared meal packaging, we mean the assembling, packaging, and shipping of single-serving, nutritious meals to a community of need.

One of the most effective ways to mobilize a large group of people around a mission cause is to organize a meal-packaging event. It provides a group that shares values around helping neighbors with a clear objective and a concrete way they can impact a large global issue in tangible, measurable ways. Rise Against Hunger, with "a mission to end hunger in our lifetime" mobilized more than 1.3 million volunteers in 2018 alone.[11] Three of the largest meal-packaging organizations—Feed My Starving Children, Rise Against Hunger,[12] and Feed the Hunger—are Christian organizations that focus on mobilizing generous Christians concerned about hungry people. All nine of the United States' largest meal-packaging organizations have registered strong growth over the past five years in an American philanthropic marketplace crowded with many competitors.

---

[8]Based on the number of meals packaged and distributed in 2018, the nine largest meal-packaging organizations in the United States are Feed My Starving Children, Rise Against Hunger, Numana, Kids Against Hunger, Meals from the Heartland, Outreach Program, Meals of Hope, Feed the Hunger, and Packaway Hunger.
[9]Based on the statistics provided on the websites of the nine organizations.
[10]Feed My Starving Children, www.fmsc.org/.
[11]From the website Rise Against Hunger, www.riseagainsthunger.org.
[12]While Rise Against Hunger is technically not a Christian organization, it was founded by a United Methodist minister and works closely with churches around the world as its local affiliates that distribute packaged meals.

More germane to our evaluation of mission programs that impact children, all nine organizations feature children prominently on their websites, promotional literature, advertising, and fundraising stories. In fact, on the websites of all nine organizations, it is rare to find a photo that *does not* include a child. As mentioned above, by portraying the images and stories of needy children, the programs are able to avoid a major hurdle in their support-raising efforts: the US Christian reticence to give a free meal to an adult living in poverty. If, as many US Christians believe, poverty is generally the result of inadequate personal choices made by an adult living in poverty, the organizations can avoid donor hesitation and lessened revenue by portraying the beneficiaries of meal-packaging program almost exclusively as children. As we examine the ways organizations serve children, we also want to be attentive to the ways they use children's images, how they strengthen and develop children's agency (the child's capacity to exert power to influence their life circumstances), and the ways they represent children in their communication. The very vulnerability of children requires that our churches ask harder questions than we might in other kinds of mission efforts. These harder questions help us keep our efforts to help children aligned with the mission of God, who not only desires improved nutrition for children but also cares that help is offered in ways that respect children and their families' dignity and build capacity to provide for their own needs in the long-term, according to the concepts of companionship, cultural humility, and co-development.

PACKAGED MEALS IN THE FIGHT AGAINST HUNGER

It is a beautiful thing when a group of Christians work together to provide food for people struggling with hunger. Mission conferences, campus ministries, Christian summer camps, church retreats, and even family reunions adopt a missional focus by including a meal-packaging event in their program. Christian parents help train their children to remember the hungry and inculcate a sense of social responsibility by including their own children in meal-packaging events. When the meal-packaging event is paired with education on the root causes of hunger, the event takes on even greater impact, using the power of experiential education to sensitize Christians to become advocates for the poor. According to the websites of the nine major US meal-packaging organizations, education about hunger's causes is not a major focus of most of the organizations' work. It seems strange to note that US Christians can participate in a successful meal-packaging event and never be invited to reflect on hunger's causes or be equipped to work against them. In this sense, efforts "to end hunger in our lifetime" through the provision of packaged meals are doomed to failure: the programs are created as stop gap responses whose powerful appeal is predicated on the urgency of the need. But if my meal-packaging efforts to feed a child in Haiti for a day do nothing to help her or her family or community to respond to the root causes of hunger in more coordinated or effective, long-term ways,[13] my efforts, at worst, may be mere Band-Aid solutions. Why does this matter?

Packaged meals can save a life when delivered in a disaster zone. But when delivered to communities suffering from chronic poverty, they ignore the root causes of hunger. Beyond missing the chance for a sustainable impact, meal-packaging programs do a more serious disservice by lulling donors into a false sense of complacency. As international hunger expert Valéry Nodem lamented, "We are inoculating an entire generation of college students to believe they are doing something to combat hunger by giving a few hours to package rice and beans."[14] Most meal-packaging programs invite volunteers to assemble rice and beans (and sometimes protein or other nutritional supplements) generally purchased in the United States or received as donations and then shipped at relatively high cost to distant communities in ways that follow a more paternalistic "donor/recipient" model, don't build relationships between the two, don't identify the causes of hunger, and don't provide a sustainable response to hunger. The Haitian child I feed today through meal packaging will be hungry again tomorrow.

If done alone—without inviting your congregation to reflect more deeply about hunger's causes—meal-packaging events can powerfully reinforce the comfortable (for *us!*) colonial-era stereotype of the relatively privileged giving charity to the poor without ever asking the question, Why are these people hungry? Giving to a world in perpetual need allows my congregation to engage in benevolent behavior and, perhaps, to feel good about its work.

---

[13]Church World Service incorporates hunger education in all of their disaster kits, "Ration Challenge," and CROP Walk activities: see https://resources.crophungerwalk.org/resources/educate-others/.
[14]Valéry Nodem, Presbyterian Hunger Program, personal interview, May 20, 2014.

Yet most of the meal-packaging organizations surveyed have repeatedly provided food to the same communities for years, and, at some point, one of your church members is going to ask, "Why do we keep giving to the same need—doesn't our help make a difference?" This question helpfully points to the question of sustainability—whether the organizations are building a community's capacity to provide for local food needs: Are they helping parents to develop the capacity to provide their children with the food they need? As we reflect on the importance of co-development, there is something deeply troubling about annually mobilizing millions of people to assemble, ship, and airdrop foreign food into communities whose desperate need is not to eat for a day but *food sovereignty*, the capacity to provide for their families' food needs over the long term.

Frankly, when we look at meal-packaging projects from a systems perspective, they appear to be a workaround operation of massive proportions. Why is it we occupy our churches with "giving a fish" to a hungry person rather than addressing the root causes of hunger: communities' access to land and water, the need for tools and agricultural technology, infrastructure needs, local economic constraints, and so on? It is difficult to imagine a project that provides food on a regular basis to a foreign community over many years that does *not* create and build dependency, reinforce stereotypical donor/beneficiary roles, and undercut the dignity and proper role of parents as primary providers for their children. For children to see that their parents need a handout day after day and that they appear to be incapable of providing for their family's needs communicates a profoundly negative future at best. By helping in the short term, are we hurting children over the long term?

Again, a packaged meal delivered to a hungry person in a disaster zone can save a life, and we give thanks to God for the good intentions of everyone participating in this kind of compassionate mission work. But if your congregation doesn't know the context into which the meals you pack are delivered—if you're not sure if the organization attends to God's concerns for human dignity and sustainability—it's time to start asking some questions. Because in some ways, meal packaging can operate as the mirror image of short-term mission (STM) construction trips: designed around donor enthusiasm rather than as a sustainable response to a community's need. How might you lead your congregation to work as mission companions in the spirit of a more sustainable co-development? More than merely packaging meals, can your congregation imagine partnering with local organizations to build food sovereignty—that is, to strengthen families' capacity to fulfill God's good intention of providing food for their children?

Dropping large quantities of free food through a large-scale meal-packaging program can depress commodity prices in localized, non-disaster contexts, potentially driving local farmers out of business and reducing local food supply. Local rice farmers in Haiti will struggle to compete with large amounts of free, imported rice, thus it becomes important to ask the meal-packaging agency if they prioritize providing food for communities facing disaster situations. Popular authors Bob Lupton (*Toxic Charity*) and Steve Corbett and Brian Fikkert (*When Helping Hurts*) draw attention to our need to be attentive to a community's transition on the continuum from *disaster* to *recovery* to *rehabilitation* to *development*. Ignoring where a community is on this continuum—that is, providing continuous disaster relief to respond to a community's chronic problems—can hurt the very people we seek to help.

This is not to say that congregations should not participate in meal-packaging efforts—nutritious meals, placed in the right hands in the right context, can literally save lives. Thus, mission leaders who seek to lead their people more deeply into more sustainable mission strategies that empower local families will ask questions of the organizations with which they partner to help their people understand the potential impacts of their actions. They will ensure that a foundation of respectful co-development is being built: one that strengthens local partners and, once the acute disaster has passed, helps them toward self-sufficiency rather than making them more dependent on outsiders; one that empowers local partners by helping them identify and respond to the real causes of hunger in their community; one that deepens long-term relationships as companions in God's mission.

Here are some starter questions that can help your congregation's mission leaders assess a meal-packaging organization (feel free to add your own questions based on your congregation's values and priorities):

- *Prioritizing disaster relief:* Does the organization prioritize communities experiencing/recovering from a disaster? If not, how does it justify sending outside food to the same community year after year?

- *Prioritizing children*: In nondisaster contexts, does the organization prioritize children whose nutritional/development needs are greater and more time-sensitive than the general population's?

- *Commitment to addressing hunger's root causes*: How does the organization educate your congregation about poverty's root causes and mobilize you to work to address them? How does the organization encourage the host community to learn about poverty's root causes in their own context? In other words, does your congregation's work in meal packaging distract you from the harder work of addressing hunger's root causes—or does it motivate and empower you to engage in this longer-term, more difficult work?

- *Commitment to local organizations/structures*: To what extent does the organization support/collaborate with local organizations? How are local distributing organizations' experience and wisdom respected by the US meal-packaging organization? Can the meal-packaging agency recall some lessons local partners have taught them?

- *Discrimination by religion*: Does the organization offer food to people without regard to church membership/religious affiliation? Giving food only to Christians—and withholding it from other hungry people—raises significant ethical questions and can be highly counterproductive: it can trigger jealousy between the local church and its surrounding community in ways that weaken its witness. In fact, offering food incentives for hungry people to join the church replicates the disastrous nineteenth-century mission policy of giving free rice to Chinese who joined the church, thus creating "rice Christians" and damaging the significance of a public commitment to Christ.

To the extent that meal-packaging programs strengthen your church's relationships with a specific community, they can bring blessing to hungry people and give public witness to a long-term relationship with the local partners: "A friend in need is a friend indeed" as the saying goes. Let us be clear: to *not* provide food to hungry mission companions in a time of disaster or crisis is not consistent with our understanding of God's mission. At the same time, a congregation should not enter into the role of providing free food to mission partners without having considered its "exit strategy":

under what circumstances will the congregation stop providing food? If you don't have an exit strategy when you begin a subsidy or "giveaway" program, you create a powerful expectation that you will continue the subsidy over the long term—or forever. What might begin as a gesture of love and concern can quickly become an unsustainable intervention that promotes unhealthy dependency and frustration and could end in disappointment when your congregation stops sending food.

What if we reimagined caring for hungry children and their families by seeking ways for our churches to use a meal-packaging event to gather mission enthusiasts, your own church members, and folks from beyond your congregation (including young people) to educate and mobilize them to work together for food sovereignty in your local community and with global mission companions? Many congregations need help to educate their members about complex issues like local and global hunger and to accompany their mission companions toward food sovereignty. By partnering with one of the following organizations, you can extend your congregation's reach and draw on the organization's decades of experience:

- *Feeding America* (www.feedingamerica.org) is a network of two hundred food banks across the United States. Contact your local food bank to begin a relationship with people in your own community who live in food insecurity. Whatever your mission priorities locally or globally, including your local food bank keeps hunger work *real* and allows people in your congregation to be exposed to—and to develop relationships with—real people struggling with hunger in your community. Note: It is sad when congregations ship food across the world without pausing to acknowledge that members of their own community go to bed hungry.

- *Bread for the World* (https://bread.org) organizes local churches to advocate for US government policies that help American and global communities to feed themselves. Partnering with Bread for the World is an excellent way to complement your congregation's disaster assistance work with long-term hunger education and advocacy work on hunger's root causes. Their online resource library (with resources in both Spanish and English) and their tools for activists provide excellent and useful resources for mission leaders.

- *World Relief* (https://worldrelief.org) understands local congregations in both the United States and overseas to be part of God's answer to the needs of the hungry. It connects US and global congregations to address hunger with an eye toward holistic, sustainable development, prioritizing people affected by disasters, violence, or extreme poverty and refugees/displaced persons. World Relief partners with congregational mission leaders in hunger education, advocacy, and a national legal services network for immigrants.

- *Catholic Charities* (www.catholiccharitiesusa.org) does effective advocacy work on issues of domestic hunger, while Catholic Relief Services (www.crs.org) educates and mobilizes US parishes around issues of global hunger. Both organizations pair "hands-on" activities with effective strategies to advocate for families struggling with hunger. By gathering the collective social and political capital of US Catholic parishes across the country, both organizations are able to make a measurable impact on US food policy.

- *CWS* (formerly Church World Service, https://cwsglobal.org) has long been an innovator in engaging local congregations (mainline Protestant, Catholic, and evangelical) with disaster assistance and long-term recovery and development in respectful ways. They combine hunger education with "hands-on" activities (like the popular CROP Walk) better than many other organizations.

- *Growing Hope Globally* (https://growinghopeglobally.org) grows lasting solutions to hunger by helping subsistence farmers grow their own food and earn an income. Through their unique Growing Project model, US farmers (rural or urban) work with their churches and surrounding communities to become part of the solution—raising money and awareness to end world hunger. Catholic, evangelical, and mainline Protestant congregations participate in this popular program.

CHILD-SPONSORSHIP PROGRAMS

Child sponsorship represents one of the most popular ways for individuals to support children in the Majority World. The scope and growth of these programs around the world is breathtaking: more than nine million children are supported through international child-sponsorship programs at a cost of more than $3.29 billion annually.[15] In just four years (from 2011 to 2015), the budgets of the fifteen child-sponsorship organizations tracked by the Evangelical Council for Financial Accountability increased 40 percent.[16] Child sponsors pay a monthly fee (generally between $25 and $40) to improve a poor child's nutrition, health care, and education and to cover program costs. Child sponsorship is immensely attractive to donors because it creates the idea of a personal relationship between a donor and a child: sponsors are provided with personal information about "their" child—from their food preferences to their hopes and dreams—exchange letters with them, and, in some cases, provide occasional gifts or even travel to visit their child.

As a fundraising strategy, there is nothing more effective than child sponsorship at moving donors to give consistently. This pattern of monthly giving generates a large, regular stream of revenue that more fickle individual donations, government contracts, and foundation grants simply cannot provide. For community workers and program leaders, this kind of dependable funding is extremely positive: they are enabled to actually plan their work, maximizing resources without the vicissitudes of easily distracted donors who often do not understand the long-term needs of the community. We'll look now at the two kinds of child-sponsorship programs based on how they support children.

Direct-sponsorship model. We will describe as the "direct sponsorship model" a program (like Compassion International and Children International) that uses funding exclusively for sponsored children in the form of "school tuition and uniforms, several nutritious meals per week, health care and tutoring . . . (and) 8 hours per week in an intensive after-school program that emphasizes their spiritual, physical, and socio-emotional development" in order to "raise the child's self-esteem, aspirations and self-expectations."[17]

---

[15]Bruce Wydick, et. al., "Does International Child Sponsorship Work? A Six Country Study of Impacts on Adult Life Outcomes," *Journal of Political Economy* 121, no. 2 (April 2013): 393.

[16]Sarah Eekhoff Zylstra, "What Current, Past, and 'Never' Child Sponsors Think," *Christianity Today*, December 19, 2017, www.christianitytoday.com/news/2017/december/child-sponsorship-donors-survey-compassion-world-vision.html.

[17]Wydick, et. al., "Does International Child Sponsorship Work?," 397. This description of program expenses is specifically for Compassion International, but many of the direct-sponsorship programs provide similar goods and services to sponsored children.

In a 2013 peer-reviewed study of more than ten thousand children in six countries, Wydick and colleagues studied children sponsored by Compassion International,[18] the largest example of the direct model of child sponsorship. The authors found that children sponsored over a ten-year period showed an increase of between 1.03 to 1.46 additional years of schooling over unsponsored children; likewise, secondary school completion was 11.6 to 16.5 percent higher for less than half of the sponsored children. The study also found a slight increase in the probability of salaried employment and white-collar employment. The study itself notes that causality is much more difficult to prove in the complexities of real-world communities. Did children sponsored by Compassion International stay in school longer and earn more money as adults *because of* their participation in the program, or was the critical variable in fact a mother's tenacious drive that pushed her child to "the front of the line"—to sign her child up for a child-sponsorship program, for a government-sponsored pre-kindergarten program, for immunizations, for homework help from neighbors? Other impact studies of the Compassion International program have found both positive and negative impacts.[19]

While the Wydick study pointed to school attendance, future employment, and future earnings as the measurable indicators of success of this example of the direct-sponsorship model, other organizations have encountered negative impacts on children and their families and have quit using the direct model despite an anticipated drop in donor support for the popular strategy. The statement made by Jeremy Moodey, the CEO of Embrace the Middle East, a British organization that built its ministry on the direct-sponsorship model but changed course because of its concerns

---

[18] Along with nonsponsored siblings, nonsponsored children living in the same community with sponsored children, and children from communities with no sponsored children. According to the study authors, Compassion International was the only child sponsorship organization that agreed to participate in the study.

[19] A smaller study on children sponsored by Compassion International in Indonesia by a graduate student from Wydick's university found mixed results among sponsored children between the ages of four and fourteen: slightly increased self-esteem and optimism and slightly decreased patience and reciprocity: Mario Carrillo, "Does Child Sponsorship Have a Positive Impact on the Quality of Life and Social Behavior of Sponsored Children? Evidence from Indonesia," May 7, 2013, https://repository.usfca.edu/cgi/viewcontent.cgi?article=1078 &context=thes.

for what it perceived as overriding negative impacts, points to some of the weaknesses of the model:

> There are much bigger problems with child sponsorship. In particular, the potentially negative impact on the wider community (including those children who do not benefit from sponsorship) and on the sponsors themselves, and the administrative burdens of running a child-sponsorship programme.
>
> It is precisely for these reasons that Embrace the Middle East (formerly Bible Lands) began phasing out its longstanding child-sponsorship programme a few years ago. This provoked quite a few complaints from some of our supporters. But we were convinced that, in moral and developmental terms, it was the right thing to do.
>
> Having visited schools in Palestine where Embrace provided child sponsorship, I have seen how potentially divisive such support can be: not only between sponsored and non-sponsored children, but even between sponsored children, where some are showered with letters, cards, and gifts, and others receive hardly anything from their sponsors. This can have a demoralising effect on the child. No wonder a 2008 study by Sussex University into child sponsorship found there was "anxiety, jealousy and disappointment among those children and families who receive no letters or gifts."
>
> Then there is the issue of the donors. Child sponsorship can create an artificial and unhealthy attachment between sponsor and child which may insulate sponsors from an understanding of the wider issues contributing to "their" child's poverty, and also create cultural confusion for the child. Indeed, there are times when child sponsorship seems to be more for the benefit of the sponsor (especially if the sponsor feels the need to "personalise" his or her charitable giving) than for the child, who may develop a close bond with his or her sponsor only for that link to be broken abruptly and traumatically on leaving school.
>
> Finally, and as pointed out in the 1989 *New Internationalist* article, child-sponsorship programmes are notoriously expensive to administer, given the need for charity staff to process letters, cards, gifts, and restricted donations. Of course there will be some benefits from child sponsorship. But the weight of evidence still suggests that these are more than offset by the significant disadvantages.[20]

---

[20]Jeremy Moodey, "Child Sponsorship Research Fails to Convince," *Church Times*, May 17, 2013, www.churchtimes.co.uk/articles/2013/17-may/comment/letters-to-the-editor/child-sponsor ship-research-fails-to-convince.

For this reason, World Vision, Embrace the Middle East, and Plan International, after years of generating billions of dollars through the direct-sponsorship model, changed directions and adopted the indirect-sponsorship model because they were convinced the direct model was not as effective and generated more negative side effects.[21]

Counterintuitive decisions like these grab our attention and give us pause. A strategic decision by experienced, savvy organizations like the three mentioned above to knowingly risk losing millions of dollars of dependable donor revenue, potentially alienating hundreds of thousands of donors, makes us ask, Why would they do this? All three organizations realized they could more adequately respond to sponsored children's needs in education, health, and nutrition by working through the child's community (through what we will call indirect sponsorship) because the direct-sponsorship model was observed to create jealousy and conflicts between sponsored and nonsponsored children within the same community and even the same family (several organizations limit the number of children from one family that can be sponsored). Using the lens of cultural humility we developed in chapter four, we can see that from a child's perspective—especially children from cultural backgrounds that are more collectivistic than individualistic[22]—it is difficult to comprehend why a foreign benefactor would choose to provide major support to their sibling or neighbor but refuse to support her or him. To see another child receive letters, visits, gifts, and attention and not receive them yourself can be damaging to a child and cause rifts and tensions in communities where social harmony is highly valued. For these reasons and more, these organizations have shifted to the indirect, or community-based, child-sponsorship model.

Indirect child-sponsorship programs. Most of these programs, including some of the largest and oldest (World Vision, Plan International, Save the Children, and Kindernuthilfe of Germany, among others) do not directly and exclusively benefit the sponsored child but rather "use funding given in the name of a sponsored child more broadly to create village-level public goods" (such as potable water projects, school construction, health projects,

---

[21]Marty, former director of funds development, World Vision International, personal interview, February 2020.
[22]See Tool 2, "Seeing into Our Blindspots: Anticipating and Addressing Cultural Differences."

and personal development programs for children).[23] Indirect sponsorship benefits all of the children in a community as well as their families. This is sometimes called a "community-based approach": it takes a more holistic view of the challenges of families living in poverty and a broader approach to lifting the entire community out of poverty by addressing infrastructure needs (to build a new school, staff a village health clinic, improve a contaminated water source, etc.) in ways that direct sponsorship simply cannot. A World Vision spokesperson reports:

> Depending on the needs of a sponsored child's community, initiatives like clean water systems, improved schools, health clinics, farming co-ops, pastor training, and community savings groups are implemented to create a vibrant, sustainable future for vulnerable children, including the individual sponsored child. Our community development approach means that for every child sponsored, at least four—and in many communities, more—children benefit also.[24]

Plan International, which sponsors 1.4 million children in forty-eight countries, is one of the few child-sponsorship organizations to have commissioned an external impact assessment study of their work. Plan International commissioned the Royal Melbourne Institute of Technology (Australia) to study the program's impact on sponsored children and their communities. The full report was published in 2019 and is available online.[25] As the study compared children in sponsored communities versus nonsponsored communities, it found the rate of school attendance was higher in communities where Plan International ran a program and that overall school attendance by sponsored children increased by roughly 2 percent each year the organization worked in a community.[26] The study could not conclude that sponsorship *caused* this positive outcome, nor could it find any link between sponsorship and higher rates of school completion.[27]

---

[23]Wydick, et. al., "Does International Child Sponsorship Work?," 397.

[24]Zylstra, "What Current, Past and 'Never' Child Sponsors Think."

[25]Royal Melbourne Institute of Technology, "Changing Lives: An Analysis of Child Sponsorship Data," https://plan-international.org/publications/changing-lives-analysis-child-sponsorship-data.

[26]Royal Melbourne Institute of Technology, "Changing Lives: An Analysis of Child Sponsorship Data," 11.

[27]To prove causality would require researchers to identify and eliminate every other potential factor that might improve school attendance—a difficult challenge in real-life settings outside a laboratory.

In 2014, World Vision conducted an internal assessment of outcomes for eight communities in five different countries where child-sponsorship funds are used to support local community development projects (e.g., water, sanitation, and hygiene projects; agricultural and food security programs; and education and health programs). Outcomes before World Vision began work in the community were compared to outcomes after several years of World Vision work in the same community. The study itself noted that findings based on the feedback of children are problematic due to the limitations to children's being able to speak for themselves, as we noted above. Likewise, the study noted that, for numerous findings, it was not possible to make direct comparisons, because differing criteria and measurements were used in the "before" and "after" studies. Several particularities of World Vision's programs in each community—determined, in principle, by the communities themselves—and the research methodology employed render making overall claims of program effectiveness more difficult than in the 2013 Compassion International study. In general, when pre- and postintervention data can be compared, it appears that World Vision's investments in the community yielded positive outcomes for sponsored children and their communities: increased access to clean water and sanitation in some communities, decreased incidence of malaria among children in some communities, increased school attendance, and so on. But it is difficult to measure the impacts on children due to the different study methodologies used and the fact that the study was not external (external, peer-reviewed studies are required to be more objective).

Some critics raise pointed questions about the "donor illusion" created by organizations using the direct model to raise funds for a specific child but the indirect (community development) model to impact communities. But a 2017 survey notes that a full 74 percent of US charitable givers believe that child-sponsorship funding doesn't help one specific child.[28] To their credit, World Vision and Plan International both have clear disclaimers acknowledging the way sponsors' funds are pooled and used to bring entire communities out of poverty. An important advantage of the indirect model of

---

[28]Sarah Eekhoff Zylstra, "What Current, Past, and 'Never' Child Sponsors Think," *Christianity Today*, December 19, 2017, www.christianitytoday.com/news/2017/december/child-sponsorship-donors-survey-compassion-world-vision.html.

sponsorship programs is that, while project impact is more diffused and therefore more difficult to measure, the model recognizes that poverty and its causes (poor health, contaminated water, inadequate schools, unvaccinated children, etc.) are community based and that solutions must be community based as well. In addition, the indirect model can touch areas of life that direct sponsorship cannot: while the provision of clean drinking water or the vaccination of children is an extremely effective intervention to improve community health, it is financially unfeasible and morally repugnant to provide clean drinking water or vaccinations *only* to the sponsored children in a community—these interventions can best be done for the entire community.

ACCOUNTABILITY IN CHILD-SPONSORSHIP PROGRAMS

It seems apparent that the $3.2 billion given annually in support of direct and indirect child-sponsorship programs may provide some benefits for sponsored children and, for the latter, for their communities. But Christian stewardship—and the "higher bar" of accountability we established earlier in the chapter for assessing programs that touch the lives of vulnerable children—require that we evaluate *all* of the impacts on children and their families.

Several of the studies noted the remarkable lack of research that characterizes this multibillion dollar flow of resources. Wydick himself states, "Given the number of individuals involved in child sponsorship relationships and the billions of dollars committed to them, *it is surprising that almost no research exists that evaluates the impacts of these programs.*"[29] Most of the child-sponsorship organizations have not made public any evaluation of how their work impacts vulnerable children, their families, and communities. Given the higher bar of accountability we established for caring for vulnerable children, we find this lack of research and transparency not just surprising, but profoundly troubling.

Likewise, the parents of some sponsored children felt the model reduced their authority in their own home.[30] This perspective should raise significant

---

[29]Wydick, et. al., "Does International Child Sponsorship Work?," 397-98, emphasis mine.
[30]"The Pros and Cons of Child Sponsorship," Develop Africa, www.developafrica.org/blog/pros
-and-cons-child-sponsorship-%E2%80%93-outsider%E2%80%99s-perspective.

concerns for sponsors and helps us reflect on a curiously under-researched perspective: How do the parents of sponsored children feel about their child's participation in a child-sponsorship program? What would they do to improve the program? And alternatively, mission leaders who understand mission as companionship would ask, What resources do parents in a specific community need—and what gifts might they already have—to provide for their children better? This is the question that draws us into missional solidarity with the people God calls us to serve.

Our concept of co-development cautions us against entering into a community and providing goods and services directly to needy members (in this case, vulnerable children) and invites us to recognize that it is God who has chosen to place children in families and communities. Our participation in God's mission is to care for all God's children by strengthening the families, the community leaders, and those ministering to children over the long haul without undermining the role mothers and fathers are called by God to play in their child's life. Yet in our review of the literature, no child-sponsorship organization has suggested that it is asking sponsored children's parents these kinds of questions.[31] Child sponsorship can easily violate parents' agency—their God-given responsibility and right to raise their children according to their values—and it can do so right in front of their children. Parents can feel humiliated before their children by a program that is intended to help but is structured in a way that undermines their role and doesn't consider their opinions. Because sponsors don't seem to be asking these questions from the parents' point of view, they can unwittingly contribute to this phenomenon.

This insight helps us perceive a "blind spot" most US sponsors have: we can be so focused on the tree that we are blind to the forest around it. Jeremy Moodey's comment describes this phenomenon succinctly: "Child sponsorship can create an artificial and unhealthy attachment between sponsor and child which may insulate sponsors from an understanding of the wider issues contributing to 'their' child's poverty."[32] By focusing our attention and

---

[31]Or if they have asked the parents these questions, they haven't published the parents' responses. This seems to us to be a critical missing component in the organizations' understanding of their relationship with communities they serve.

[32]Moodey, "Child Sponsorship Research Fails to Convince."

soliciting a monthly contribution from us to make a difference in one child's life and not engaging us in deeper reflection on the causes of poverty, direct child-sponsorship programs are distracting millions of sponsors from understanding *why* children go to bed hungry at night and from strategizing with their parents and community leaders to end hunger, improve education, and strengthen families. The *Chicago Tribune* published a critique of child-sponsorship programs in 1998 that served as an early wake-up call most of us have ignored: "Child sponsorship organizations are often better at promising miracles than delivering them. Potential sponsors may find it irresistible to change a child's life with a few dollars a week. However, reality is not that simple and help is not that cheap."

The organizations that have done some evaluative work have generally asked the questions that *donors* would pose—questions about increased education and income—but not the questions that sponsored children's parents might ask. Between 1998 and 2014, I conducted a series of semi-structured focus group interviews with some of the parents of sponsored children and employees of the child-sponsorship programs in Central and South America. The question that generated the most energetic responses in all three parent groups was this: What questions do you wish the child-sponsorship agency would ask you as a parent? These are some of their responses: How is child sponsorship affecting our community? Are the benefits to some individual children outweighed by the jealousies and conflicts generated in our community's life? Is the relationship with a foreign sponsor negatively impacting my ability to raise my child? (One Peruvian mother asked me, "Would you want a foreign adult writing regularly to your seven-year-old daughter?" I simply couldn't reply.) Are direct-sponsorship relationships creating jealousies between sponsored and nonsponsored children? How are specific child-sponsorship program practices (for example, the rule limiting the number of sponsored children in the same family to three) impacting family unity and our ability to raise our children? How do the parents—especially those who practice a religion other than Christianity or no religion—feel about the organization's evangelistic work with their children? Does the poverty of non-Christian parents force them to set aside their concerns for proselytism of their children so they can receive program benefits? Do large, multinational child-sponsorship agencies take the time necessary to truly listen to community leaders' assessment of their own needs or do they enter a community with predetermined, "one size fits all" solutions?[33] Our research in this area has not found that child-sponsorship organizations are asking these kinds of child- and community-centered questions and transparently sharing the results (and methodologies) of their research.

A second area of concern is the costliness of "donor care," which can siphon off needed support for the child. The CEO of Embrace the Middle East, the British organization that abandoned child sponsorship due to its negative impacts, noted that child-sponsorship programs are "notoriously expensive to administer, given the need for charity staff to process letters, cards, gifts, and restricted donations." If the costs to create and maintain the "feeling of connection" between sponsor and child are as high as some allege, integrity requires us to ask, Could I, as sponsor, forgo that expensive program benefit and allow my contributions to support programs that empower an entire community? The impact would be powerful.

A NEEDED COURSE CORRECTION

While some child-sponsorship programs may improve children's nutrition and health and help them stay in school longer, we have noted numerous inherent challenges to these programs' capacity to strengthen families to care for their children in sustainable ways.

In chapter six, we saw that, rather than condemning short-term mission (STM) for its shortcomings, it is critical that we redeem the energy, the deep sense of connection, and the powerful space of missional formation that STM can provide and use STM trips as instruments of transformation of the ways that congregations and communities work together to address the causes of hunger and violence.

In the same way, it is an undeniable fact that child-sponsorship programs have uncovered the power behind one of the most successful strategies of fundraising known: by creating the powerful notion of connection between

---

[33]These questions were articulated in interviews conducted in March 2007 and October 2014 with employees and the parents of sponsored children of a major US child sponsorship organization working in two Latin American cities. The employees and most of the parents asked not to be identified.

a child and a sponsor, child-sponsorship programs galvanize millions of sponsors to set aside disinterest, apathy, and donor fatigue and give, sometimes sacrificially, in support of vulnerable children. There is no reason to criticize your members or anyone who is seeking to help children through child sponsorship. Their intentions are good. But we are not merely philanthropists. As congregational mission leaders, we bear a special responsibility to lead our people to help vulnerable children in ways consistent with how God cares for all God's children: appropriately, respectfully, and by working through families.

Child-sponsorship programs have been shaped by the US philanthropic marketplace over time through millions of interactions between the organizations' representations of needy children and the multibillion dollar response of caring sponsors. These programs are large and complex products of the consumer market, and some would throw up their hands and claim we are powerless to impact them. But, in fact, it is the sponsors themselves—more than the children or their families—who hold remarkable power to help shape child-sponsorship programs' methodologies and impacts every time they contribute, contact the organization with a question, or demand greater accountability. Child-sponsorship organizations will exercise greater accountability as sponsors demand it. World Vision and Plan International's paradigm shifts from direct to indirect sponsorship show the power of sponsors asking questions and expressing concerns that eventually redirected their programs.[34] When hundreds of child sponsors begin to require less "care" and press the organizations to support children in more sustainable ways that contribute to co-development, child sponsorship will become a more effective and faithful way to engage in God's mission with vulnerable children and their families. Or are we such demanding consumers that we insist on the satisfying experience of child sponsorship rather than more effective companionship work of empowering families to provide for the needs of their children?

Improving the quality of life of vulnerable children is obviously not a simple or short-term task, and it would be unfair to condemn child sponsorship out of hand since we, the consumers, have given it its power. But it

---

[34]Emily Buchanan, "What's It like to Be a Sponsored Child?," June 10, 2011, www.bbc.com/news /world-13697855.

is problematic for child-sponsorship organizations to work with other people's children without attending to the questions of impact, independent
evaluation, parent/family agency, and transparency we have lifted up in this
section. For congregations and individuals not yet sponsoring a child, we'd
encourage you to consider other programs that work to strengthen the families and communities of vulnerable children. For those currently sponsoring a child, you may want to identify the questions that your experience
and the reading of this book raise in your mind and communicate them to
your child-sponsorship agency. If you decide to support children in a different way, you should give the agency ample warning before moving your
support to a different program or agency. If you are supporting "your child"
in a direct child-sponsorship program or a community through an indirect-
sponsorship program, you may want to continue to support work in the
child's community through a different kind of program if possible. Individuals and congregations who decide to continue to support a child or
community through a child-sponsorship program are encouraged to communicate their questions and concerns to the child-sponsorship program.
We humbly offer these suggestions in the spirit of mission companionship
because we believe that vulnerable children should not have to bear the cost
of connection with US Christians who want to help.

CARING FOR ORPHANS

In the 1950s, Catholic and private orphanages were a common sight in cities
and towns across the United States and Europe. But by the turn of the
century these institutions were shut down in response to the continuing
reports of child abuse in orphanages and the growing body of research
which indicated that institutionalized care had numerous detrimental impacts on child well-being, especially on children's cognitive and emotional
development.[35] These negative effects of institutional care for children—
especially for children living in an orphanage for many years or for those
institutionalized early in their life—have led to an important shift in how we

---

[35]The most influential study, the Bucharest Early Intervention Project, is reviewed in Charles
Nelson et al., "Cognitive Recovery in Socially Deprived Young Children: The Bucharest Early Intervention Project," *Science* 318, no. 5858 (2007): 1937-40, www.bucharestearlyinterventionpro
ject.org/Nelson_et_al__combined__2007_.pdf.

care for vulnerable children. Today there are almost no orphanages left in the United States or the European Union,[36] and you will find few child experts or advocates who would support placing a child in the institutionalized setting of an orphanage. Why the dramatic turnaround in a primary strategy for caring for orphans?

Simply put, children do not thrive in orphanages. The Faith to Action Initiative, a leading coalition of major actors in global child welfare including World Vision, Catholic Relief Services, World Relief, Australian Council of Churches International Relief, and Christian Alliance for Orphans, notes in its guiding principles that (1) children grow best in families and thrive in community and (2) an orphanage cannot replace family care:

> The family is the most essential source of love, belonging, emotional support, cognition, physical sustenance, and spiritual guidance in the lives of children. The best way to meet the needs of vulnerable children is to strengthen the capacity of their families and communities to permanently care for their well being and every effort should be made to do so.[37]

Not only do children not thrive in an orphanage, but children in institutional care, including government-run facilities, can be easy targets for traffickers.[38] Pragmatically, the cost of raising a child in an orphanage is five to ten times higher than supporting a child in a family.[39] For these reasons, the United States, Europe, and Australia have largely eliminated orphanages and now rely on reunification, kinship care, temporary foster family care, and adoption to care for orphaned children. None of these more modern strategies is perfect, but in most cases, all are improvements over the orphanage model.

In striking contrast, the situation in countries like Haiti, Malawi, Zimbabwe, Cambodia, and Nepal and across the Majority World is quite

---

[36]While some children are cared for in smaller "group residential homes," the vast majority are placed with families through foster care programs.

[37]"About Us: Guiding Principles," Faith to Action Initiative, www.faithtoaction.org/guiding-principles/.

[38]US State Department, "Child Institutionalization and Human Trafficking," June 2018. The report continues: "Even when a child leaves or ages out of a residential institution, the vulnerability to human trafficking continues, in part due to the physical and psychological damage many of these children have suffered. Some traffickers, in recognizing the heightened vulnerability of these children, wait for and target those who leave or age out of institutions." www.state.gov/wp-content/uploads/2019/02/283784.pdf.

[39]"Start Here," Faith to Action Initiative, www.faithtoaction.org/start-here/, accessed May 18, 2021.

different: millions of children are housed in privately run orphanages, most of which are virtually unregulated by the state. Why this massive disparity in the treatment of vulnerable children? Given the negative impacts of orphanages on children's IQ, emotional development, and their capacity to form trusting relationships—not to mention the increased potential for abuse—by what rationale are millions of the children of the Majority World institutionalized in orphanages when we would never accept such treatment for *our* children? The answer will shock you:

> There are an estimated eight million children residing in orphanages, or residential care facilities, globally and it is estimated that four out of five of these children are not orphans. It is well documented that many of these children are taken from their families by recruiters and sold into orphanages for the purpose of profit. These children are known as "paper orphans."[40]

Paper orphans, reports Australian lawyer and child advocate Kathryn van Doore, are children, generally from economically disadvantaged families in the Majority World, who have been legally classified as orphans, sometimes through unscrupulous means, for the purpose of filling overseas orphanages:

> "Recruiters" target families in rural areas with limited access to education for their children. They convince the family that their child will receive a better education and future in a boarding school. The recruiters often collect several children from a village under this guise and then depart with the children to a city.
>
> In the city, the children are often sold into orphanages (if not into another form of exploitation). Once in an orphanage, the children become "paper orphans," with names changed, death certificates for parents forged and requests for family contact denied.[41]

In theory, orphanages should function as an option of last resort for children in the Global South; but in reality, millions of children have been sent to orphanages despite having one or more parents, and the practice is only growing. Van Doore was deeply committed to caring for vulnerable children and founded an orphanage in Nepal. But her observations caused her to stop in her tracks and change how she cares for children:

---

[40]Kathryn E. van Doore, "Paper Orphans: Exploring Child Trafficking for the Purpose of Orphanages," *International Journal of Children's Rights* 24 (2016): 378-407.

[41]Kathryn E. van Doore, "The Business of Orphanages," Brewminate, https://brewminate.com/the-business-of-orphanages/.

After Australian lawyer Kate van Doore set up an orphanage in Nepal and took over another in Uganda she was astounded to find that the children she thought she was helping were not orphans at all. They were "paper orphans"— children given fake identities after being taken from their families and placed in orphanages to attract funding from foreign donors, volunteers and tourists. "The kids started saying to us, 'Can I go home to mum now?'" said van Doore who runs the charity Forget Me Not. "It was devastating to discover these children had been exploited for profit. I was horrified and determined to fix it," said van Doore.[42]

Another troubling fact is that orphanages attract "voluntourists"—people from the United States, Europe, and Australia, including many Christians, who plan an international trip around a visit to an orphanage to care for children. Voluntourists often contribute money—hard currency—which, in struggling economies can represent a significant portion of the annual income of an orphanage: "The U.S. State Department first identified orphan trafficking as a form of modern slavery in a 2017 report. It said the industry was fueled by demand from tourists to visit or volunteer in orphanages, often for a fee or donation."[43] The Australian Parliament's Joint Standing Committee on Foreign Affairs, Defence and Trade defines orphan trafficking as "the active recruitment of children from families and communities into residential care institutions for the purpose of foreign funding and voluntourism."

These disconcerting facts should challenge the way many of our congregations care for children through orphanages because, tragically, "unscrupulous orphanage operators . . . [have] adopted a business model where the centres [orphanages] got more money from international donors if they had more children."[44] Thus, our STM groups can unintentionally contribute to the growth of the global orphan trafficking industry by visiting or contributing

---

[42]Emma Batha, "Calls Mount to Stop Orphanages Exploiting Poor Children to Lure Money, Tourists," Reuters, November 13, 2018, www.reuters.com/article/us-slavery-conference-orphanages /calls-mount-to-stop-orphanages-exploiting-poor-children-to-lure-money-tourists-idUS KCN1NJ0AE.

[43]Batha, "Calls Mount to Stop Orphanages."

[44]Lindsay Murdoch, "Stealing a Generation: Cambodia's Unfolding Tragedy," *Sydney Morning Herald*, April 7, 2013, www.smh.com.au/world/stealing-a-generation-cambodias-unfolding -tragedy-20130406-2hdy2.html.

funding to orphanages.[45] Christians in the United States, Europe, and Australia provide significant support to orphanages in the Majority World: US Christian giving to orphan care has grown roughly three times faster than all charitable giving by Americans for each of the past four years, and a 2017 study showed that a majority (51 percent) of all church attendees in Australia are contributing funding to institutional care overseas.[46]

The growing demand by US congregations' STM teams for orphanages to visit[47] and the deep satisfaction they report of those experiences raise serious questions about our theology of mission: God's mission is, of course, not really about our personal satisfaction. We cannot engage in mission in the self-emptying way of Jesus Christ if we prioritize activities because they make us feel good. John 13:1-20 reminds us that Jesus' model of mission calls us to *servanthood*, the intentional placing of others' needs ahead of our own: "So if I, your Lord and Teacher, have washed your feet, you also ought to wash one another's feet." Mission in the way of Jesus Christ invites us as leaders to be wholly committed to giving voice to vulnerable children and their families. We must ask hard questions of beloved mission activities like short-term mission trips, meal-packaging projects, child-sponsorship programs, support for orphanages, and other market-based mission strategies— and that can bring us into some tension—even conflict—with other members of our church.

But the good news is, as you seek to reform the way your congregation understands and engages in mission, you are not alone: as the reality of the negative consequences of orphanage care for children have come to light and as news of the shadowy circuit of child trafficking being unwittingly supported by mission dollars has spread, a growing number of organizations and individuals have stepped up to raise awareness of the problem among US congregations. Excellent resources are available to congregational mission leaders who seek to educate their congregations on the potential

---

[45]Christopher Knaus, "Australia to Curb Tourism to Foreign Orphanages That Exploit Children for Profit," *The Guardian*, February 28, 2018, www.theguardian.com/world/2018/mar/01/australia -to-curb-tourism-to-foreign-orphanages-that-exploit-children-for-profit.

[46]Christopher Knaus, "The Race to Rescue Cambodia's Children from Orphanages Exploiting Them for Profit," *The Guardian*, August 18, 2017, www.theguardian.com/world/2017/aug/19/the -race-to-rescue-cambodian-children-from-orphanages-exploiting-them-for-profit.

[47]In addition, several meal-packaging programs donate large quantities of prepared meals to orphanages, enabling the institutions to survive.

dangers of supporting orphanages in other countries. The Australian Council of Churches International Relief (www.kinnected.org.au) has developed some outstanding materials (including well-designed educational videos for youth and adults) to help congregations understand the unintended consequences of visiting or supporting orphanages. The Faith to Action Initiative (www.faithtoaction.org), which includes global experts such as Catholic Relief Services, World Relief, World Vision, and the Christian Alliance for Orphans, provides well-designed, compelling resources on the plight of orphans and has lent significant social capital and leadership to the "de-institutionalization movement"—helping children get out of orphanages and into families.

LEVERAGING THE POWER OF CONNECTION TO REFORM ORPHAN CARE

In chapter six, we saw that STM trips have grown exponentially in popularity in recent years because they tap into our members' legitimate need to feel connection with other church members and with their siblings in Christ in culturally different communities. In a similar way, child-sponsorship and orphan-care programs have exploded in growth because they tap into the power of connection and Christians' valid need to find meaning by making a difference in the life of one child. The good news is that the same personal needs that have powered the rapid growth of these congregational mission activities can be leveraged into highly effective mission strategies: STM can become the crucible where your members are transformed to see mission as the church's reason for being through the power of connection. Strategies of care for vulnerable children cause our members to see the culturally "other" through the eyes of kinship in Christ. To the Peruvian pastor's incredulous question, "Can you imagine if these (lead-poisoned) children were *our* children?," local and global mission companions are answering as La Oroya's Esther Hinostroza did: "But these *are* your children!" By God's grace, we are surrounded by a "great cloud of witnesses"—individuals, organizations, and coalitions of people who have encountered these troubling mission practices that are, in fact, hurting vulnerable children and who have had the courage to change course. We have witnesses such as Ravy Keo and Cathleen Jones.

In 1992, American missionary Cathleen Jones and her husband were assigned to be directors of a denominational orphanage start-up in Cambodia.

While developing and running the orphanage, the Joneses became convinced there must be a better way to care for vulnerable children. Jones teamed up with Ravy Keo, a Cambodian Christian social worker, and they resolved to work together to try to forge a better solution for children labeled as orphans—even though they might have one or even two living parents, whose poverty seemed to be their sole barrier to providing for their children.

Keo and Jones's story represents a highly significant turnaround, because when mission leaders change course after years of pursuing specific mission strategies, their decision makes us stop and take notice. These women had more than a desire to change course for themselves: they had a vision to change how a nation cares for its vulnerable children. Thus Children in Families (CIF) was born. CIF is a local Cambodian nonprofit organization that has done internationally recognized work to develop systems that strengthen families in Cambodia as an alternative to the rapid increase of orphanages. CIF also educates Christians on how best to provide for vulnerable children through emergency care, kinship care, foster care, domestic adoption, and disabled children's services. Rather than removing children from poor families, CIF screens, trains, and supports extended family members to care for their family's children. In addition, they screen, train, and partner alongside Cambodian families who provide long-term foster care or adoption.

It can be awkward and even embarrassing for leaders to have to publicly change strategies. You will likely face adversity from the Christian and mission communities, as Keo and Jones did. Yet their example inspires us to find the courage to change course in our congregation's mission practices when new information emerges. *Without the attitude of prayerful, critical reflection on our mission practices that Jones exhibited, we can entertain and satisfy our congregations at a superficial level, but we may not be leading them into the deeper commitment that God's mission requires.*

Faithful participation in the *missio Dei* demands that we ask the hard questions of our mission activities: *What is motivating us to engage in this work? Who profits from this activity? To what extent is there a sense of co-development where children's voices and those of their families have the first word? What are the potential negative impacts of our work?* Mission work is done by imperfect humans like us: though our participation in God's mission will never be completely free from mixed motives or our needs for affirmation and meaning, it is the God of grace who chose to include us in the *missio Dei*. By asking these critical questions, we can lessen the negative impacts of our work and bring blessing to many people around the world, including ourselves.

In this "great cloud of witnesses," you'll find leaders and organizations that have turned their mission practice around to better serve vulnerable children. We understand the challenge of telling mission-minded Christians that they should stop supporting orphanages. ACCI Relief helpfully proposes that congregational mission leaders focus on two strategies: (1) educate your congregation on the potentially negative impacts of institutionalized orphan care (see Kinnected.org) and (2) propose these alternative activities for congregations desiring to help orphans:

- Volunteer in a program that seeks to preserve families and prevent family separation. Volunteers could work with whole families or parents to strengthen their capacity to look after their own children.

- Volunteer within family reunification programs. Help a family prepare for their child's return by helping them renovate their house, get access to a water source, or set up a small business or a veggie patch.

- Volunteer in programs run in the community that everyone can access. Examples might be English programs, sports programs, creative workshops, or educational support programs.

- Use your skills to build the capacity of staff working with children. This might be in areas of promotions, websites, English, management, accounting, or games and activities.

- Focus on learning so that you are better equipped to advocate for a project or the needs of children when you return to your own country.[48]

FREEING YOUR CONGREGATION TO CARE FOR VULNERABLE CHILDREN

Throughout history, caring for children has been an important part of Christian mission, precisely because children are so very close to the heart

---

[48]"Ethical Volunteering," Kinnected, www.kinnected.org.au/for-volunteers.

of God. But their fragility and their highly impressionable nature require us to set higher standards for ourselves as we lead our congregations to care for them. Whether our members have been accustomed to packaging meals, sponsoring a child, supporting an orphanage, or even making children the focus of our STM trips, we have the knowledge and tools to help our congregations equip families to provide for their own children. This may mean that we choose to reframe a stand-alone meal-packaging event into a hunger-education event with prayer, education, a videoconference conversation with mission companions and a hands-on food activity (working in a neighborhood soup kitchen, delivering meals to sick or elderly, meal packaging or gardening). We may choose to not travel to an orphanage but partner with one of the holistic development agencies cited to help our congregation develop a long-term "twinning" relationship where your mission companions and your congregation agree to learn about each other and to use each one's resources to address your shared needs. And we may channel the funds we have been personally giving each month to child sponsorship to support an organization that is working to empower families to better care for their children. But remember, our congregations' understandings and practices of mission have been so profoundly shaped by the marketplace—by what "sells"—that the reformation we advocate will not happen easily.

By recognizing children *and their families* as our companions in mission; by adopting a posture of cultural humility as we dream, plan, execute, and evaluate our work together; and by committing together to co-development, we lead our congregations into a deeper engagement in the mission of God. Engaging in God's mission together, mission companions are led to discover the power of connection based on the gospel truth that they are, in fact, members of the same family: "For in Christ Jesus you are all children of God through faith. As many of you as were baptized into Christ have clothed yourselves with Christ. There is no longer Jew or Greek, there is no longer slave or free, there is no longer male and female; for all of you are one in Christ Jesus" (Gal 3:26-28). La Oroya's Esther Hinostroza got it right: she understood that as members of the same family, our calling into God's mission is about caring for lead-poisoned kids, orphans and "paper orphans," and hungry children and their families just as we care for our own, because in Christ they *are* our family.

This biblical truth liberates us from the marketplace's power to twist God's mission into a satisfying version of "selfie mission" that is all about us. This is why wise congregational mission leaders will seek to channel their people's enthusiasm for helping children into strategies that help them grow in their sense of unity in Christ with mission companions across the city and across the globe. In the final chapter, we will look at mission leadership and suggest several strategies to work for the reformation of congregational mission practice in ways that can reform our church.

FOR REFLECTION

1. What surprised you the most about the way orphanages interact with vulnerable children and their families? Why did this surprise you?

2. According to a 2017 Kaiser Family Foundation / *Washington Post* poll, "46% of all U.S. Christians said that a lack of effort is generally to blame for a person's poverty, compared with 29% of all non-Christians." How might this understanding of the causes of poverty affect the ways your congregation works against it?

3. From the perspective of your congregation's core values, how do you weigh the strengths and weaknesses of the "direct" and "indirect" types of child-sponsorship programs? What concerns raised by the book about child-sponsorship programs resonate with you? How do you think vulnerable children can best be supported?

4. The book notes that American Christians' visits and financial support contribute to the growth in the number of orphanages in other parts of the world despite widespread agreement that children do not thrive in orphanages. How might you educate your congregation and propose alternatives to orphanage support?

EIGHT

UNBINDING MISSION LEADERSHIP

I WAS WORKING IN THE CHURCH OFFICES in the city of Kananga in what is now the DR Congo late one afternoon when General Secretary Dr. Tshihamba Mukome Luendu came to the door and said, "We have an American visitor scheduled to meet with some pastors over at the Ndesha Church . . . could you translate for us?" I hopped in the church's beat-up Toyota Land Cruiser with a group of pastors who had gathered to catch a ride to the meeting. As we headed to the Ndesha district, I remember feeling a sense of respect for these pastors: none of them made more than $150 a month, yet each one was leading his church with a level of commitment that inspired me. Pastor Diese led a downtown congregation where four choirs artfully translated gospel truth into Congolese harmonies and rhythms. Pastor Manyayi was one of the most gifted preachers I'd ever heard. He could recite long biblical passages from memory and wove stories of healing or miracles together with our region's traditional story forms that would delight and challenge worshipers. He was a master of "call and response" and engaged worshipers so deeply in the Word that the entire congregation would be on its feet by the end of the sermon. I felt blessed to work with these leaders and was grateful to be included in the sense of shared purpose that characterized the group.

When we arrived at the Ndesha church, we were welcomed by several of the elders, offered a place to sit and given a glass of orange-colored Bako, the local soft drink. Dr. Tshihamba introduced the American visitor and then excused himself and departed for another meeting. I translated the introductions and opening pleasantries around the table as accurately as I could, but, after a pause, the visitor did something that left me speechless. He reached into his pocket and pulled out a thick envelope and placed it on the table and said, "My church gave me $500 and sent me here to find the congregation with the best project that we can support. Can you share with me what you are doing in your churches?" At first, there was an awkward silence. Then the room was suddenly transformed into an audition for TV's *The Voice*: pastor after pastor joined into the "song and dance" format, spinning their best project idea in hopes of earning for their congregation the coveted prize. What had begun as a space of Christian intercultural fellowship quickly became something akin to a mudwrestling contest from which only one pastor would emerge victorious to claim the visitor's prize. Word would spread quickly across the city of one pastor's victory—and of the losers' defeat. What would their congregation say if their pastor didn't deliver? The pressure was intense.

I felt pulled in two directions. I had learned a few things about Congolese culture: its high valuing of group unity and harmony and its disdain for competitiveness—even the word *outstanding* had a highly negative connotation, as it suggested someone had selfishly sacrificed the common good for individual achievement. I knew from my own cultural background that the elder was merely trying to be faithful to his congregation's request by taking advantage of his brief time in the city to identify the *best* project. I should have said something. I could have explained to the elder some of the implications of his request. If he had known the negative impacts, I imagine he would have stopped in his tracks and asked for suggestions as to how to proceed. I could have asked the Congolese pastors if they needed "caucus time" to formulate a response to the request that respected their more collectivist culture and, if so, I could have invited the elder to step outside with me and explained things to him. But I was silent. I feared saying something that might cause the elder to take his money off the table. I feared the pastors would be disappointed in me if my words or actions kept one of their churches from benefiting.

The surreal audition ended. The elder thanked everyone and gave the envelope to one of the pastors. I was so disappointed in the whole episode I can't even remember who "won." All I remember is the raw jealousy that emerged that afternoon and the fissures it left behind. And my own inability to act.

As I recall the events of that afternoon in the Ndesha church, I realize each of us was responsible for our own actions—the elder, the pastors, me— and each of us was doing the best we could in an intercultural space where none of us had a completely clear vision. But reflecting back on that afternoon, I realize now that my intercultural experience and role allowed me to see the approaching "train wreck." But I allowed myself to be bound by traditional patterns of donor/recipient relationships rather than advocating for companionship when I neglected to raise the questions that could have averted the divisive results.

SLOW MISSION

Perhaps in your role as a mission leader in your church, you have occupied that uncomfortable position between your well-intended members and your mission companions. You see the energy and excitement that a particular initiative or project is generating among your people, but perhaps you have an inkling—or even a dreaded certainty—that the impacts in the companion community will not be positive. The last thing you want to do is derail your congregation's enthusiasm. They are good people working with the best of intentions. Yet you sense the direction they're going could hurt rather than help.

Sometimes our most powerful tool is to be able to raise a question, to identify an unvoiced assumption, to ask whose voice is missing from the conversation. As leaders, we have the power to slow down a decision-making process, to enrich it with the missing complexity that we know from experience is always present in intercultural relationships, communication, and ministry. When mission is companionship rather than task completion, the quality of our relationship and the warmth and respectfulness of our interactions become more important than the speed of our movement forward. Sometimes the only step needed to avoid the proverbial train wreck is slowing the train down: to allow your decision-makers to see an intercultural situation in more of its rich complexity. Just as the "slow food" movement slows us down to restore mindfulness and a respect for traditional ways of connecting the earth with hungry consumers, the concept of "slow mission" invites us toward greater mindfulness as we engage in God's mission: slowing down to remember human relationships in all their intercultural complexity and blessed potential. What a gift you as a leader give to your congregation when you ask questions about a project's sustainability *before* your congregation begins, when you inquire about the potential unintended consequences of a particular intervention, when you wonder aloud how other members of another community might perceive your congregation's actions. Merely raising these good questions can be a powerful blessing to your congregation because, in a complex, intercultural world for which there are no maps, slow is good.

All of us know that a beautiful strength of our churches is that they preserve long-held beliefs and practices—our very identity. This is precisely why a church's sanctuary is a natural place to gather in times of grief or tragedy. But the challenge to "change leaders" like you and me is that this same preservation role generates powerful resistance against change. Even something as "simple" as proposing a change in worship music can become a major conflict! In congregational mission, to raise questions about some of the time-honored pillars of your congregation's mission practice (its partners, its allocations, or its mission activities) can create conflict. Drawing the attention of your congregation's other mission leaders to current practices that appear to be based on selfie mission ("I wonder if this activity isn't benefiting us more than our companions?") or colonial-era assumptions ("Our proposal reads like we know more about their context than they do") is an action that must be taken very seriously—or you may feel like you've stepped in front of a bus! We've put off these honest, difficult conversations in our congregations for so long, there is deep sensitivity when the subject is broached. Yet my experience is that there is a desire among mission leaders in many congregations—from traditional to avant garde, from conservative to progressive—to probe the questions of what to them has never made sense about mission as they practice it:

- Why do we do similar activities each year with few sustainable results?

- How would it feel if someone did these same mission activities to our children or to us?

- If the gospel is primarily about restoring our relationship with God and with neighbor, why do our mission efforts not seem to result in deepening relationships?

How will this difficult change to "slow mission" begin? Today, having solid ideas and a winsome style qualifies one for leadership perhaps as much as the traditional path of academic degrees and years of practical experience did in an earlier era. My research with congregational mission leaders has shown that their congregations are less interested in "top-down" learning from a scholar or professor but are very interested in practical learning, "best practices," and the chance to learn from the intercultural mission experiences of congregations like theirs. In fact, 49.6 percent of the 649 mainline Protestant, Catholic, and evangelical congregational mission leaders we surveyed in 2019 ranked "access to the 'best practices' of other local churches to network with them and learn from their experiences" as the tool they *most* needed for leading their congregation in mission.[1] This "horizontal learning" is highly prized by congregational mission leaders regardless of their particular denominational affiliation. This is why your role as local mission leader has become so important: your congregation ascribes authority to you and looks to you for leadership in mission—your ideas, your respect for their values, your willingness to "do the work." In today's flattened landscape of mission, *you* are better placed than a professor of mission history to help your congregation's members avoid "reinventing the wheel" when they proceed, unaware of the lessons of the past. *You* are more likely to be called on than a mission agency executive to help their work be more coordinated (to avoid unintentionally "double-funding" an already sponsored international student at your town's seminary!). *You* are more likely to be asked to help align your congregation's mission work with its core values than any outside consultant. This book was written for congregational mission leaders who sense responsibility for helping their congregation accompany God into mission in more faithful and effective ways—and leadership today requires some skills in leading change.

Change for human beings, even at the individual level, is slow and difficult. A hoped for change during the Lenten season, for example, begins with simple, repeated practices that over time grow into changed behaviors. For organizations like a local congregation, the change process is more complex,

---

[1] B. Hunter Farrell and S. Balajiedlang Khyllep, "Survey of Local Church Mission Leaders," World Mission Initiative, January 2019 (n = 649 mainline Protestant, evangelical, and Catholic mission leaders).

to be sure, but mindful leaders can create a process of change in which congregational members' experiences, reflections, decision-making, and learnings mutually reinforce each other and draw the congregation toward a new understanding and practice of mission. This slow, critically important process can happen when a leader like you is praying, listening, planning, observing, and leading your members through the action/reflection model[2] into new hopes, commitments, practices, and behaviors. Through your teaching, through experiential learning opportunities (especially, as noted in chapter six, through STM and other community-based, liminal experiences), through your shepherding of relationships with mission companions (by including mission companions in times of joint Bible study, prayer, and worship), and by shifting the structures of missional engagement from transactional to companionship, you create a space of missional transformation for your congregation.

What does it look like when mission leaders prayerfully and intentionally slow down their congregations to go deeper in God's mission? Here are four brief cameos of innovative mission leaders that may help you imagine the possibilities in your own congregation.

REFRAMING MISSION EXPERIENCES

As congregational mission leaders, as long as we frame STM as "a work trip" designed to build a house or provide dental care for children—or we frame service at a neighborhood homeless shelter as "volunteer" or "charity" work—we may fall into the pattern Haynes described as "transactional": we give time, labor, and money to purchase a mission-wrapped experience that often ends when we return home.[3] But one mission leader decided to shift the way her congregation framed missional experiences.

The Reverend Dr. Ashley Goad, the global missions pastor at the First United Methodist Church of Shreveport, Louisiana, centered her doctor of

[2]Described by Brazilian educator Paulo Freire in his seminal *Pedagogy of the Oppressed* (New York: Seabury, 1968), which invites the learner to engage in a cyclical movement that begins with practical experiences (action) followed by critical reflection on the action (reflection). The initial reflection leads to the next action, deeper reflection, and so forth. Intercultural mission experiences at a local shelter or soup kitchen or during an STM experience create a space for action/reflection cycle to lead congregation members into deep learning and transformation.
[3]Robert Ellis Haynes, *Consuming Mission: Towards a Theology of Short-Term Mission and Pilgrimage* (Eugene, OR: Pickwick, 2019), 251, 255.

ministry project on improving STM in her own congregation. We quote her at length as she summarizes the change process she implemented as a mission leader in her own congregation:

> In 2013, First United Methodist Church Shreveport changed its mission mindset from transactional to transformative. We made the distinctive decision that no short-term mission trip should happen outside a long-term partnership. Thus, we set out on a journey to discover what a partnership truly is . . . our mission statement became: *Our vision as a Global Missions ministry team is to come alongside leaders all over the world who are making a difference in their communities and empower them to live into their callings to make disciples.* This took away the presumption that we had all the answers and that we needed to figure out solutions to the problems of the world. Instead, we sought out leaders/missionaries/pastors to come alongside—to lift up, encourage, affirm, love, help, etc. Our mission trips are now "family visits" . . .
>
> Our local missions director and I have taught a series of classes based on the books *When Helping Hurts* by Fikkert and Corbett, *Ministering Cross-Culturally* by Sherwood Lingenfelter, and *Cross-Cultural Servanthood* by Duane Elmer. We've found that education is the key.
>
> Our mission trips have turned into pastoral care trips. Anyone can be a friend . . . it does not take special skills or special degrees. If you need a project or need to hold a hammer, these trips are not for you. We can put you to work with Fuller Center for Housing or another one of our local mission partnerships.[4]

Goad is an example of a mission leader whose concerns about the short-comings of STM motivated her to engage in an action/reflection cycle: after her years of experience, she began engaging in intentional reflection and dedicated study to assess STM and design strategies for improving it. Her hands-on experience in her Louisiana congregation reveals the fruit of her learnings:

1. **Change takes time:** Personal change is hard. Changes in group behavior are a more complex and longer-term process that requires "a long obedience in the same direction," to quote Eugene Peterson's classic phrase. Changing group behavior is akin to putting braces on teeth and results in slow, deep change. Any change process in a congregation is a medium- to long-term project that requires clarity of vision,

---

[4]Ashley Purcelle Goad, "Mind the Gap: Navigating the Pitfalls of Cross-Cultural Partnership," DMin project, 2016, https://digitalcommons.georgefox.edu/dmin/129.

commitment, and discipline on the part of the leader. Goad understood this change process as a five-year exercise and didn't grow impatient when the needed changes were not implemented in the first year.

2. **Reframing STM:** Simply by naming the previous model as "transactional," Goad sensitized her congregation to the inadvertent commodification that had occurred in their engagement in mission. She
invited them to consider changing their STM model by offering precisely what people sought in STM: deep transformation of mission
partners and themselves. Rather than going to "do" or to "fix partners'
problems," Goad invited church members to "come alongside local
leaders." Trip objectives are intentionally shifted from "work trips" to
"pastoral care visits" that support frontline Christians.

3. **Embedding STM in long-term relationships:** Goad challenged the
congregation to organize STM exclusively in the context of its longer-
term mission partnerships. This prevents the "one and done" mode
whereby US congregations seek the "new" over the "known" (a
practice referred to disparagingly by some mission critics as "voluntourism" or "drive-by mission"). In her Shreveport congregation, STM
has become a tool to deepen relationships and their understanding of
specific contexts, and it creates the space where bonding, bridging,
and linking social capitals can empower joint work.

4. **Mission formation:** Many mission leaders look at the existing
function of STM in their congregation's mission program and can't
imagine how to change its direction. Goad and her colleagues saw that
for the congregation to "do differently" they had to "think differently,"
thus she launched several book studies to deepen her congregation's
reflections on mission: "We've found that education is the key." An
axiom of effective pedagogy is the Latin proverb, "Nihil volitum nisi
praecognitum" ("Nothing is desired unless it is preknown"); that is,
when we approach a book knowing what we're looking for, we're more
apt to find it. Learners need a hook on which to hang new knowledge.
Congregations engaging in a general book study will have mixed results, but when a leader focuses the group's attention with a challenge
to read a book to ascertain how it can help them improve their STM
work, tangible results become possible.

REPURPOSING STM AS CONTEXT LEARNING

Kim Lamberty is the director of Justice, Peace, and Integrity of Creation for the Society of the Sacred Heart in the United States and Canada and regularly consults with Catholic parishes across the country about effective mission engagement. She shares the example of how the St. Thomas Aquinas Parish in Lafayette, Indiana, channeled its strong need to "do" into a strategically important task: getting to know their partners and their context. The parish sent an STM group of parishioners and Purdue University students to Haiti with a clear methodology consisting of portable tape recorders and a set of questions Kim and Haitian leaders had prepared in collaboration with the Haitian mission companions. The responses to the questionnaire and resulting conversations helped the two groups to map out short-term interventions in three specific areas: the quality of beans used for seed, the storage of harvested beans, and how to mitigate the impact of natural disasters on bean production. By repurposing the parish's desire to accomplish a task into a listening exercise, Lamberty and Haitian companions put the group on the road toward a shared objective—and mission companionship was the result.[5]

INVESTING IN MISSION LEADER FORMATION

Susan Buenger is the retired associate for Global Engagement of First Presbyterian Church of Colorado Springs (FPC), a 3,500-member church of the Evangelical Covenant Order of Presbyterians. FPC is a church with a long and storied history of local and global mission involvement—the kind that would present a daunting task to a mission leader with a desire for change. But Buenger is a sensitive change leader. Under her leadership, FPC has come to use STM as a tool to support the congregation's larger mission objectives to form missional leaders. She credits her congregation's transition to more faithful and effective STM to the initiative of a small group of lay leaders and long-term missionaries who are part of the congregation. The change strategy emphasized a grassroots effort that would give congregants a deep sense of ownership of the congregation's five international partnerships.

---

[5]Kim Lamberty, personal interview, September 3, 2019.

It was a Spirit-lead process that surprised the mission leaders. There was no well-informed, or comprehensive plan. They used prayer, group discernment, listening well and learning together to affect change in addition to leadership from the church staff. All of this has resulted in significant, long-term relationships with local churches and ministries. These partnerships are lay-led, and while they are primarily "owned" by the congregants who participate, most of the congregation knows what the focus areas are, and have heard and read about, or met the international partner leaders.[6]

Buenger intentionally sought out opportunities for missional leader formation: the Chalmers Center (Lookout Mountain, GA) provided training for a large number of the congregation's mission leaders (FPC covered half the cost of the Center's STM Leadership and Assets-Based Community Development courses), and the congregation hired a consultant to provide intensive training in healthy partnerships and STM leadership for many of FPC's mission leaders.[7] This included contextualized training where congregants joined international partners in their country for mutual learning. Rather than understanding STM as an end in itself, FPC used the trips to form leaders, build relationship with a few national and global partners, and deepen congregational "buy-in" and mutual transformation in Christ.

CONGREGATIONAL TWINNING: LONG-TERM COMPANIONSHIP THAT LEADS TO JUSTICE

A major strategy by US Catholic parishes and many evangelical and Lutheran congregations is to establish long-term "twinning" relationships with a parish in another country or in another region of the United States and STM has been a key tool in slowing mission down and establishing and nurturing long-term companionship relationships. Parish twinning is a "process where a parish/church seeks to integrate global concerns into their parish life by developing a faith-filled relationship with another parish within or outside of the U.S."[8] Two Catholic grassroots mission leaders,

---

[6]Susan Buenger, personal correspondence, January 10, 2019, and July 21, 2020.

[7]The Chalmers Institute was founded by *When Helping Hurts* coauthor Dr. Brian Fikkert, and works to "move churches and ministries from short-term hand-outs to lasting transformation": https://chalmers.org/.

[8]"What Is Twinning?," Archdiocese of Cincinnati, https://resources.catholicaoc.org/offices/mission -and-pontificial-mission-societies/parish-twinning.

Dr. Mike Gable and Michael Haasl, of the Archdioceses of Cincinnati and Saint Paul & Minneapolis, respectively, have been developing the parish twinning model for more than twenty years each through the action/ reflection model and have developed some extremely useful resources for congregational mission leaders.[9] We have reproduced at the end of this chapter as Tool 6 their Checklist for Healthy Parish Twinning Relationships. Gable, a Catholic layman with a rich history of mission experience in Honduras, leads the Archdiocese of Cincinnati's mission program and has engaged forty of the archdiocese's two hundred parishes in long-term twinning relationships. He shares his insights into STM as a strategy for mission leaders to engage in the slow and deep work of justice:

> In the Archdiocese, we seek to turn STM into a tool for social analysis and for social justice. Through multiple trips to the same parish over time, our people realize that there is less need to "help the poor" and a bigger need to remove the barriers preventing the poor from developing themselves. We have several parishes twinned with Ghanaian parishes. While it's nice to raise $1,000 for our friends, if you do your homework, you'll find that the U.S. government was ignoring a bill to support a $1 billion program of the U.N. Millennium Development Fund to build highway and seaport infrastructures. However, a Cincinnati twinning parish lobbied their congressperson and the bill was finally passed shortly thereafter. We've learned that it's much better to deal with the root causes of poverty and advocate for rights of people.[10]

These four cameos show how innovative mainline Protestant, evangelical, and Catholic mission leaders are using the transformative space of missional experiences to form their congregations' leaders, deepen relationships, and make a sustainable impact in host and home communities.

---

[9] The Roman Catholic Church has been particularly attentive to the growth of the grassroots mission movement present in many of their parishes and dioceses, denoted as the "third wave of mission," a term from Catholic missiologist Fr. Robert Schreiter that explains how this form of mission is directly related to the third wave of globalization. Catholic missiologist Fr. Roger Schroeder elaborates on this form of mission in his book *What Is the Mission of the Church: A Guide for Catholics*. A group of Catholic missionaries and former missionaries have established the Third Wave of Mission Institute to provide high-quality resources (a video series and downloadable workbooks) to help mission leaders lead their congregations into long-term relationships. Michael Haasl, personal correspondence, April 7, 2021.

[10] Michael Gable, personal correspondence, April 7, 2021, and May 19, 2021.

SLOW MISSION AND CONGREGATIONAL RENEWAL

Our research with more than 1,200 Catholic, evangelical, and mainline Protestant congregational mission leaders indicates that a majority of the mission leaders surveyed understood congregational renewal and revitalization to be inherently linked to the congregation's engagement in mission. The Lilly Endowment has dedicated decades of research and hundreds of millions of dollars of funding to understanding what contributes to vital, thriving congregations. Lilly's "Thriving Congregations Initiative" articulates the fruits of their extensive research in three succinct characteristics of healthy congregations that confirms what our local mission leaders anticipated as the role of mission in congregational renewal. For Lilly, thriving, vital congregations engage in three specific practices: they (1) explore and understand the rapidly changing contexts in which they minister, (2) gain clarity about their own values and missions, and (3) draw on practices from their theological and ecclesial traditions to adapt their ministries to their changing contexts.[11] We will lift up the stories of two Midwestern US congregations to illuminate these practices.

CONNECTING TO CONTEXT

The Lilly Endowment research notes the critically important relationship between a congregation and its context: vital congregations "explore and understand the rapidly changing contexts in which they minister." We would argue that the gospel must be incarnated to be understood; that is, the *text* of the gospel—the core message of God's unconditional love and forgiveness and the beloved community God's love creates—cannot be understood outside the specific context of personal/community life. Developing practices that help your congregation connect deeply to the context of your own neighborhood or that of an overseas community is a goal worthy of significant prayer and effort. Let's look at how the Rev. John Edgar, the founding pastor of the United Methodist Church for All People in Columbus, Ohio, led his leaders to engage with their South Side neighborhood in intentional, humble, and iterative ways.

---

[11]"Thriving Congregations Initiative," Lilly Endowment, https://lillyendowment.org/thriving congregations/.

In January 1999, the Columbus South District of the United Methodist Church launched the United Methodist Free Store as a direct service ministry of the district. At that point in time there was no intention to birth a local church. Initially this was an initiative designed to get people who were members of the seventy-eight United Methodist Churches in the district to invest themselves and their resources in a ministry serving low-income people in the inner city of Columbus. Edgar said they began with the belief in "radical hospitality" and were "helping people from our churches get a little bit out of our comfort zone by establishing relationships of hospitality" with neighborhood residents. Conversations with residents led to deepening relationships that, through the lens of Assets-Based Community Development principles,[12] helped both church and community see tremendous potential rather than merely bottomless need.

The three needed shifts. These initial conversations led to the creation of a "free store" where community members shopped in a store stocked with donated items. It was a tremendous success and forced the congregation to wonder, "Why didn't we run out of things to give away?" The Free Store, in itself, was a partially formed intuition on the district's part that arose directly out of what they had learned when they listened to the hopes and dreams of the neighborhood. It represented a fledgling attempt to create a space where meaningful relationships could begin. Perhaps a community development expert might well have counseled church members against giving things away for free as a first point of connection with the neighborhood by noting the possibility of creating dependent relationships on both sides of the Free Store cash register (community members who needed free goods and church members who needed to be needed). But so important was the creation of a space for encounter and study that the church's effort proved to be the perfect "misstep" with which to begin! (Pastor Edgar understands the Free Store not as a development "misstep," but as a tangible way for people in the neighborhood to "touch grace": "free gifts offered in the name and with the

---

[12]Assets-Based Community Development (ABCD) "insists on beginning with a clear commitment to discovering a community's capacities and assets." John Kretzmann and John P. McKnight, "Assets-Based Community Development," *National Civic Review* 85, no. 4 (1996): 23-29, https://comdev.osu.edu/sites/comdev/files/d6/files/Assets-Based%20Community%20Development%20-%20Article.pdf.

love of the Living Christ."[13]) Because the study of their context required deep listening and the daily practice of showing up for neighbors and allowing what they learned to challenge them theologically, Edgar and the congregation grew to understand this space of connection between church and community as "the front porch of God's kingdom"—a liminal space where both church and community members could sit together, develop relationships, and together enjoy a foretaste of the kingdom. It was in this space that three essential shifts occurred in the congregation's self-understanding that knit the church tightly together with its surrounding South Side community.

Shifting the "who." Church members grew in cultural humility as "binocular" (able to see both the community and the church) and "bilingual" (able to speak the languages of both community and church) community members. These new capacities led to a shift in the congregation's identity and values in missional directions: the congregation's identity began to be understood in relation to their surrounding community—they were becoming mission companions.

Shifting the "what." If mission had previously been understood as an activity good Christians did for needy folks in the community and beyond, now mission became a way of life that drew church and community members into a deepening web of relationships, shared concerns, and joint action. Church members began to see the community not as the *objects* of the church's mission but as their *companions* in God's mission. Congregational efforts to "develop" the community gave way to a more mutual yearning for co-development. Both groups saw how much they needed each other for their own development: when a ministry of benevolence gives way to a mutual relationship, companionship blooms.

Shifting the "where." The evocative image of a church seeking to become "the front porch of God's kingdom" shifted the congregation's focus beyond the four walls of the church building. Rather than waiting for the community to come to church, Pastor Edgar and church members placed themselves in the "in-between spaces" where deep desires about a different kind of future were shared: the places where mothers sought better nutrition for their children and where parents prayed and worked for safe housing for their families.

---

[13]Rev. John Edgar, personal communication, April 19, 2021.

The action/reflection cycle. Engaging in an action/reflection cycle, neighbors gathered and reflected on the achievements and mistakes of the Free Store in the "front porch" spaces, and as they reflected, possible new actions emerged. The subject of access to healthy food at reasonable prices kept appearing in multiple conversations. "By listening to people's aspirational goals," Pastor Edgar noted, "the church started to explore access to healthy food. They heard that people wanted to eat healthier but that it's expensive." This led them to develop healthy eating and living initiatives. Through action and reflection, local initiative was tapped and blended with church inputs and in time became the All People's Fresh Market, community gardens, a primary health care center (created in partnership with a national Catholic health care system), and a number of health and wellness programs—programs that benefit community and church members alike and created more spaces of encounter and relationship: two women can meet at the weekly produce market, sign up to take an exercise class together, and be drawn into deepening friendship. Community members share their stories on the All People Podcast, an ingenious innovation where community members can find their voice, articulate their hopes and learnings, and together write the future of South Side.

Continued action and reflection surfaced new opportunities for joint action. In numerous "front porch" conversations, affordable housing surfaced as a concern and community members helped the congregation understand that safe and secure housing is the lynchpin of all human development: education and nutritious food can't be utilized without a safe place to live. Together they began to grapple with this larger, more complex issue that both considered essential to just and equitable relationships in their neighborhood. Today, the ministry that grew out of the church is called Community Development for All People, an organization that has attracted more than $70 million in investment for sustainable, mixed-income housing, in addition to its health and wellness ministries, a bike shop, an arts initiative, leadership academy, and youth development. UMC and Community Development for All People have taken seriously their role as innovation leaders and have shared their experience with dozens of congregations around the country. Southside UMC Church in Kalamazoo, Michigan, and several others trace their own stories of renewal and a recentering in their own context to their visit and their initial conversations on the "front porch" of the United Methodist Church for All People in Columbus, Ohio. While this Midwest American experience grew up around a US congregation whose context had changed, their lessons about mission companionship, their development of attitudes of cultural humility (evidenced in their role as learners), the action/reflection model, and use of intercultural liminal spaces (powerfully framed as their "front porch of the kingdom" image) will be helpful for congregations seeking to engage locally or globally.

CLARITY OF VISION

For the Lilly Endowment, the second characteristic of a thriving congregation is the work it does to gain clarity about the congregation's own values and mission:

> Thriving congregations have a striking clarity about their values and mission. Drawing on their theological and ecclesial traditions, they have developed a strong sense of identity and are able to articulate "why" they are called to love God and serve those in their congregations, neighborhoods, regions and across the globe. This clarity enables a thriving congregation to identify specific areas of interest and then align its ministries and activities around those priorities.[14]

Sixth Presbyterian Church in Pittsburgh, Pennsylvania, was for many years the home congregation of Presbyterian minister Fred Rogers, the creator and producer of *Mr. Rogers' Neighborhood*, one of the most beloved and impactful children's television shows in American history. The values of unconditional love, equality, and justice that Fred Rogers shared in millions of American homes represent the church's DNA and are still quite present today at "Sixth Pres": you can hear it in Rev. Vincent Kolb's preaching, in the Christian education classes offered, and in the culture of community activism the church has created. Sixth has always been a generous supporter of organizations that minister to human need. After Pittsburgh Seminary's

---

[14]"Thriving Congregations Initiative."

World Mission Initiative did a two-session series to invite the congregation to reflect critically on their mission engagement, the mission committee asked us to accompany them in a process by which they could identify their congregation's values and align their mission financial grants with these foundational values. Mission committee chair Tom Twiss explains:

> In recent years, Sixth had deepened its commitment to social justice work. But our mission allocations didn't fully reflect this shift in our values. Despite a gradual increase in the emphasis of our mission allocations to social justice, most of our allocations were still to fairly traditional charities. We began thinking about this discrepancy more seriously after [the World Mission Initiative] led two programs at Sixth on the "charitable industrial complex." The programs also helped us realize that we didn't have any clear criteria for comparing the organizations we were assisting . . . and that we might be able to create a process that would ensure a closer match between our values and our allocations.[15]

In the values/mission alignment process we developed with Sixth Presbyterian mission leaders, they agreed overwhelmingly that, while they wanted to continue to support various charities, they sensed a call to shift the focus of their financial support from direct assistance to advocacy—toward the *prevention* of the human suffering to which their charitable giving was responding. The outcome reflected this sense: after working to identify the congregation's shared values and creating a "Word Cloud" to illustrate them (fig. 8.1), the mission leaders developed a set of criteria that reflected these values and assessed their current mission allocations and pressing new needs. This was the result:[16]

> Early in our discussions I proposed that we use 40% of our budget for "direct service" and 50% for "advocacy" (retaining 10% for a "Rainy Day fund" for emergency needs). I was pleasantly surprised when my proposal was rejected by the committee in favor of one that would allocate just 30% of our budget to "direct service," and 60% to "advocacy."[17]

---

[15]Thomas Marshall Twiss, personal email, May 31, 2020.
[16]You can find a review of several free versions of WordCloud at https://monkeylearn.com/blog/word-cloud-generator/#wordclouds.
[17]Thomas Marshall Twiss, personal correspondence, May 31, 2020.

Figure 8.1. Congregational values word cloud

Some leaders expressed their doubts about an "overly bureaucratic" process that might trigger the defunding of long-term partners, but "at the end of the process [they] told me they felt their initial concerns had turned out to be unfounded, and that they were very happy with the outcome."[18] Because the process was slow, intentional, and transparent, Twiss and Sixth Presbyterian's mission leaders created a space of trust where mission supporters grew to imagine new possibilities for their church—in ways that their mission work could align with and support their common values. We have included as Tool 7 ("Aligning Hearts and Hands: Connecting Congregational Values to Mission Funding Allocations") the exercise that emerged from this experience with Sixth Presbyterian Church.

MISSIONAL PRACTICES AS SEEDBEDS

According to Lilly, the third characteristic of a thriving congregation is one that draws on practices from their theological and ecclesial traditions to adapt their ministries to their changing contexts. Most of us can empathize with the congregational mission leader who asks for the list of "best practices"—a curated collection of strategies that are guaranteed to "work" in every context. But we know from experience that the shiny new approaches from the latest bestselling book that worked in one place and time can never serve as a rigid blueprint for change in other congregations.

---

[18]Thomas Marshall Twiss, personal correspondence, May 31, 2020.

Each congregation has its own DNA, values, relationship with its own context, and understanding and practice of mission. There is no such thing as "best practices," but "better practices" from other contexts can help open your congregation's eyes to broader horizons and kindle its imagination to new possibilities.

The fruits of Lilly Endowment research invite us to identify the practices that grow the skills and insights needed for mission companionship, cultural humility, and co-development. These three stones—well-selected and placed—become the hearth around which companions gather and where new behaviors, learnings, and insights can be kindled and fanned into radiant life. Drawing from previous chapters of the book, we propose practices like these:

- "Crossing over experiences": Intentionally placing your leaders and emerging leaders in intercultural places of service, such as a homeless shelter or soup kitchen in your community, creates a liminal space where leaders can bring a learning posture, appropriate levels of risk, and the energy generated by the action/reflection that allows companionship to take root in your leaders' hearts. What if your next mission/outreach committee meeting began by serving dinner to neighbors struggling with homelessness, followed by half an hour of reflection on the experience and prayer for discernment? The power of "crossing over" experiences can change the direction of even a church committee (smile)!

- Intercultural worship services: Whether together in the same location or virtually (using technology to beam into each other's worship spaces), worship binds hearts together. Even the act of working together on the shared task of creating worship that communicates the cultural diversity of companions allows mission companions to shift into learners: bringing greetings, sharing prayer requests, lifting up ways companions are engaging in God's mission and upholding them in prayer, sharing in the preaching and hearing of the Word.

- Joint testimony: Whether in public worship, an evangelistic campaign, or in smaller fellowship groups, the sharing of personal testimonies—the story of God's mighty acts in a person's life—across lines of cultural difference creates a radically leveled playing field. Participants are confronted with the greatness of our God, who is powerful and merciful to each and every person but in different ways.

- Prayer: Lifting up mission companions consistently in public worship and in group or personal prayer times often creates the connective tissue that binds two groups of people together. Exchanging prayer requests keeps mission companions in the center of our prayers.

- Joint campaigns for co-development and justice: Now that we have gotten to the point of knowing and trusting each other—of loving each other—we can't sit idly by while our mission partners struggle with inhumane conditions that defy God's good intentions for the world. Channeling your congregation's missional calling to accompany mission companions in their struggle against hunger and injustice can galvanize a local congregation in profound ways.[19] It can also open your eyes to injustice in your own neighborhood and complete the circle of God's mutual mission by bringing mission companions to work in your context.

- Intercultural Bible study: To study Scripture together, particularly texts that are understood differently in different cultural perspectives, deepens our respect for God, who speaks every language. To illustrate this to your mission leaders, read the following illustration and invite your mission leaders to participate in this reflection.

INTERCULTURAL BIBLE STUDY

When you engage in Bible study with your mission companions, invite the group to read Jesus' parable of the prodigal son in Luke 15:11-32, then have them shut their Bibles and ask them, "Can you recall the reason the younger son goes hungry?" Ask them to write their response in one phrase. Allow several people from different cultural backgrounds to read their response. Ask the group what they notice about the pattern of responses. Then share with them this reflection:

---

[19]See my "From Short-Term Mission to Global Discipleship: A Peruvian Case Study," *Missiology: An International Review* 41, no. 2 (April 2013): 163-78, for an example of a global justice campaign that made a difference for thousands of lead-poisoned children in Peru and helped many North American Christians find greater relevance to their faith.

Lutheran New Testament scholar Mark Allan Powell asked a diverse group of Americans, Russians, and Tanzanians to read the story. Afterward, each participant was asked, "Why did the younger son go hungry?"

Here's what Powell discovered:

- 100 percent of the Americans said that the son had squandered his inheritance.

- 84 percent of the Russians said it was "because of the famine" (N.B., only 6 percent of the Americans even mentioned the famine in their retelling of the parable).

- A majority of the Tanzanians said it was because "no one gave him anything to eat." In much of sub-Saharan Africa, it is shameful for a community to allow a member to go hungry.

Powell then looked back at what Luke 15 actually says. In verse 13 it says the prodigal son "squandered his property." In verse 14 it attributes his hunger to "a severe famine . . . throughout that country." In verse 16 it states, "no one gave him anything [to eat]." Thus, all three interpretations were correct, but all three were *incomplete*. Americans tend to stress individual responsibility. The Russians' cultural memory of food shortages and famine is so present that they aren't able not to empathize with the famine-stricken young man. The Tanzanians understand implicitly that we owe it to each other to keep each other from starving to death.[20] In fact, the main point of the parable is not how the young man got into trouble but that the loving father drops everything to race toward his son and embrace him. Intercultural Bible study can be the first step in the journey toward cultural humility by helping us remember that it is God's Word that is inspired, not our culturally limited interpretations.[21]

THE POWER OF SLOW MISSION

As we discussed earlier in this chapter, Catholic and Protestant mission leaders have used "parish twinning" (or "congregational twinning") in ways that have slowed their engagement in mission, allowing a congregation to

---

[20]Mark Allan Powell, *What Do They Hear? Bridging the Gap Between Pulpit and Pew* (Nashville: Abingdon, 2007).

[21]A helpful resource for mission leaders wanting to engage their people in intercultural Bible study is E. Randolph Richards and Brandon J. O'Brien, *Misreading Scripture with Western Eyes: Removing Cultural Blinders to Better Understand the Bible* (Downers Grove, IL: Intervarsity Press, 2012).

engage in deeper relationships and "study up" on their companions' context. In a different ecclesial context, the Evangelical Lutheran Church in America has developed an important set of long-term missional relationships through their "companion synod program." Many evangelical and other congregations have developed long-term relationships with a specific local or global partner congregation.

Another strategy is the mission networks developed by the Presbyterian Church (USA): in 1995, forty representatives from congregations in Trinity and Shenango presbyteries (central South Carolina and northwest Pennsylvania, respectively) gathered in Washington, DC, to meet leaders of the Sudanese church, pray and worship together, receive updates from Sudanese partners, and engage in joint planning together. A single congregation could not have paid the travel costs of the Sudanese visitors, but by working with a network of churches they were able to gather, listen to Sudanese leadership in formal presentation and informal conversation, and together get a larger vision for what God was doing in Sudan. Prayerful, strategic reflection and better-coordinated work were the results. In the first decade following that meeting, more than thirty country mission networks were formed across the denomination in response to grassroots interest in engaging better in mission.[22] It has been the congregational mission leaders and global mission companions who have taken the initiative and shaped the networks to be spaces of strategic reflection, shared Bible study and worship, and joint planning. Twinning parishes/synods and mission networks create spaces where slow mission fosters the creation of mission companionship.

Why is slow mission so important? Because sometimes, as novelist Chinua Achebe noted, "when we are comfortable and inattentive, we run the risk of committing grave injustices absentmindedly,"[23] as we see in the following reflection:

> Beginning in 1984, the world was confronted with horrendous televised images
> of starving children and their weeping mothers, victims of the now-infamous

---

[22]For an article on the characteristics of highly successful mission networks, see B. Hunter Farrell, "Multiplying the Gifts: Habits of Highly Effective Mission Networks," *Presbyterians Today*, 2016, www.presbyterianmission.org/wp-content/uploads/MultiplyingtheGiftsHunterFarrellJuly _Aug16PT.pdf.

[23]Chinua Achebe, *The Education of a British Protected Child: Essays* (New York: Knopf-Doubleday, 2009).

Ethiopian famine that eventually claimed more than one million lives. Christian churches responded generously, including Ethiopian famine relief as a mission priority. Together with a wide array of governments and non-profit organizations, the international community quickly generated more than $100 million to provide direct food aid.

But as media attention moved elsewhere, some troubling facts began to emerge. Although the humanitarian crisis had been framed as a famine, throughout the 1980s there was actually enough food produced in Ethiopia to feed its entire population. But in the national context of the rebellion of the Tigray, Eritrea, and Wollo regions against the brutal Derg regime, the root problem was one of food distribution. The Derg government, after engineering widespread starvation to punish the rebels, adeptly diverted the donated food aid from the needy to feed its own army. The end result was chilling: "The humanitarian effort prolonged the war and, with it, human suffering," concluded renowned British researcher Alex de Waal after his exhaustive study of the international response to the famine. Because well-intended Christian mission efforts had ignored the underlying structural injustices, well-intended help was misdirected, and tens of thousands of Ethiopians died needlessly. Mission without justice ceased to be God's mission at all.[24]

Slow mission allows us to listen to mission companions, step back, and take a broader view of the complex contexts in which we are called to serve. We are tempted to succumb to our American cultural tendencies (our short-term focus, our fascination with "newness," and our love of problem-solving challenges) to react to disasters with well-intended but absent-minded generosity without ever "connecting the dots" to ask why these disasters continue to happen. If the Methodists and their mission companions on Columbus's South Side had not paused to connect the dots and only responded to their neighbors' need for "free stuff," they never would have seen the needs or the assets (the energy and resources the local community would bring) to address the deeper issues of the lack of affordable, nutritious food or safe housing. If the Catholics and Presbyterians in Peru had only provided a feeding program or Vacation Bible School for La Oroya's children who were struggling with excessive lead in their bodies, they would have been missing the mark.

---

[24]B. Hunter Farrell, "When Mission and Justice Embrace," in *That They All May Be One: Celebrating the World Communion of Reformed Churches*, ed. Neal D. Presa (Louisville: Westminster/John Knox Press, 2010), 32.

Perhaps it makes more sense now why STM trips and programs to care for vulnerable children are so popular in our US church culture. Our challenge as mission leaders is to slow mission down—to prayerfully lead a change movement in our own congregation using STM, companionship relationships, the action/reflection model to deepen mission thinking, intercultural Bible study and worship, and members' desire to care for vulnerable children as transformative—then lead them to reflect on more sustainable, empowering mission strategies. You will encounter resistance—often strong and at times seemingly unyielding. "Selfie mission" strategies are shaped by the marketplace's uncanny ability to provide a sense of consumer satisfaction. They may even temporarily assuage our feelings of guilt as we behold the massive and growing inequities of our nation and our world. But "selfie mission" silently invisibilizes the humanity and agency of mission companions and reduces companionship to mere consumerism. Many of our congregation members have been raised to understand mission as an experience the church should provide rather than as God's gracious invitation to join God in "turning the world upside-down" in the name of Jesus Christ.

This book has attempted to expose the crisis affecting much of US congregational mission. Yet the myth of "mission from a position of power" from our colonial heritage is as enticing—and addictive—as it is unbiblical. The crisis our congregations find themselves in has been centuries in the making. It requires more than just adding another organization to the congregation's mission partner list or adjusting the budget for a new annual emphasis. Our congregations' understanding and practice of mission have carefully—if unknowingly—been built on the shifting sands of power, the assumptions of racial and cultural superiority, and Western notions of development. As those sands have begun to shift under the mission programs we have built, many are beginning to realize that massive change—a reformation—is required in the way our congregations understand and practice God's mission. The needed reformation will not come from academia, from denominational headquarters, from the offices of the independent mission agencies, or from the halls of the great Catholic missionary orders—despite all the good these mission structures have done in years past.

In the emerging landscape of mission, it is mission leaders like you who in God's plan hold the keys to shifting the thinking of your congregation and channel its energy to walk with mission companions as together we change the world. This urgent call to reformation is being heard and heeded in local congregations across the country—mainline Protestant, evangelical, and Catholic—where mission leaders have begun to recognize the troubling contradictions between God's mission and the benevolent—but neocolonial and donor-satisfying—activities of what passes for mission today. With the three-stone hearth we've proposed in this book—a theology of companionship, a heart attitude of cultural humility, and the principles of co-development—and the strategies and tools we've described, a congregational mission leader can gather her or his key church members together and begin to prayerfully imagine a new way.[25]

But leadership in times of change is never easy. As leaders, we will often be tempted to keep silent and just "go with the flow" as I did when the church representative put the envelope of cash on the table in front of the pastors' group in Congo. We will feel the pressure to plan mission activities and portray our work as if it were *our* mission. But the depth of our relationship with our mission companions—our commitment to working with them to share God's love and improve the quality of life for us all—motivates us to educate ourselves, to find the strategies and tools we need, and to seek out allies who can help us engage better in this life-giving work. The good news is that it is the same Spirit who first planted a question in your heart and drew you to read this book who urges us all to look beyond the superficial answers and to ask a deeper question. By God's grace, it is the same Spirit who will walk with us through the difficult but critically important work of this reformation in congregational mission.

Across the country, a growing number of congregational mission leaders are prayerfully raising questions, deepening relationships, and redirecting mission energy in life-giving ways that respect neighbors and glorify the One who calls us to engage in God's mission.

Will you join us?

---

[25]For next steps for your congregation, join us at www.freeingmission.com.

CHECKLIST FOR HEALTHY PARISH TWINNING RELATIONSHIPS

BACKGROUND

Have you considered how your church could develop deep, impactful relationships with other churches or parishes to personalize mission? A twinning relationship is one solution. Twinning relationships are well-known within Catholic, Lutheran, and evangelical churches as a "process where a parish/church seeks to integrate global concerns into their parish life by developing a faith-filled relationship with another parish within or outside of the U.S."[26] It's a coming together of God's people to develop Christ-centered, mission-oriented faith communities that may flourish in mutual solidarity.

OBJECTIVES: This checklist will guide congregational mission leaders through a step-by-step process for their congregation to engage in a mutual twinning relationship with a local or global partner.

ACKNOWLEDGMENT: The following checklist was adapted with permission from guidelines developed by Michael Haasl, Center for Mission, Roman Catholic Archdiocese of Minneapolis/St. Paul.

To initiate parish/church partnership

▶ Form a team of at least five to ten parishioners

▶ Seek the support of the pastor and parish council

---

[26]"Parish Twinning," Archdiocese of Cincinnati, accessed July 15, 2021, https://resources.catholicaoc
.org/offices/mission-and-pontifical-mission-societies/parish-twinning.

▶ Plan initial orientation of team

- Watch and reflect on Third Wave of Mission video (especially the parish twinning) modules, using the accompanying booklets (https://thirdwave ofmission.org/video-modules/)

- Select preparatory readings and have your team read and reflect on one or all of the following resources:

  - Pope Francis's Joy of the Gospel

  - U.S. Bishops' Called to Global Solidarity (1997)

  - Sherron Kay George's Called as Partners in Christ's Service (esp. pp. 16-83)

  - Pakisa Tshimika and Tim Lind's Sharing Gifts in the Global Family of Faith

▶ The team identifies clear understandings and goals of what the parish needs from the partnership:

- Establish criteria for identifying a partner (have personal connection with global partner, share values of community co-development and mission, stand in solidarity with marginalized people in the community, etc.)

- Communicate with potential partners through email or videoconference

- A Counterpart Team at partner parish undergoes initial formation, developing its criteria for twinning relationship

- Make decision based on criteria

After agreement reached with partner

▶ Plan activities to help groups get to know one another, including

- Each group shares its history, core values, and stories that illustrate the parish living out its core values

- Jointly establish vision/goals of partnership, including motivations and expectations of each partner

- Establish communication protocol, ensuring equal, honest participation of both sides, attentive to cultural difference in communication styles (see chapter four of *Freeing Congregational Mission*)

▶ Establish mutual structures

- Establish leadership committees on both sides of partnership (five to fifteen people)

- Mutual ongoing formation and learning on both sides

- Common vision and mission statements ("covenant"), mutually developed

- Mutually agreed-on goals, activities, and timelines as relationship proceeds (see "Projects" below)

- Reciprocal visits (see below)

- Mutual annual evaluation (see "Regular evaluation" below)

▶ Broad-based involvement from both sides

- Many facets of parish life on both sides (represented in effort)

- Liturgy, youth, school, faith formation, justice/outreach groups, women's groups, men's groups, small faith communities, etc.

▶ Reciprocal visits

- Mutually agreed-on group size and frequency

- An application/selection process that includes a commitment to work with partnership for at least some period of time upon return from a visit

- Orientation using Third Wave of Mission videos (faith foundation; hopes; roles; expectations; input regarding historical, cultural, political, social, and religious considerations; preparation for encounter; liability and insurance issues; and logistical concerns for visit)

- Mutually defined objectives and mutual planning for visit

- Visits by parish leadership

- Invite new parish members to participate in visit

- Journaling during preparation, during visit, and upon return

- Maximize opportunities to have real encounters with local people—personal stories, day-to-day life, faith stories (staying in local homes is always a challenge to organize but often results in the deepest relationships and most impactful experiences)

- Large group times for deepened sharing (intentional conversations, with translators as necessary), including reflection on Scriptures or other writings

- Joint time to reflect on and evaluate relationship: past years' experiences, hopes and plans for the future, joys and struggles of the relationship

- Intentional sensitivity to cultural difference and power imbalance (see chapter four of *Freeing Congregational Mission*)

- Visits to local NGOs that are working to address structural injustices

- Joint time for debriefing and evaluation of visit, via videoconference/ Skype

- Sharing your stories of trips upon return with friends and home church

► Multifaceted education of and communication to parish

- Communication of partnership purpose, personal stories of parishioners' journeys and of the people of partnering parish, of increased capacity of partners

- Invite others to participate

  - Special Sunday(s) each year

  - Newsletters

  - Commissioning service, prayers at services

  - Webpage

  - Ongoing displays

  - Forums

  - Sunday school / adult education

► Projects

- Review Third Wave module on sustainability (www.youtube.com/watch?v =hLG8scQYaBM&list=PL2ngI1Rl5k-7Y2jjpbbNXOgZt2NtpcyO&index=2)

- Social/economic projects derive from relationship, are secondary to the relationship

- Should enhance esteem and sustainability of community, should build on local assets, should draw on already existing plans and resources including people and organizational resources, should capacitate the local people, potential effects regarding potential dependency addressed up front (see chapter five and Tool 3 of *Freeing Congregational Mission*)

- "Do no harm" principle, attentive to possible negative impact

- Project idea initiated by local companions; design, planning, implementation by local companions; US parish primarily in support role

- Only community-to-community projects, *not* individual-to-individual assistance: build the common good on both sides

- Reflected on by both parish twinning committees, with broad-based consensus

- Spiritual and relationship-building projects as well as socioeconomic

- Campaigns that address systemic injustice:

  - mutually define with partner an issue of concern

  - educate both parishes

  - act together (letter-writing campaigns, visiting delegations meet with government officials when appropriate, etc.)

- Regularly communicate stories, joint actions to parish, including formation and capacity-building

▶ Accountability of mutual commitments if funds or goods are involved

- Be clear on the mechanisms and expectations regarding accountability

▶ Regular evaluation of partnership including mission statement, goals

- How are our goals being met/addressed? Does our mission statement need changing?

- How have our activities deepened our mutual relationship and understanding of one another?

- Has deepening our relationship remained central and intentional, or has it been tangential to "doing a project"?

- How have our activities and our relationship broken down historic feelings of superiority and inferiority? How have they reinforced these feelings?

- Have decisions by the two core committees been made mutually with equal participation of each side?

- Is the partnership creating dependency in any way? Is it paternalistic or creating tension/divisiveness in any way?

- How has the partnership enriched the faith life of each parish?

- To what extent have we engaged many people (of both parishes of the partnership), and what can we do to engage more?

- What has the partnership done to address systemic injustice or poverty in the community or region? How might we together advocate with governments or nongovernmental organizations to do so?

- How has the partnership led to deepened connection to and understanding of immigrants, disenfranchised people, and the evil of racism in our own US community?

ALIGNING HEARTS AND HANDS

Connecting Mission Funding Allocations to Congregational Values

BACKGROUND

Many congregations struggle to allocate mission funding in ways that reflect their values. The reasons are numerous: the pressure of diminishing resources and growing demands, members functioning as advocates for outside organizations, or even a lack of clarity of the purpose of the congregation's mission. Most leaders believe their congregation's mission funds are allocated haphazardly rather than in a prayerful, strategic manner.

This process will provide a congregation's decision-making body with a clear methodology to align mission funding decisions with the congregation's values—and increase congregation-wide "buy-in," participation, and support.

OBJECTIVE

To help a congregation's decision-makers identify the congregation's core values and align mission funding decisions with those values. In general, the closer the alignment between congregational values and funding allocations, the more a congregation's members will support the mission.

PROCESS

This process calls for three sessions: (1) First, a session will be held with your congregation members that will identify the core values that undergird your congregation. (2) Second, a working group of three to five people is chosen because they are knowledgeable of current mission activities but have no or few conflicts of interests with potential mission partners or organizations considered for funding. This group will meet to develop criteria that can help discern shared values of the church community with potential partners. Based on alignment with the church's values, the working group will construct an initial proposal for mission allocations. (3) Finally, the working group will present their proposal for funding programs and confirm the allocations plan with the decision-makers of mission allocations. This is a general process, so please adjust it to fit your church's structure.

CHALLENGES TO BE EXPECTED

Any prioritization process for the allocation of finite resources can create tension among members. It is very important to engage the entire congregation from the beginning of the process and work transparently so everyone feels a sense of ownership in the process. Make sure to elicit input and opinions from those who cannot participate in person, especially in getting their input into what they see as the church's values that was asked of congregational members in the first session. This process cannot be rushed, and leadership must intentionally "over communicate"—providing information and process updates more frequently than they might assume are needed.

SESSION 1: IDENTIFY VALUES

Before the session, strategically invite participants and gather all needed materials:

- Send an invitation to all congregation members and include the congregation's various groups (women, men, youth, committees, Sunday school classes, mission and outreach groups) and all financial contributors.
- Have sticky notes (several for each individual), pen or pencil, and a board or wall for notes to be posted.
- Print and post on wall your congregation's mission statement, if you have one.

After welcoming everyone and opening the session in prayer for the Spirit to lead discernment, the facilitator leads the group using the following steps.

▼ SHARING STORIES

- Invite participants to reflect on their positive experience of the church and identify one story that shows the congregation at its best (allow three to four minutes).

- Invite participants in groups of two to share their chosen story. Give about three minutes for everyone to share in pairs. Then invite participants to share their stories in the larger group. Encourage everyone that stories be summarized in just a few sentences so that more people can share their stories.

▼ WRITING UP VALUES

- Based on the stories shared, ask participants to write on provided sticky notes the top two values (principles that guide your church to function in specific ways) they see at the core of the church's identity (this might be something mentioned by someone in their stories or something that individuals understand that undergirds the church). See below for examples of values.

- Examples of congregational values (the number of values can vary)

Inclusiveness	Evangelism	Respect	Equality
Justice Seeking	Outreach	Compassion	Hospitality
Human Development	Openness	Worship	Earth Care
Racial Justice	Reconciliation	Education	Serving the Poor
Progressiveness	Spiritual Growth	Diversity	Discipleship
Stewardship	Family	Community Service	Partnership
Christ-centeredness	Crosscultural Mission		

▼ SORTING VALUES

- After everyone has written down their top two values for the church, have each participant share and post them on the board or wall. After the last person has shared, sort them into a few categories. See below for examples of general categories of values.

- Combine and condense all the values into three to four general categories that will help clarify your values. Confirm these values with the group, asking, "Do these values represent the core values that we share?" Seek a show of hands to confirm or adjust these general values and pray, giving thanks to God for the values that bind your congregation together.

Example of general categories of values: try to condense as much as possible into three to four categories

Evangelism/Witness	Social Justice	Development	Inclusivity
Outreach	Progressive	Community Service	Multicultural
Worship	Sanctuary	Partnership	Diversity
Mission	Reconciliation	Family	Bible-Believing
Jesus Christ	Racial Justice	Stewardship	Hospitality
Discipleship	Earth Care	Education	Inclusiveness
Spiritual Growth	Equality	Human Development	Respect
			Compassion

SESSION 2: WORKING GROUP CLARIFIES CRITERIA AND SCORES THE ORGANIZATIONS

Before the session:

- Remind people that only those selected for the working group will participate in this session.

- Invite others not able to be present at session one to submit their top two values before the working group meets. Make sure to add these values to the list and WordCloud so you can post it for the final session.

- Publish all the submitted values in the form of a WordCloud (see sample below) that portrays all the values cited, prioritizing those most frequently cited. You can create one here (https://wordart.com/). Display prominently around the church (and in a newsletter) for everyone to see.

- Bring a list of all the currently supported organizations and the amount each has received annually for the last three years. You will be using these lists to assess each organization's alignment with congregational values. It will be good to include any potential organizations to support here.

After welcoming everyone and opening the session in prayer for the Spirit to lead discernment, the facilitator leads the group using the following steps:

▼ IDENTIFY CRITERIA

- Working group will brainstorm criteria for each of the three to four general categories of values to measure an organization's alignment with the church's values. For example, if the value is "evangelism," then the possible criteria would be an organization that regularly shares the gospel.
- Working group will come up with two succinct questions to rate each organization based on how they meet your criteria. Each working group member will rate each organization according to the question. *Please see some example questions for each of the categories below.*

Questions: Develop clear, succinct questions to rate each organization based on how they align with your congregation's values. Make sure to have equal numbers of questions for each category. Two questions will be sufficient for each category. Please rate with: 1—not at all, 2—slightly, 3—somewhat, 4—quite a bit, and 5—always. Here are some sample questions for each of the categories above. Develop all questions in the positive so that "5—always" would be the most desirable goal as this makes comparing scores easier.

Evangelism/Witness

1. Does the organization intentionally share its Christian faith with the community it serves?

2. Does the organization regularly promote and nurture the spiritual growth of its clients?

Social Justice

1. Does the organization address the root causes of social injustice and poverty?

2. Does the organization/church prioritize immigrants, the underprivileged, persons of color, or other oppressed groups?

Development

1. Does the organization work toward partnership and collaboration with the community it serves?

2. Does the organization work for the reunification of families and not support the separation of families, especially by putting vulnerable children in orphanages?

Inclusivity

1. Does the organization have adequate representation of persons of color and women on its board of directors or staff?

2. Does the organization offer its services to a wide variety of people or focus its services only to some groups of people?

▼ **SCORING PROCEDURE**

■ For every organization you evaluate/assess, score it using the questions you develop.

■ Rank the organizations from the most aligned to the least aligned with your congregation's values.

■ Taking note of the last three years' funding pattern, allocate funding to the organizations accordingly. Remember this is an initial/draft proposal that will be decided on by decision-makers. After the Working Group has tabulated and confirmed its draft proposal, then you are ready to move on to the next session.

SESSION 3: PRESENTING AND CONFIRMING THE ALLOCATIONS

Before the session:

- The working group, pastor(s), mission leaders, session and council members, and any others who are responsible for the church's decision making in mission allocations are encouraged to participate in this session.

- The working group will prepare to present:
  - the shared congregational values developed in the first session (using the word cloud)
  - the general categories of values developed in the first session
  - questions developed used to rate each organization that was considered for funding

- the results of the scoring

- the final allocation proposal

- a list of all organizations (both current and potential) and the amount comparison from last year's allocation to the new allocation proposal

After welcoming everyone and opening the session in prayer for the Spirit to lead discernment, the facilitator leads the group using the following steps:

▼ PRESENT ALLOCATIONS

- Working group will present to the committee members, session, or council their proposal of allocations and their rating of each organization.

- Working group will then share how each organization was rated based on the values and the categories of values developed (in the first session with the congregation members), the questions used to rate the organizations, and the results of scoring.

▼ CONFIRM ALLOCATIONS

- Invite decision-makers to comment on, modify, or affirm the proposal. Facilitators are encouraged to recommend that decision-makers advance amendment proposals that take the congregational values into consideration.

- After determining how much each organization will receive in the next year, present a comparison chart of allocations in both the past year and the current proposal for each organization so decision-makers can vote to approve the final allocations.

- After the allocations have been approved, have the decision-making group develop a brief statement that explains how the process moved from values to decisions. Share this statement when presenting the allocation plan to the congregation.

Note: Because this is a human process, you will have to allow space for the group to hear and decide on "exceptions" to the criteria it has established. But the movement of the process and its building on widely shared values predisposes participants to find common ground. In general, the tighter the connection between congregational values and funding allocations, the more that members will support the congregation's mission.

GENERAL INDEX

SCRIPTURE INDEX